I0821273

THE MODERNIST ARCHITECTURE

of Samuel G. and William B. Wiener

Municipal Incinerator.

Courtesy of LSU-Shreveport Archives and Special Collections.

THE MODERNIST ARCHITECTURE of Samuel G. and William B. Wiener

SHREVEPORT, LOUISIANA 1920–1960

Karen Kingsley and Guy W. Carwile

LOUISIANA STATE UNIVERSITY PRESS
BATON ROUGE

Grateful acknowledgment is made to Furthermore: A Program of the J. M. Kaplan Fund for its generous assistance in publishing this book.

Published by Louisiana State University Press

Manufactured in the United States of America
First printing

Designer: Michelle A. Neustrom
Typefaces: Cinta, diplay; Sentinel, text
Printer and binder: Walsworth

Library of Congress Cataloging-in-Publication Data

Kingsley, Karen, and Guy W. Carwile, authors.
The modernist architecture of Samuel G. and William B. Wiener : Shreveport, Louisiana, 1920–1960 / Karen Kingsley and Guy W. Carwile.
pages cm
Includes bibliographical references and index.
ISBN 978-0-8071-6162-3 (cloth : alk. paper) — ISBN 978-0-8071-6163-0 (pdf) — ISBN 978-0-8071-6164-7 (epub) — ISBN 978-0-8071-6165-4 (mobi)
1. Wiener, Sam'l. G. (Samuel Gross)—Criticism and interpretation. 2. Wiener, William B., 1907–1981—Criticism and interpretation. 3. Modern movement (Architecture)—Louisiana—Shreveport. 4. Shreveport (La.)—Buildings, structures, etc. I. Carwile, Guy W., 1957, author. II. Title.
NA737.W522K56 2016
720.9763'99—dc23
2015035561

The paper in this book meets the guidelines for permanence and durability of the Committee on Production Guidelines for Book Longevity of the Council on Library Resources. ♾

CONTENTS

Big Chain Store, Broadmoor.
Courtesy of LSU-Shreveport Archives and Special Collections.

ACKNOWLEDGMENTS

Like the community that fostered the architectural work of Samuel G. and William B. Wiener, there are many people who generously gave their time and provided information in the preparation of this book. First, of course, are members of the Wiener family—Bill Wiener Jr., Jay L. Wiener, Kathryn L. Wiener, Marion Wiener Weiss, and Samuel G. Wiener Jr.

Essential to our research was the staff at the LSUS Archives and Special Collections of the Noel Memorial Library, Louisiana State University, Shreveport, the guardians of the Samuel G. Wiener Collection and other significant holdings. We heartily thank the director, Laura Lyons McLemore, and archivists Shawn M. Bohannon, Fermand M. Garlington, and Domenica B. Carriere for their unfailing guidance and patience on many occasions.

We are particularly grateful to the owners of Wiener-designed homes and gardens, who graciously invited us in: William Atkins Jr., Stephanie Busbea, Christopher Coe, John Hansen, Warren and Meighan Maley, Kim Mitchell, James Jr. and Jeanne F. Muslow, Craig Nicholson, James Osborne and Bryan Sullivan, Roy and Bonnie Parish, Kenneth and Virginia Paul, and Joe and Susan Pierce.

Others who have helped by providing information, anecdotes, or showing and talking about the buildings described in this book are Phillip Aught, Karen Brewer, the late Eric Brock, Nita Cole, Rabbi Janna L. DeBenedetti, Trey Freeze, Robert Ginsburg, Jim Hayes, Eric Hill, the late Emily Wile Hussey, John Hussey, Diann London, Richard Longstreth, Seisel Wile Maibach, Joy Powell, Randall Ross, Lois Flesh Rosenfield, and Sutton, Mitchell, Beebe, and Babin Architects, and the Caddo Parish School Board. We thank them all.

At Louisiana Tech in Ruston we received important support from Edward Jacobs, dean emeritus, and Donald Kaczvinsky, dean, both of the College of Liberal Arts, and Karl S. Puljak, director of the School of Design. Important contributions were made by the many students who over the years have assisted Guy Carwile in the documentation of several Wiener-designed buildings for the Historic American Buildings Survey (HABS) of the National Park Service.

Additional support came from the State of Louisiana Department of Culture, Recreation and Tourism's Office of Cultural Development, Division of Historic Preservation, through the funding of a number of HABS documentary efforts at Louisiana Tech between 2002 and 2015. The staff at the Division of Historic Preservation, and in particular Mike Varnado, was most helpful.

We both join in thanking our editors at Louisiana State University Press, Margaret Lovecraft and Neal Novak, designer Michelle Neustrom, copyeditor Stan Ivester, and the anonymous peer reviewer who offered many valuable suggestions.

Finally, Guy is indebted to his family—wife Stephanie and daughters Mary Taylor and Parker—for their support, and to the memory of Mary Durr Stodghill and Floyd H. Carwile Jr. Karen is grateful to her family and to Lake Douglas, Pauline Saliga, and Mark Mones.

THE MODERNIST ARCHITECTURE

of Samuel G. and William B. Wiener

Weekend House, Cross Lake.
Courtesy of LSU-Shreveport Archives and Special Collections.

INTRODUCTION

In 1933, William B. Wiener in collaboration with his brother Samuel G. Wiener designed a weekend house for his family on the shore of Cross Lake, just outside Shreveport, Louisiana. This house was featured in *Architectural Forum* in 1934 and described as "Le Corbusier's 'machine for living' in full flower."[1] Wiener's inspiration for the Cross Lake house clearly was Le Corbusier and Pierre Jeanneret's Villa Savoie built in Poissy, France, between 1929 and 1930, photographs of which were featured in architectural journals as well as Henry-Russell Hitchcock and Philip Johnson's book *The International Style: Architecture Since 1922.*[2] The Cross Lake house is one of the earliest modernist buildings in the United States and was the first in a series of buildings—residential, commercial, and institutional—designed by William (1907–1981) and his half-brother Samuel (1896–1977) in accordance with the forms and materials of the new architecture of Europe, or the International Style as it came to be known in the United States. What is extraordinary about the buildings the Wieners designed, mostly in Shreveport and its vicinity, is that they form one of the largest and earliest clusters of modernist buildings by American-born architects in the United States. The Wieners' designs place northern Louisiana in the forefront of architectural innovation in the twentieth century.

These buildings are both unexpected and remarkable for they were constructed in a state that had a strong architectural tradition of its own and, from the late nineteenth century, had tended to lag behind such high-fashion centers as New York City, Chicago, and Los Angeles. The most prominent modernist architects—Richard Neutra and Rudolf Schindler, who practiced primarily in California—were European born and, before immigrating to the United States, were exposed to the architectural revolution spreading across Europe. But a set of circumstances produced a sudden and vigorous culture—an uneven development in American architecture—in Shreveport at this particular time.

This study examines the institutional, commercial, and residential work of the Wiener brothers from the 1920s to the 1960s. It explores how and why modern architecture appeared so early in Shreveport, the impact of the Wieners' travel in Europe in 1927 and 1931, the importance of family and the Jewish community in their client base and commissions, and how the Wieners adapted European modernism to the demands of building in Louisiana. The book investigates how the Wieners' designs evolved in the post–World War II period in response to changing ideas about architectural form, technical advances, and new materials.

When fascism in Europe in the 1930s suppressed modern architecture and Jewish architects, many of the architects fled to the safe harbor of the United States, reconstituting their work as part of a national aesthetic that came to be known as the International Style. The Wieners, however, had already introduced this new manner of design into the American South, drawing in large part for commissions on their personal and professional networks. Thus, the clients who welcomed such innovative designs are a significant aspect of this story. Houses the architects created in Mississippi and Texas are included.

While the focus is on the work of Sam and William Wiener, this study examines their work in the context of their contemporaries in Shreveport and elsewhere in the state who also embraced the ideas of modern architecture, and discusses the Wieners' place in modernist architectural trends in the nation as a whole. Both architects were at the forefront of American modernism, and many of their buildings were extensively published in architectural and related journals, yet they never achieved a national profile or became influential beyond their region. Some reasons for this are also considered.

Although some of the buildings have been demolished or altered, most of the Wieners' large body of work survives. Many of the designs, especially residences and schools, remain as originally designed. For all the buildings, including those that have been lost, archival and published sources, along with photographs and interviews with family members and former clients, provide insight into the projects and the architects' ideas and goals.

1
BEGINNINGS

Architects Samuel Gross Wiener and William Benjamin Wiener Sr. (identified as Sam and William in this book) were half-brothers, sons of second-generation German Jewish immigrant Sam Wiener Jr. (1864–1942; identified as Sam Jr.). Sam's mother was Tillie Loeb (1870–1897), whose parents immigrated from France and who died when he was only one year old. Sam and his brother Earl Loeb Wiener (1894–1946), both of whom were born in Monroe, Louisiana, were sent to live with relatives in Canton, Mississippi. Their father, Sam Jr., relocated from Monroe to Shreveport and married Florence Loeb Wile (1874–1967), a widow and the younger sister of Tillie. They had two sons, William Benjamin and Jacques Loeb Wiener Sr. (1909–1988). Sam and William and their brothers grew up in a prosperous family that was part of the thriving, culturally rich Jewish community in Shreveport.

Shreveport in the Early Twentieth Century

In the early twentieth century, Shreveport and northwest Louisiana were experiencing an economic boom, and the city strengthened its place as a commercial and transportation center in a three-state region—Louisiana, Arkansas, and east Texas. Founded in 1836 and laid out by the Shreve Town Company on the west bank of the Red River, the town was named for Captain Henry Miller Shreve, one of the company's investors. Shreveport was a center of the southern pine belt and quickly became a distribution point for lumber. Cotton also fostered Shreveport's growth in the nineteenth century, with steamboats shipping it along the Red to the Mississippi River and on to New Orleans. By the 1860s the city had become second only to New Orleans for the number of cotton factors in the state, and a cotton exchange was established in 1880. The seven railroads that came through Shreveport at the turn of the twentieth century cemented its place as a regional transportation center. The city served as a transfer point from one line to another.

It was the discovery of oil north of the city in 1904 that fully propelled Shreveport's growth and wealth. Drilling for oil began in what came to be known as the Caddo–Pine Island Field in 1905 and, in 1911, in Caddo Lake, where what is thought to be the first offshore drilling platform was established. The onset of World War I further stimulated a demand for petroleum products, and by 1919 Louisiana took third place in the nation after Texas and Oklahoma for oil production. Meanwhile, in 1906, natural gas had been detected in an area approximately thirty miles

Aerial view of downtown Shreveport, 1930s.
Courtesy of LSU-Shreveport Archives and Special Collections.

north of Shreveport, and the first pipeline from the Caddo Field was laid in 1908. Additional gas fields in the region were found and exploited in the following years and contributed to Shreveport's prosperity, notably, in 1921, the Haynesville Gas Field. The discovery in 1930 of what became known as the Rodessa Field lessened the impact of the Great Depression on Shreveport.

From the beginning of the twentieth century, people flocked to the city to work or profit from these resources, setting off a financial, commercial, and construction surge. New houses, subdivisions, office buildings, and shops and commercial centers testified to the flourishing economy. Shreveport's population jumped from 16,013 in 1900 to 28,015 in 1910, and it continued to increase, reaching 43,874 in 1930.

It is in this context of a rapidly expanding and changing city that architects Sam and William grew up. In the twentieth century's second decade alone they saw stylish new commercial and institutional buildings begin to replace many of downtown's low-rise mid- and late-nineteenth-century structures. Among the new structures were John Y. Snyder's steel-framed six-story Hutchinson Building of 1910, which is sheathed in white glazed terra-cotta, as is Mann and Stern's ten-story building completed in 1911 for the former Commercial National Bank. A three-story Renaissance Revival U.S. Post Office and Federal Building (now the Shreve Memorial Library) from the office of James Knox Taylor, supervising architect of the U.S. Treasury, was built between 1910 and 1912. But business was so busy that the building soon proved inadequate and it was doubled in size, in the same style, in 1931.

Shreveport native Edward F. Neild and New Orleans–born Clarence Olschner designed two handsome Beaux-Arts classical buildings that face each other across Cotton Street on the edge of downtown. The first, built in 1914, is the former B'nai Zion Temple, and in 1916 the architects repeated the style for the Scottish Rite Temple. The Wieners were members of the B'nai Zion congregation, and Sam was soon to have a connection with Olschner when in 1923 he joined the architectural firm of Jones, Roessle and Olschner and became a partner.

New buildings, bigger and grander, continued to go up well into the 1920s, including in 1924 the seventeen-story steel-framed Slattery Building by Mann and Stern. This Gothic Revival–detailed structure was probably inspired by Hood and Howells's celebrated Tribune Building in Chicago, then under construction. And in 1928 Edward F. Neild and Dewey Somdal's Caddo Parish Courthouse was a significant and massive addition to the city's downtown, occupying an entire city block. By then Sam had become a partner of Jones, Roessle, Olschner and Wiener and was ready to embark on a career that would place Shreveport in the forefront of avant-garde architecture. In 1933 William established his architectural practice in Shreveport and joined Sam in effecting this transformation.

The Wiener Family: Their Beginnings in the United States

Sam and William's father, Sam Wiener Jr., a son of Samson and Caroline Wiener, Jewish immigrants from Germany, grew up in Canton, Mississippi. In the early 1880s he took the position of manager for the new railroad station in Lufkin, Texas.[1] While living there and along with two friends (Simon W. Henderson Sr. and Joseph H. Kurth Sr.) he founded the Angelina County Lumber Company in 1890 and followed that by establishing the Angelina and Neches River Railroad to carry the lumber. Not only did his interests in the timber industry make him prosperous, he also became a significant landowner in east Texas. Sam Jr.'s brother Eli Wiener joined him in Lufkin and, with a Mr. Trout, a Lufkin mechanical engineer, who had invented a geared oilfield pump, they established the Lufkin Foundry Company to manufacture a fifteen-foot-diameter flywheel for pumping systems. This added to the families' wealth, for the timber-rich land later proved to be abundant in oil. In another venture, Sam and Eli partnered with a chemist from Alabama who had created a method of making paper from southern pine, and they also made plywood from the pine trees. By this time, according to Bill Wiener Jr., Sam Jr.'s grandson, there was "nothing left to do in Lufkin" and Sam left for Monroe, Louisiana, where he married Tillie Loeb and had two sons, Sam and Earl.[2] Nevertheless, connections with the town of Lufkin remained in the family and, in the late 1960s, Sam Jr.'s son William opened an architecture office there as a branch of the main Shreveport office.

Moving to Shreveport, Sam Jr. continued on his entrepreneurial path, buying and developing land in the city's central business district. He also established a steam laundry and, in 1897, with his brother William B. Wiener Sr. and Leon B. Loeb, the Wiener-Loeb Grocery Company and the subsidiary Big Chain Grocery Company, which he sold to his nephew I. Edward (Ed) Wile in 1923. Sam Jr. became a part owner of Feibleman's Department Store in downtown Shreveport. The design of the store was one of the first major projects for his son, architect Sam. In Shreveport the Wiener family became part of a vibrant Jewish community and, through business affairs and through marriage, intertwined with the Loeb and Wile families, who later proved central to the early success of Sam and William as architects.

ABBREVIATED WIENER FAMILY TREE

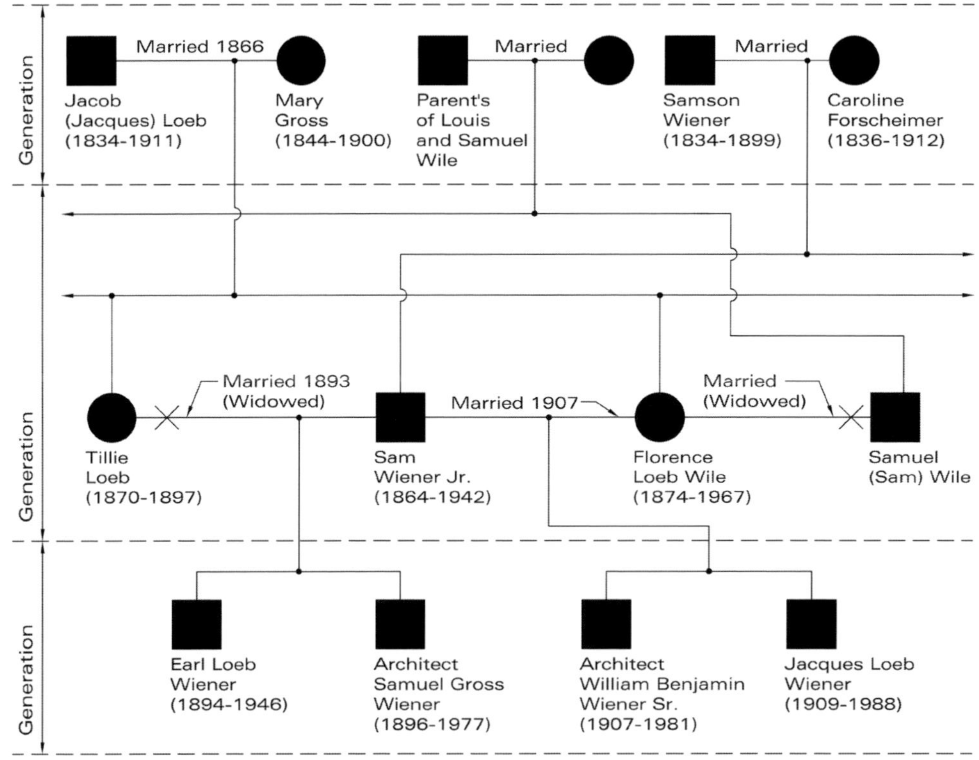

Illustration by Guy W. Carwile.

THE COUSINS: THE LOEBS AND THE WILES

Sam Jr.'s second wife, Florence Loeb, was first married to a member of the Wile family, and another of her sisters, Emily Loeb, also married into that family. Emily's son, Ed Wile, became owner of the Big Chain Grocery Company stores, and her daughter Mary T. Wile married Hyman B. Badt, who worked for his brother-in-law, Ed Wile, as a manager for the store. Architect Sam created houses for both of his cousins, the Wiles and the Badts, and, over the years, Sam and William designed a number of Big Chain grocery stores for Ed Wile.

Carrie Loeb, the younger sister of Tillie, Florence, and Emily, who married Sam Jr.'s younger brother William B. Wiener Sr., had two sons, William B. Wiener Jr. and Julian Wiener, who both became physicians, practicing in Mississippi. William B. Wiener Jr. married Carolyn Loeb in 1943, and Julian Wiener married Kathryn Loeb in 1952 (these two Loebs were not related). Sam and William designed a house for their cousin William and Carolyn in Jackson, Mississippi, and Sam designed a house for cousin Julian and his wife, Kathryn, which also is located in Jackson.

This intricate web of family relationships, made difficult to untangle because of the Wiener family's preference for recycling first names, nonetheless illustrates how crucial this network was to the success and prominence of architects Sam and William. The closely knit Wiener, Loeb, and Wile families were central in the acceptance and encouragement of modern architecture in Shreveport.

THE ARCHITECTS: SAMUEL G. AND WILLIAM B. WIENER

Sam, born in Monroe on December 26, 1896, and raised with relatives in Canton, Mississippi, following his mother's death in 1897, rejoined his father and his father's new wife, Florence Loeb, who were then living in Shreveport in 1907. William was born on December 4, 1907, in that city. The Wieners' family home, at 738 Austen Place, was on a fashionable residential street only a few blocks south of downtown in a subdivision platted in 1870. The house, a blend of Queen Anne and Colonial Revival styles and built in 1896, is typical of the homes owned by the neighborhood's affluent residents. As Shreveport grew and new residential subdivisions spread south to create the Broadmoor and Highland districts, Austen Place and its vicinity suffered the decline experienced in many American inner-city neighborhoods between the world wars. The Wieners' childhood home survives, as do a few nearby grand houses, but the area is now characterized by vacant lots and commercial and light industrial buildings.

Sam and William attended public schools in Shreveport. Their father, Sam Jr., had made his fortune without the advantages of higher education, but he was determined to send his sons to college. In 1915 Sam left for Ann Arbor to attend the University of Michigan, graduating with a bachelor of science degree in architecture in 1920. Sam may have selected the University of Michigan because his brother, Earl, was a student there. William also studied architecture at the University of Michigan, completing a BS in 1929. It is not known why Sam and William chose architecture as a profession. Clearly it was Sam's decision first, and his enjoyment of the field might have influenced William, or perhaps a younger brother just followed in the footsteps of an older brother. Certainly it was not the choice of their brothers Earl and Jacques, who entered the more traditionally aspirational career of law, or their cousins, who became physicians.

Sam married Marion Pfeifer (1903–1987) in 1926. They had two sons born in Shreveport—Samuel Gross Wiener Jr. (b. 1928) and Earl Wiener (1933–2013). The former, an artist currently living in New York City, designed artwork for several of his father and uncle's projects in Shreveport,

left
Samuel G. Wiener.
Courtesy of Bonnie and Roy Parish.

right
William B. Wiener.
Courtesy of Kim Mitchell.

most importantly mosaics for Woodlawn High School and a mural for the Julian and Kathryn Wiener House in Jackson, Mississippi.

William married Babette Levy (1911–1986) in 1934. William and Babette also had two children born in Shreveport, William Benjamin Wiener Jr. (b. 1936; known as Bill Wiener Jr.) and Karen (Kay) Wiener Freyer (b. 1938). Bill Jr. is an architect and was affiliated with the successor firm started by his father, William. For many years Bill Jr. was active in preservation issues in Shreveport and nationally, but now he mostly spends his time as a sculptor and lives in Santa Fe, New Mexico.

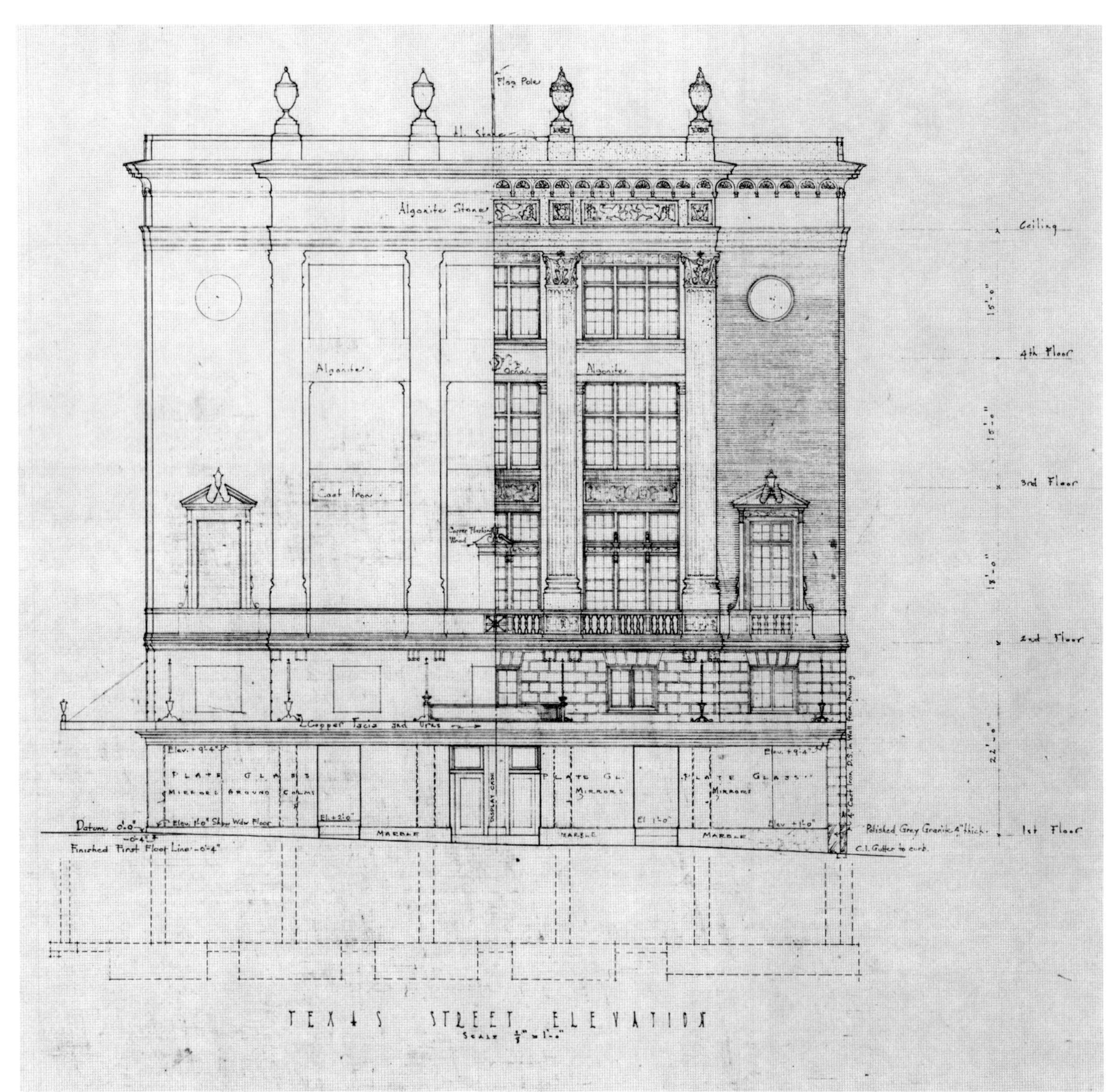

Feibleman's Department Store.

Courtesy of LSU-Shreveport Archives and Special Collections.

2

EARLY DESIGNS AND TRAVEL IN THE 1920s

In 1919, the year before he graduated from the University of Michigan, Sam was gaining professional skills as a draftsman in the firm of Esselstyn and Murphy in Detroit. That same year he also worked for a short time as a draftsman with the New York City firm of MacKenzie and Coffin. Following graduation in 1920 Sam relocated to New York City and enrolled as a student in the Atelier Corbett-Gugler. This *atelier* (studio or workshop) was based on the French system of architectural education practiced at the Ecole des Beaux-Arts in Paris, where students learned through studio projects, lectures, and design reviews (juries). Simultaneously and ever eager to learn, Sam was gaining practical experience as chief draftsman in the office of the J. Dall Construction Company.

In 1921 Sam decided to broaden his architectural education in Europe and enrolled as a student in the Atelier Gromort-Expert in Paris, established by Georges Gromort and Roger-Henri Expert, two architects active in the practice of architecture as well as teaching in the Ecole des Beaux-Arts. Gromort, who also published numerous books in the 1920s and 1930s on a wide range of architectural topics, spoke English, probably helpful for Sam's learning experience, though Sam did read French.[1] While Gromort remained committed to the rational planning principles and classicism taught at the Ecole des Beaux-Arts, Expert leaned towards a more modern interpretation of classicism and became a leading Art Deco designer in France. Sam's time in the atelier, along with travel in France and Italy, furthered his knowledge of European architecture, both historic and modern.

On his return to the United States in 1923, Sam took a postgraduate course in city and group planning under renowned architect and planner Eliel Saarinen at the University of Michigan. Saarinen had just immigrated to America from Finland, where he had been the foremost city planner. In the previous year (1922), Saarinen had submitted a modern design for the Chicago Tribune Tower competition, which won second place. Several European architects, including Walter Gropius with Adolf Meyer, submitted designs for this competition, but the *Tribune* newspaper was not ready for such a radical look and opted for a Gothic Revival design. For Sam, Saarinen offered a way forward and a new vision.

Sam's education in the United States and France, his European travel, and his experience as a draftsman in several offices had prepared him significantly more than most architectural students on the threshold of their careers. Late in 1923 Sam returned to Shreveport and joined the firm of Jones, Roessle and Olschner. He was made a full partner, and the firm's name was changed to Jones, Roessle, Olschner and Wiener.

Establishing an Architectural Practice (JRO&W)

The firm, with offices in New Orleans as well as Shreveport, began as a partnership between Ernest W. Jones (1888–1955) and Rudolph B. Roessle (1889–1967). Both were born in New Orleans, and both had worked as draftsmen in the office of Dannenman and Charlton (Frank Dannenman and John F. Charlton) from 1906 to 1911. In 1911, Jones and Roessle formed a partnership and established an office at 921 Canal Street in New Orleans. Jones served primarily as office manager and supervised construction and specifications while Roessle focused on design and was in charge of work outside the cities of New Orleans and Shreveport.

Clarence E. Oslchner (1888–1981) also was born in New Orleans, but followed a different early path. From 1909 he was a draftsman with firms in New Orleans and Beaumont, Texas, then moved to Shreveport in 1911 and became chief draftsman for Edward F. Neild (1884–1995), one of the city's leading architects. Neild and Olschner collaborated on projects, and both were given credit, but they never formed an official partnership. Olschner had an office in Suite 1206 of the Merchant's Building from 1918 until he joined Jones and Roessle in 1922 as a partner. There his responsibilities lay primarily in the preparation of plans and specifications. In 1935 in the midst of the Great Depression when commissions were thin and his work on the Municipal Incinerator with Sam was completed (the incinerator is discussed in chapter 4), Olschner was hired as an engineering inspector for the Federal Emergency Relief Administration (FERA) in Fort Worth, Texas.

When Sam joined Jones, Roessle and Olschner in 1923 the firm had offices in Shreveport in Suite 219 of the Ardis Building (they expanded to adjacent suites in 1924) and, in New Orleans, on the tenth floor of the Maison Blanche Building on Canal Street. Sam worked most closely with Olschner in the years that followed. They were both based in Shreveport whereas Jones and Roessle operated out of the New Orleans office. The mid-1920s were favorable for architectural firms, especially in Shreveport, which was experiencing the benefits of the region's booming oil and gas industry. The city's commercial heart demonstrated its status and wealth architecturally in many new buildings, from banks and office buildings to institutional buildings, car dealerships, exclusive shops, and department stores. Handsome residences were built along leafy streets in new and growing subdivisions. In 1925 Sam joined the architect's professional association, the American Institute of Architects (AIA).

FEIBLEMAN'S DEPARTMENT STORE

One of Sam's first projects with Jones, Roessle, Olschner and Wiener was Feibleman's Department Store at the corner of Texas and Louisiana streets in downtown Shreveport. Sam's father, Sam Wiener Jr., with his brother-in-law Leon Loeb, was a part-owner of the building, and Feibleman's leased it. The building was designed in 1923 and completed in 1924. Olschner was responsible for the building's plan, and Sam designed the exterior. The Feibleman family of New Orleans already owned a store on Canal Street (replaced in 1931 with a Moderne building designed by Moise Goldstein at Baronne and Common streets; it has since been converted into a hotel), and Olschner went to New Orleans to study the plans and organization of the Canal Street store.

Feibleman's in Shreveport opened with much fanfare on Saturday, October 4, 1924, only one month after the originally planned date. The previous day the event was announced with a headline on the front page of the *Shreveport Times,* and the newspaper was filled with advertisements heralding the wares to be found within. The newspaper described the building as palatial and "one of the most pretentious of the city. It is a commercial institution, yet it breathes from the very lines of its exterior a Welcome, an invitation to the purchasing public to make this store the headquarters for its manifold wants."[2] The newspaper's description continued for several paragraphs in the same florid prose, describing the various sales departments and proclaiming that shoppers would be "greeted by a vision of beauty unsurpassed in this and virtually any other city of the south and southwest."[3]

The five-story "vision of beauty" certainly evoked the splendor and opulence of an Italian Renaissance palace, and testified to Shreveport's flourishing economy and well-heeled customers. The reinforced-concrete-framed building, which occupies a corner location to present two handsome facades, is faced with rusticated stone on the lower levels, pressed brick and smooth stone above, and terra-cotta trim. The three upper stories had large windows between fluted Corinthian pilasters, and the building is dotted with extravagant Beaux-Arts ornamentation. Roundels at each corner of the fifth story are filled with terra-cotta representations of the arts, and long horizontal panels just below the projecting cornice feature urns flanked by griffins molded in low-relief. Four large urns crown the roofline of the Texas Street facade. This ornamentation set the stage for the elaborate and luxurious interior with fixtures and finished of English mahogany on the two lower floors and rosewood on the upper. The principal entrance was on the store's narrower Texas Street side and, typically of the 1920s, was located in the center of the facade and flanked by large display windows. A continuous canopy above the first-floor level shaded the display windows and sheltered pedestrians. Inside, the store had English mahogany furnishings, three elevators, ceiling fans on every floor for cooling, and refrigerated water fountains. The basement was reserved for a variety of more-economically priced goods and clothes, and the store included a nursery and playground where children could be left while their parents shopped. A roof garden and a cafeteria were reserved for employees.

In 1930, Sears, Roebuck and Company purchased the store, though it retained the Feibleman name. Sears was expanding in Louisiana, and the following year it acquired the Feibleman store in New Orleans.[4] In the following years Sears made many changes to the Shreveport store, notably in 1946 when the interior was remodeled with a new fifth floor to give the store six sales floors. More significantly, especially for the building's exterior appearance, the store was air-conditioned and the windows on the upper stories that had been essential for ventilation as well as light were now redundant and were bricked up. The introduction of air-conditioning, cheap fluorescent lighting, and acoustical ceilings had a profound impact on the design of department stores, as well as many other types of buildings. The elimination of windows provided solid perimeter walls for office and storage space, fitting rooms, and for the display of the increasing variety of wares available after World War II. Sears became a pioneer in the 1930s for building air-conditioned windowless stores and, for most customers, these changes were appreciated as an improved shopping experience.

Nevertheless, within a couple of decades the store was a victim of the next revolution in shopping patterns. In 1961, Sears relocated to one of Shreveport's new suburban malls, a shift common to downtown emporiums in many cities. Among the forces that generated such changes were the increased ownership and use of automobiles and shoppers' need for parking. Parking meters had been installed in the downtown in September 1939 in order to control and time-limit parking, and Sears added a garage to its store in 1947, but by 1961 Sears saw more profits in a suburban mall and moved out. The building became a discount store for a few years, after which it remained vacant until it was acquired by the state in 2001.

KINGS HIGHWAY CHRISTIAN CHURCH

When he was studying in Paris in the early 1920s, Sam made a trip to Italy. The impact of that journey is evident in his design of 1925 with Jones, Roessle, Olschner and Wiener for the Kings Highway Christian Church (see Plate 1).[5] The Italian Romanesque character is revealed first in its blocky gable-fronted massing and cruciform plan. On closer inspection, Italian influences are more apparent. Exterior walls are a tapestry of various shades of red brick interwoven with dark blue brick and colored marble, and every sixth row of the bricks is emphasized by alternating between protruding headers and sawtooth projections. Along with diaper patterning and blind arcades below the roof, the exterior has a richly tactile surface, an effect reminiscent of medieval craftwork. A small gabled entrance portico is supported on four columns with Byzantine-influenced block capitals of the kind Sam would have seen in Italy.

Exhibiting as much character as the exterior, but inverting the custom in religious buildings for an interior more richly decorated than the exterior, here the nave is austere in character. Stocky square piers with plain impost blocks instead of capitals support a six-bay round-arched arcade, transverse arches of alternating bands of brick and stone span the nave, and the church is covered by an exposed timber-frame roof. Small paired clerestory windows admit light, but the limited illumination adds an aura of mystery.

The square bell tower to the rear of the church was part of Sam's original design but not constructed until 1951 when Shreveport architect Julian Sokoloski made a compatible addition to the church. His treatment of the walls, however, is much simpler, reflecting postwar taste—and perhaps, budgets.

The church was one of several buildings in the mid-1920s from the Jones, Roessle, Olschner and Wiener office that incorporated patterning and alternating colors in their brick walls. Another, the gable-fronted Bossier City Municipal Building (now occupied by Bossier Arts Council) of 1926 also has a strong Italian flavor though mixed here with cast-stone Spanish-styled scrolls and a large cartouche outlining the round-arched portico. Much of the building's beauty, like that of the Kings Highway church, lies in the tapestry brickwork, here laid in Flemish bond in shades of ochers and browns. Another medieval Italian-influenced structure is the former McKinley High School (now McKinley High School Alumni Center) in Baton Rouge. Only Jones, Roessle and Olschner are credited on a 1974 wall plaque with the school's design although it was built in 1926, when Sam was already a partner in the firm.

The European Voyage of 1927

In 1926, Sam married Marion Pfeifer (they met in 1923), and the following year they traveled in Europe. William, who was then a student at the University of Michigan, accompanied them for part of the trip. The full extent of this trip's itinerary is not known, but Spain, Algeria, Tunis, and Italy were included on the journey, and they spent enough time in Venice to collect material for a book on the city's architecture. Sam's *Venetian Houses and Details,* published in 1929, included photographs, freehand sketches by Sam, and hard line drawings by William.[6] The drawings in particular show in intimate detail the close study that both architects made of the buildings and their ornament. On their return, William returned to Michigan, where in 1929 he completed a BS in architecture, and Sam went to Shreveport. The impact of their European travel is revealed in Sam's design of 1928 for the Municipal Memorial Auditorium (now the Municipal Auditorium). However, Bill Wiener Jr., William's son, remembered that Sam wanted something more contemporary for the Municipal Auditorium, something more modern European, but the clients could not be swayed.[7] This dissatisfaction suggests that Sam had seen and been excited by the modern buildings then going up in Europe and was looking for a new direction in his own work.

MUNICIPAL MEMORIAL AUDITORIUM

The influence of the rich decorative traditions of Venice and North Africa is perhaps more evident in the Municipal Memorial Auditorium than in any other building Sam designed.[8] Shreveport-based Seymour Van Os was an associate architect on this project with Jones, Roessle, Olschner and Wiener. The auditorium also exhibits a new influence on the firm's work—Art Deco. This eye-catching and often colorful style, inspired by and taking its name from the Exposition International des Arts Décoratifs et Industriels Moderne held in Paris in 1925, is primarily found on commercial buildings of the late 1920s and the 1930s in America. At the auditorium, the abstraction of forms, the geometric stacking of parts, and the extravagant stylized "modern" decorative treatment are characteristics of Art Deco.

In March 1927, Shreveport's city council placed a $500,000 bond issue on the ballot asking voters to fund construction of a municipal auditorium; the vote passed with an overwhelming majority. The auditorium was conceived as a memorial honoring Americans who had fought in World War I and a venue for theatrical productions and public gatherings. A long limestone panel across the facade inscribed with the words "Dedicated To Those Who Served In The World War" proclaimed its memorial role. The building's cornerstone was laid on February 3, 1929, and the dedication took place on November 11, 1929, the eleventh anniversary of Armistice Day.

The auditorium is located on the southwest edge of downtown, bordering a formerly residential neighborhood and one block away from where Sam and William were raised as children. The building is a massive symmetrical building in a composition of large and small blocks that gives an indication of the interior spaces and their use.

Municipal Memorial Auditorium. *Photo by Guy W. Carwile.*

At the center front, the lobby is set forward from the body of the building, is five bays wide with five sets of entrance doors, and is framed by slightly projecting vertical pier-like elements. These piers, which encase secondary staircases that give access to the ballroom above the entrance lobby, conclude with limestone banners with inscriptions and stylized eagles, popular motifs at the time for civic buildings. Lower recessed wings, which flank this central section, contain municipal meeting rooms. The mass of the auditorium rises behind the gable-fronted facade. The building is constructed mostly of red brick in a Flemish and in English bond on structural clay tile over a reinforced concrete frame, though the base is granite. Structural steel is used for the long-span trusses crossing the auditorium space and to support the seating risers.

The auditorium departs from the literal Italian Romanesque of the Kings Highway Christian Church into a more abstracted expression in the decorative potential of combining brick, stone, and terra-cotta. The central section of the facade is the most elaborately ornamented, where seven courses of brick with alternating long face blocks (stretchers) and headers alternate with two courses of headers, which give horizontal emphasis. These headers project and recede to give an extraordinary textural quality to the walls. The effect is most dramatic when viewed from afar rather than close-up. The horizontal patterning of the walls is balanced by the verticality of the doors and, above them, the large steel-framed casement windows that open from the ballroom.

The principal entrance to the lobby is through five pairs of decorative steel-grille security gates in front of paneled doors that are framed by a tall limestone surround with horizontal reveals to increase their monumentality. Above them are bulky limestone brackets carrying diminutive limestone balconies in front of the multi-light ballroom windows. This central section of the facade concludes with a massive entablature carrying the dedication inscription and incorporating the building's most elaborate enrichment. A row of eleven eight-pointed stone stars are outlined in terra-cotta with marble accents and filled with geometric and floral motifs; similar eight-pointed stars occur throughout the building. Although the facade teems with ornament, the effect is not restless, but disciplined by the repetition of pilasters, friezes, and patterns to give the impression of an enormous intricate tapestry. Along the parapet is a continuous row of five-pointed stars, each set within a circle, a simplified version of the American Legion emblem (see Plate 2).

Rather than finishing abruptly at an angle, the corners of the facade's central section are chamfered, as are the end wings. Consequently, the building appears to curve around to its sides, which helps alleviate the sense of its physical mass. The sides of the building are more or less identical and typically are less elaborate. Above each set of three upper windows is a roundel surrounding a geometric cast-iron grille which allows fresh air to enter the attic after the accumulated hot air is vented. This section is articulated by five colossally scaled pilasters that relate to the scale of the auditorium housed within. The modular quality of this central element was necessary because the initial design had only three bays, with the option to add a bay, which was done in order to increase seating capacity. At the auditorium's rear, the tall fly loft rises above the stage, and lower wings, similar in height and exterior character to those at the front, contain dressing rooms. Sam gave interest to the fly loft, which is usually a plain box-like shape, by articulating its height with four full-height pilasters each capped with a limestone scupper.

Inside, the lobby creates a grand sense of occasion with its open beams and pendant Art Deco–styled light fixtures in bronze and brass. Sam designed these, and the Bailey Reynolds Company of Kansas City manufactured them. Perhaps in part to save money or because it is particularly hard-wearing, the lobby floor and the concourse off of it are of colored concrete instead of the usual terrazzo or stone, which made it the earliest major building in Louisiana to feature colored concrete. The lobby gives way to a foyer (concourse) and then the vast auditorium. These interior spaces were designed to transport the audience from their daily routine into a more glamorous or exciting world. Built shortly after Shreveport's Strand Theater (designed by New Orleans architect Emile Weil), which opened in 1925 and is located just a few city blocks away, the auditorium was planned to accommodate more than that theater's original 2,250 seating capacity. Initially, the auditorium had a seating capacity of nearly 5,000, but over the years, wider seats (from seventeen inches to twenty inches), accessibility requirements, and fire-code restrictions have reduced this to about 3,300. Drawings for the auditorium do not indicate if there was a separate entrance for black patrons, as was often the case for public buildings in this era of racial segregation, but they do show that the "colored" restrooms for both men and women were on the southeast side of the second floor, the balcony level, and that these restrooms have fewer fixtures than those for whites. It was usual in this time period for black patrons to be restricted to balcony seating.

As Shreveport's largest indoor venue, the auditorium was planned to be multipurpose, able to accommodate theatrical and musical performances, motion pictures, conventions, and athletic events. Removable seating on the arena floor, which is wood, allowed for stage performances and conventions or athletic events. Fixed seating is on two balconies. The seats originally had cast-iron end panels decorated with the American Legion emblem and garlands. The most visually striking element in the auditorium is the large coffered ceiling with nine light fixtures based on an eight-pointed star. A suspended acoustical ceiling was installed below the ornate original when the auditorium was air-conditioned in 1956, but was removed in the 1990s. Sam was the architect for the 1956 renovation. The interior is peppered with arabesque details executed in plaster, a material commonly used to decorate theater interiors because of its relatively lightweight nature and ability to be molded inexpensively into elaborate shapes.

The auditorium is known more for its role accommodating a wide range of significant public events and entertainments than for its equally significant design. From 1948 to 1960 it was the host location of Shreveport radio station KWKH's nationally broadcast program, *Louisiana Hayride,* which was pivotal in launching the careers of Hank Williams, Kitty Wells, Johnny Cash, and Elvis Presley. It was the auditorium's relationship to the *Hayride* that led to its designation as a National Historic Landmark (NHL) by the National Park Service in 2008. The *Hayride* was second in importance only to the *Grand Ole Opry* in Nashville, and the auditorium was the entertainment mecca for the Louisiana, Texas, and Arkansas corner. The auditorium's imposing size and appearance, interior grandeur, and modern facilities communicated Shreveport's

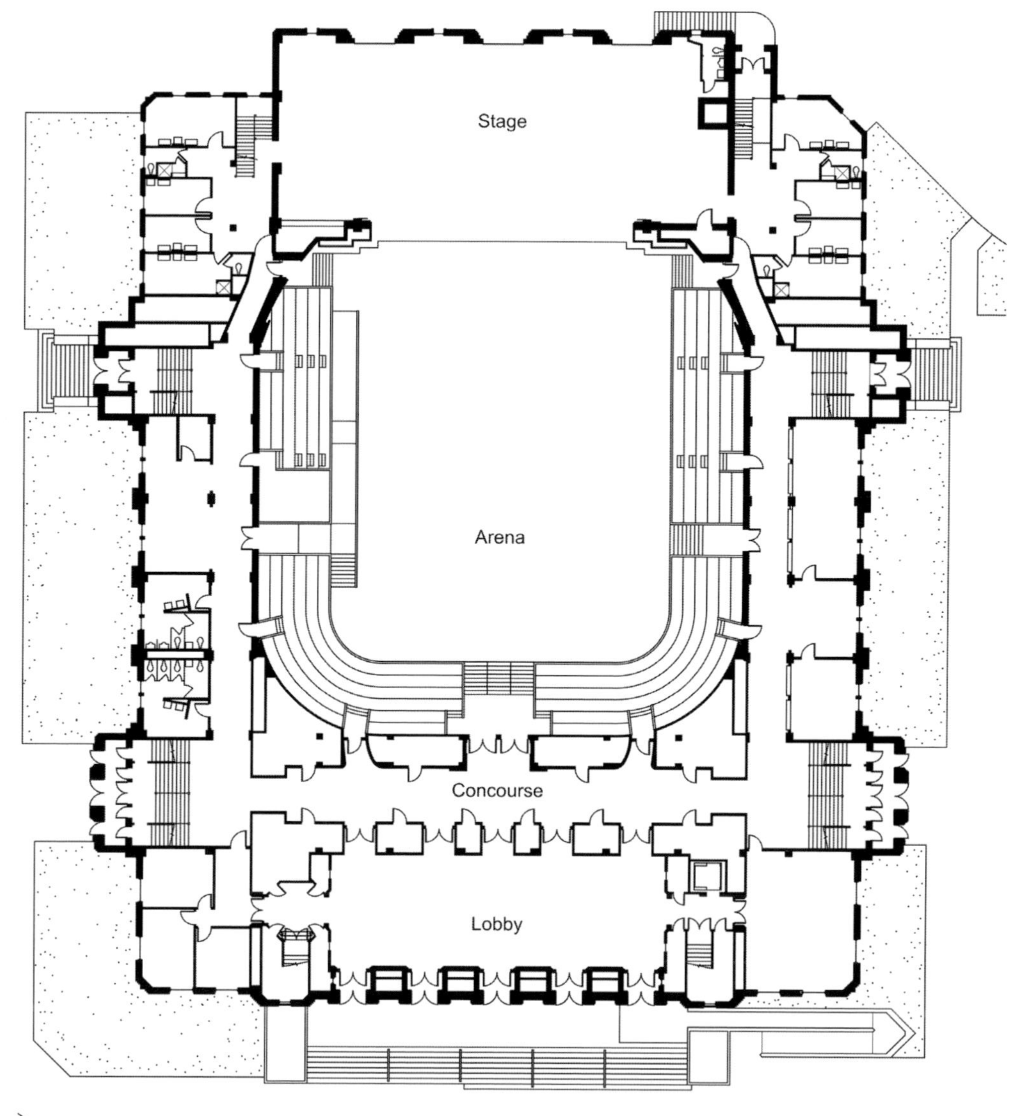

First Floor Plan

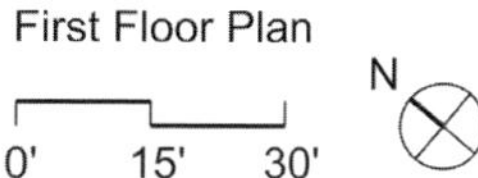

Municipal Memorial Auditorium, first-floor plan.
Drawing by Guy W. Carwile.

Panoramic view of Big Chain Store, Fairfield.
Courtesy of Emily (Mimi) Wile Hussey.

aspirations as a major regional and cultural center. The oil city had come of age.

In 1975 the auditorium was included in a photographic exhibition in New York City as one of fifty-four buildings representing the best of American Art Deco. Although often identified as an Art Deco building, the auditorium is too blocky and insufficiently angular and sleek, its walls are too textured, and the ornamental motifs remain too close to historic Venetian and Moorish sources than Art Deco's typically stylized and colorful forms. An acknowledgment of the Mediterranean medievalizing tendencies of the auditorium is revealed in a letter (January 16, 1974) from Olschner to Sam where he comments that in this building Sam was "using brickwork patterns as a Spaniard would."[9] Yet, despite Sam's facility with the expressive qualities of brick and ornament at this stage of his career, his design preferences were already shifting to something less rich.

As for Art Deco, Sam's design for the Big Chain grocery store in the Fairfield neighborhood, designed the same year as the auditorium, exhibits all the appropriate and popular stylized floral patterns, zigzags, and brilliant color. Big Chain's owner Ed Wile told Sam that he wanted Big Chain Fairfield to look like a World's Fair. Apparently Sam did not like the decorative appearance of the Big Chain store any more than he appreciated the over-elaborate qualities of the Municipal Auditorium.[10]

BIG CHAIN STORE, FAIRFIELD

Only five years separates Feibleman's department store in downtown Shreveport from the Big Chain Company supermarket, but the contrast is startling. Instead of a handsome Renaissance palace, Sam fashioned the Big Chain store in brick and plastered it with Art Deco ornament. In addition to its stylish facade, the design and siting of the Fairfield Big Chain store signals the impact the automobile was beginning to have on shopping habits. Designed in 1928, the store opened in 1929.

The Big Chain company was founded in 1922 by Ed Wile as a subsidiary of the Wiener-Loeb Grocery Company that had been established in 1896 by Sam Jr. (father of Sam and William), William B. Wiener Sr., and Leon B. Loeb. In 1908 at the age of twelve, Wile, a cousin of Sam and William, started working at the grocery as a delivery boy. In 1923, Wile and a group of investors, among whom were Louie Levy (relative of Babette Levy, who married William) and Dewey R. Sandifur, purchased the Wiener-Loeb Grocery Company and merged it with Big Chain. The new company's first store (1922) was located in the Levy Building at the junction of Texas and Edwards streets (the Petroleum Tower of 1958 now occupies this site). A year later the store moved to Texas and Market streets. By 1924 another grocery store had opened at 404 Marshall Street and a bakery was established at 503 Travis Street. All these stores were in downtown Shreveport. The first store in Shreveport's developing suburbs came in 1926 at 3016 Highland Avenue (now altered) and was followed in 1928 by Sam's design for Jones, Roessle, Olschner and Wiener on the 1500 block of Fairfield Avenue. Big Chain, which grew to a total of eight stores in Shreveport and Bossier City, was for many years the premier supermarket in Shreveport, and the Wieners were the architects for all their stores from 1928 on. Plans and photographs of the Big Chain stores were widely published in national books and trade magazines as exemplary solutions to supermarket design. In 1956 the Kroger Company purchased Big Chain.

The Fairfield Big Chain grocery store was the centerpiece of a strip of four shops—the other three were leased to a drugstore, a beauty salon, and a laundry—that were unified by their Art Deco design. A service station, in a low-key cottage style, stood at the end of the row. Physically the grocery store was much wider and taller than its flanking buildings, and its facade presented a dazzling display of brickwork, terra-cotta, zigzag cornices, tinted stucco, and lavender, blue, and green glazed tiles, to create, as the trade journal *Chain Store Review* noted, "a striking effect that would serve to make the store a landmark and guiding point for the residential section in which it is located."[11] While maintaining the residential scale of the neighborhood, the row of shops was conspicuous, flamboyant, and in a style that conveyed modernity. Although today the former grocery store's facade is masked by a metal false front to serve its current occupant (a paint store), the smaller end shops show some of their original ornamentation; the service station has been demolished. Two stylized "flames" that stood atop Big Chain's parapet were saved by Bill Wiener Jr.; one was placed in the rear garden of the house of former Shreveport mayor John Hussey and his wife, Emily (known as Mimi), who was Ed Wile's youngest daughter, and the other behind the Broadmoor shopping center of the former Big Chain Broadmoor, which can still be seen near the corner of Youree and Ockley drives at Albert Avenue.

Big Chain's interior was as contemporary and glamorous as its exterior, with floors of polished terrazzo, mirrors, colorful fittings, and display and refrigerated cases from the Hussmann Refrigerator Company. The store's interior was so up-to-date that the Hussmann Company featured it, with six photographs, in a full-page advertisement for its products in the trade journal *Chain Store Age.*[12]

Shops, Shopping, and Parking

As well as in its novel style, the store broke new ground in other significant ways. As *Chain Store Review* noted, Big Chain was "not only a new store but actually a new commercial center."[13] It was in embryonic form a shopping strip, laid out in a linear fashion and providing several shopping resources in one location.

Besides creating a retail complex, the grocery store itself embodied changing grocery-shopping practices. *Chain Store Review* described Big Chain as a complete food market "equipped and stocked to meet all the food needs of the housewife."[14] Besides gathering most food needs in one location—from produce, to meat, to baked goods—the store included a delicatessen, a rotisserie, and offered pre-prepared meals, which were displayed on steam tables. Such comprehensive offerings, along with the improvements in home refrigeration that allowed foods to be maintained for longer periods, increasingly resulted in bulk buying, and weekly shopping trips began to take precedence over daily errands. Consequently, transportation of such increasingly cumbersome purchases needed to be addressed, and the solution was the addition of parking areas for automobiles. *Chain Store Review* approvingly commented that "emphasis has been placed on convenience to motorists."[15] The store and its flanking shops were set back from the sidewalk to provide a row of parking spaces in front. Underscoring the centrality of the automobile to emerging shopping patterns, the gas station was conveniently located at the end of the strip.

Parking lots had begun to accompany newly constructed commercial strips in many towns, though usually they were located to the rear. And while the Big Chain complex also provided a large parking area to one side of the row of shops, the provision of spaces in front emphasized convenience to motorists and illustrated the changing nature of shopping from the 1920s on. Country Club Plaza in Kansas City, which opened in 1923, is thought to be the first shopping center to provide designated parking areas, and Westwood Village in Los Angeles soon followed in 1929. The Park and Shop complex designed by Arthur B. Heaton, which opened in 1931 in the Cleveland Park neighborhood of Washington, D.C., is often held up as the eastern prototype for the auto-oriented shopping center, and while it is a larger complex with a more expansive forecourt parking area than Big Chain, the Shreveport example precedes it. Big Chain Fairfield was one of the earliest in the nation. Architectural historian Richard Longstreth has noted that when the Big Chain complex opened it "represented one of the most advanced designs for a store group oriented to motorists to be found outside California."[16] As the numbers and use of automobiles increased in the 1930s the provision of parking spaces for all kinds of activities became a pressing challenge for architects and town planners. For a shopping center, Sam addressed the issue again in the Big Chain Broadmoor store that opened in 1941.

MUNICIPAL AIRPORT (DOWNTOWN) AND ANDRESS MOTOR COMPANY

As the 1920s came to an end, Shreveport could boast two more handsome Art Deco buildings. One was Sam's design for Jones, Roessle, Olschner and Wiener for a terminal building for the Municipal Airport (later known as the Downtown Airport), which opened on July 13, 1931. In 1929, Shreveport's voters approved a bond issue to build the airport on the site of the former Free State Plantation just to the north of downtown. Art Deco proved popular for airport terminals nationwide from the late 1920s into the 1930s. Shreveport's building was stylishly sleek and angular, with a smooth white stuccoed exterior, and lively zigzag yellow and black terra-cotta ornament that seemed to visually represent the speed and modernity of air travel. Now demolished, the terminal building was symmetrical in outline and dominated in its center by a sixty-foot observation tower built of aluminum panels on a steel frame. Setbacks at the top of the tower enclosed a revolving beacon. A waiting room occupied the center of the ground floor of the terminal, with a restaurant and kitchen to one side and offices and space for an ambulance, a fire truck, and a mail-sorting room on the other. In April 1931, the Department of Commerce's Aeronautics Branch sent Sam a set of Airway information bulletins and the necessary forms to give the airport an official rating.[17]

The other building, the gloriously decorated former brick-and-tile Andress Motor Company on Crockett Street, also opened in 1931. Although there is little documentary evidence, this too is acknowledged as a design by Sam for Jones, Roessle, Olschner and Wiener. Colorful Art Deco ornament in a wide band between the building's lower and upper floors is modeled in high relief with zigzags and scrolls, similar to the Big Chain Fairfield store's

Municipal Airport (Downtown).
Courtesy of LSU-Shreveport Archives and Special Collections.

ornamentation, and stylized Ionic piers provided an eye-catching frame for the display windows. The building is empty and in a deteriorating state.

In New Orleans another Jones, Roessle, Olschner and Wiener commercial building is given an equally colorful Art Deco treatment, and like the Andress Company, it is empty and in poor condition. This is the former General Laundry at 2512 St. Peter Street, which opened in 1930. Because the structure is in New Orleans, it may have been a design of Jones or Roessle, but if so, its decoration with bands of zigzag multicolored glazed terra-cotta is remarkably like that of Andress and Big Chain.

Looking Ahead

The stock market crash in October 1929 and the subsequent Great Depression had a profound impact nationwide on the building trades and, consequently, for architects. For William the year 1929 marked his graduation from the University of Michigan. He decided to continue his architectural studies in the graduate program at Columbia University, but disenchanted with the traditional Beaux-Arts curriculum then being taught, he left before completing a degree. William returned to Shreveport in 1930 and joined the office of Jones, Roessle, Olschner and Wiener, but work was becoming scarce, and in 1932 he was hired by Green, LaRoche and Dahl in Texas. In the meantime he had been applying for traveling fellowships. In 1931 he placed second in a design competition sponsored by his alma mater, the University of Michigan.[18] However, the extraordinary European-influenced modernist design he submitted in 1932 for the George C. Booth Traveling Fellowship Competition did not place, perhaps proving too radical for the committee. In 1933 William returned to Shreveport and established his own architectural practice. He worked out of his parents' house on Austen Place until 1935 when he moved into suite 1401–2 of the Slattery Building. One year later he rose a couple of floors to Suite 1628 of the building, and he remained there until he moved to the Commercial National Bank Building in the early 1950s.

Sam, meanwhile, was becoming increasingly fascinated with the new architecture of Europe, which he saw illustrated in architectural journals. In 1931, he revisited the Continent to see the buildings firsthand. This trip was not so much a leisurely tour, but more a pilgrimage, a voyage of discovery, and the buildings he visited and architects he spoke to all had a major impact on his work. If his buildings of the 1920s were dominated by brick, the 1930s were quite different, and the new decade saw Sam and William in the ranks of the most innovative architects in America.

In the difficult economy of the 1930s, the brothers understood that the key to growing their respective businesses was to have their work visible to the public. Since the American Institute of Architects' (AIA) code of ethics forbade architects from advertising, the only way they could showcase their work was through publication in the periodicals. In the 1920s these were primarily regional publications or trade journals, but in the 1930s the brothers gained recognition in national and international journals. Many of their projects were published and have established a primary record of Sam and William's work and careers. Design awards were equally important, and they garnered several over the course of the years, including an Architectural Record Award of Excellence in 1956 for the James Muslow House as one the most significant houses of the year in the nation. But first they had to navigate the uncertain economy of the Great Depression.

3

GOING MODERN IN THE 1930s

In 1932 Henry-Russell Hitchcock and Philip Johnson's book *The International Style* and the accompanying exhibition held at the Museum of Modern Art (MOMA) in New York City largely introduced European modern architecture to the United States. The book began with a short text outlining the formal and aesthetic qualities of modernism and was followed by 138 photographs and drawings of buildings that conformed to the definition. The social ideals and principles that informed much of European modernism, however, were not part of the thesis. In his introduction to the book, art historian and then director of MOMA Alfred Barr claimed that "there exists today a modern style as original, as consistent, as logical, and as widely distributed as any in the past. The authors have called it the International Style."[1] Barr's claim of wide distribution in 1932 in the United States was an exaggeration. While pockets of modern houses by Rudolf Schindler and Richard Neutra existed in Los Angeles and Southern California and there were several buildings on the East Coast, there were few modernist buildings nationwide, and Hitchcock and Johnson could muster only eleven images of six American buildings to illustrate, and more than half of the architects for these buildings were immigrants from Europe. Knowledge of the new European architecture became somewhat more widespread after a small number of photographs drawn from the MOMA exhibition were shown in eleven cities, although the farthest south that the exhibition reached east of the Rocky Mountains was Cincinnati (it went to Los Angeles). The exhibition concluded its tour in 1934.

On a more popular level, modern design was spread through the Century of Progress Fair held in Chicago in 1933–34, which included a special section featuring experimental houses, notably the House of Tomorrow and the Crystal House designed by George Fred Keck with steel framing and glass walls. But these were speculative projects and hardly expected to be replicated.

Even before the Chicago fair was held and Hitchcock and Johnson's book was published, Sam and William Wiener had become fascinated by the new architecture of Europe. Buildings by European modernists were featured occasionally in American architectural journals, notably *Architectural Forum* and *Architectural Record.* For example, in 1928, the former published photographs of modern houses in Paris designed by Robert Mallet Stevens and housing by Walter Gropius in 1930. *Architectural Record* fairly regularly included tiny images of European buildings in a section titled "Foreign Periodicals," reviewed by Henry-Russell Hitchcock. Here, tantalizingly and all too briefly, the Wieners saw a new architecture and a visual language that expressed modern life and the twentieth century. Their inspiration was not filtered, for example, through the buildings at the Chicago fair but inspired directly by those in Europe.

The Second European Voyage, 1931

In 1931 Sam decided he must return to Europe to see firsthand the modern buildings that he had seen illustrated in architectural journals. Only rarely did the journals feature more than a single black-and-white image of any given building, which limited an understanding of structure, materials, details, and interiors, and, of course, color. Thus, Sam and his wife, Marion, who were joined during a part of their trip by architect and friend Theodore Flaxman, embarked on a voyage through Europe. William was in the graduate architecture program at Columbia University and did not accompany his brother this time.

Most of their time was spent in Germany, Holland, and France, but they also visited Denmark, Sweden, Portugal, and Spain. They rented a car and "drove all over."[2] Much of what they chose to see were buildings that had been featured or mentioned in *Architectural Forum, Architectural Record,* and *Pencil Points* journals. They were particularly interested in residential work, and in Stuttgart they visited the Weissenhof Housing estate, studying prototypical examples of houses by Mies van der Rohe, Peter Behrens, Le Corbusier, and J. J. P. Oud. In Berlin they attended the 1931 Building Exposition, which featured works by many of the same architects as the Stuttgart estate, and sought out architect Erich Mendelsohn and visited his Universum Cinema (1928). Sam and Marion visited the Bauhaus at Dessau, where Sam spoke with Walter Gropius, who had designed the school and several of the houses occupied by Bauhaus teachers. Later, in 1937, Gropius immigrated to the United States, to teach at the Graduate School of Design (GSD) at Harvard University and introduce the principles of European modernism in the American architectural curriculum. They saw the just-completed I. G. Farben factory in Frankfurt. In Holland, the birthplace in the early 1920s of the De Stijl movement, Sam discovered that primary colors played an essential role in a building's composition. He met Gerrit Rietveld, architect of the Schroder House (1924) in Utrecht, a house that had supports and window bars highlighted in red, yellow, or black. Willem Dudok's Bathhouse (1920) and his just completed City Hall, both in Hilversum, were also on the tour. In Sweden, Marion remembered they saw the City Hall of 1923 in Stockholm, and she recalled they visited a house on the outskirts of Paris, which probably was Le Corbusier's Villa Savoie.

An invaluable record of their trip is revealed in the postcards Flaxman purchased that featured many of his favorite buildings. Flaxman especially liked the curved streamlined forms of Dudok's Bijenkorf department stores in The Hague (1926) and Rotterdam (1930), and those of the Schocken stores in Stuttgart (1928) and Chemnitz (1930) designed by Mendelsohn. The influence of these buildings was particularly powerful in Flaxman's later designs in Shreveport. In Rotterdam, Flaxman visited the Van Nelle tobacco, tea, and coffee factory completed by the firm of Brinkman and Van der Vlugt in 1931, and he was thrilled to find that he could take a tour of the building. Flaxman recalled that the person who led the tour spoke perfect English.[3] The factory was published in Norman N. Rice's *T-Square Club* in 1931. As well as acquiring postcard views of the buildings he saw, Flaxman also sketched several of the buildings in a small notebook; it is not known what happened to the notebook after Flaxman's death.

The trip, then, was not the typical European tour visiting cathedrals and castles, but instead a modern Grand Tour in the tradition of those made in the eighteenth and nineteenth centuries to Italy and Greece by aspiring architects in search of ancient classical monuments. For this tour, the buildings were modern, not historic. It was a pilgrimage that Marion Wiener described as a "voyage of discovery" and affirmed "we *had* to go. We couldn't see modern architecture here in America and they weren't teaching it in the architecture schools. There was no other way we could find out about it."[4] According to Flaxman, who studied architecture at Rice University in Houston, but was speaking in general about the conservative nature of American architecture programs rooted in Beaux-Arts classicism, "we had the urge to clean our shelves of classical training." And he recalled "to change then took a real effort on the part of young architects."[5]

On their return to Shreveport, Sam and Flaxman applied what they had learned. (Flaxman's architectural work is discussed in chapter 9.) The formal, functional, and material aspects of progressive European work seemed to them perfectly attuned to modern modes of living. Their buildings are not copies, but rather a distillation and reinterpretation for a southern American city. What is important is that they had insisted on going to the source—to see the buildings.

EL KARUBAH CLUB HOUSE

The first building Sam designed on his return to Jones, Roessle, Olschner and Wiener was the El Karubah Club House for the Shriners, which is located on the south shore of Cross Lake, just west of Shreveport.[6] The building is a first step away from the rich tactile and ornamented surfaces of the Municipal Auditorium and the Big Chain Fairfield store. Instead it emphasizes form and the expression of function, ideas Sam had absorbed from the buildings he saw on his European trip, especially the Bauhaus in Germany with the various structures—teaching and studio block, administration building, and dormitory—each clearly expressing its particular purpose. The lively outline of the building, especially the zigzag shape of the first-floor dining room overlooking the lake, reveals the impact of the expressionistic work of Willem Dudok he had seen in Holland. Ornamentation resides mostly in the manipulation of the brick to express form rather than ornamental detail. The railings of the terrace above the dining-room elevation convey a nautical image recalling the prow of a ship, appropriate for the lakeside location. It is likely the railings were inspired by similar ones he had seen in Europe, including those on the Schroder House. That most of the brick building was painted white enhanced the water-related imagery. Although it has suffered later modifications and additions, including the loss of a one-story screened porch to the side of the dining room, the clubhouse's original central portion survives. The building's crisp angular forms are not disturbed by intricate ornament; instead, the functional elements—railings, steel-casement windows, and the brick staircase tower with its vertical window—enriched

El Karubah Club House.
Courtesy of LSU-Shreveport Archives and Special Collections.

Weekend House, Cross Lake.
Courtesy of LSU-Shreveport Archives and Special Collections.

the building. Sam first used steel-framed casement windows here, as well as a screened porch for functional and aesthetic effect.

WEEKEND HOUSE, CROSS LAKE

In 1933, William Wiener with Sam (although Sam was not credited in the article published in *Architectural Forum* in 1934) designed a weekend house for their families on the north shore of Cross Lake, just outside Shreveport. The article's anonymous author exclaimed "This is Le Corbusier's 'machine for living' in full flower."[7] The house's inspiration clearly was Le Corbusier's Villa Savoie of 1929–31, which was featured in Hitchcock and Johnson's *The International Style* of 1932 and which Sam probably visited while in Europe in 1931. Like its prototype, the principal living area of the Cross Lake house was elevated on pilotis with parking space beneath. The exterior, sleek and smooth with white walls and a flat roof, was defined by its extended horizontal form and, lifted off the ground, the house seemed to defy gravity. The Villa Savoie was a prototype for a house that addressed, among other things, cheap and efficient structural systems through concrete framing, and healthful and efficient living. The relationship between health and architectural design was an increasing concern from the 1920s not just in Europe, but was also addressed by such architects as Richard Neutra in California, as most evident in the house he completed for physician and naturopath Philip Lovell and his family in Los Angeles that came to be known as the Health House. By lifting the house's main living areas from the ground to the second level, a house's occupants could escape unhealthy ground-level air and damp, and bring them into living spaces filled with sun, light, and fresh air through large windows. While getting sufficient exposure to the sun was an important consideration in northern Europe, avoiding it was more important in Louisiana in the summer. But a raised living area would better allow fresh air and breezes to flow through the house. And lifted above the landscape with a view across the water, like the terrace of the El Karubah Club House, the house communicated a sense of freedom.

At ground level an automobile could be parked in the shade underneath the raised living area—in the Villa Savoie the automobile was accommodated on the ground floor. The ground level also included a small bachelor apartment composed of a bedroom and bath for William. This space initially was planned as a storage room, but was commandeered for an additional bedroom without adding square footage. The rooms on the upper story of the long narrow house were organized in a linear progression in a staggered plan. On one side were the entrance staircase, kitchen, bathroom, and a master bedroom, and on the other, the lake side, a second bedroom, and a combination living-dining room. At its western end the house concluded with a screened porch. The exterior freestanding staircase, set in a reentrant angle of the house, gave access to the living-dining room and, through an adjacent door, to the kitchen. The house was sited with its long side toward the lake and, because of the staggered plan, offered views to the water from the living-dining room and the screened porch.

The house's upper walls, like those of the Villa Savoie, appeared as a skin stretched tight around the skeleton. These walls were of wood stud construction with wood sheathing and covered with white-painted stucco. To keep it from cracking, the stucco was divided into small panels by strips of sheet metal to form expansion joints. Steel-framed casement windows replaced the original double-hung windows in wooden frames. When an extension to the house was built a few years later, the casement windows were not inserted into the walls, but instead projected slightly from the surface to give a more waterproof construction. At the same time this indicated that the walls were not load bearing and visually reduced the sense of thickness and therefore the mass and weight of the wall.

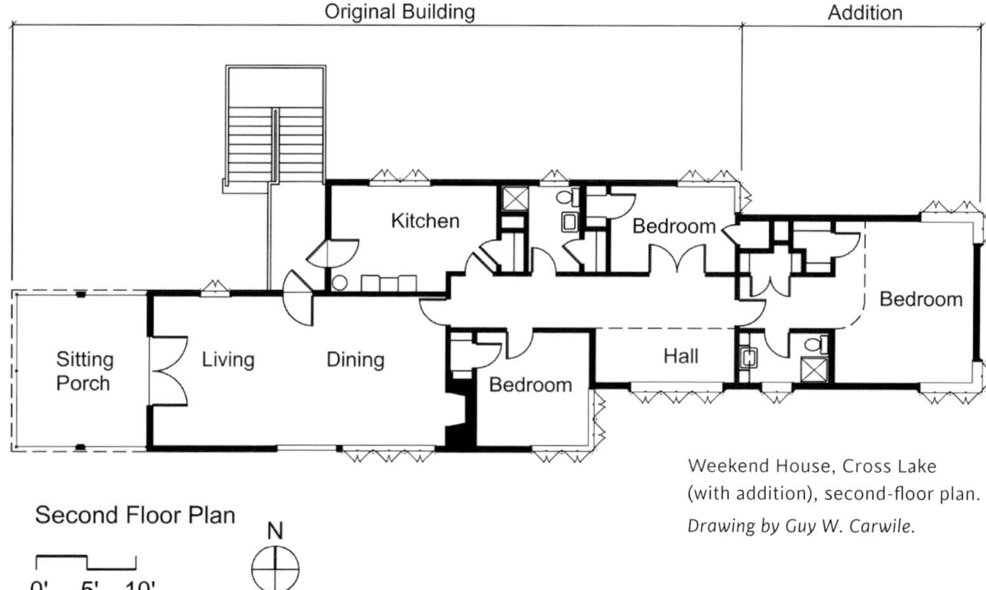

Weekend House, Cross Lake (with addition), second-floor plan. *Drawing by Guy W. Carwile.*

Despite its radically different appearance from traditional summer cottages, the house was adapted to local conditions and building types. The *Architectural Forum* author was puzzled by the house's plan and evidently unfamiliar with the southern climate and the need for cross-ventilation. The linear plan not only recalled the familiar spatial organization of the southern shotgun house but, like that house type, it responded to the heat and humidity of the Louisiana summer in the days before modern air-conditioning. The corner windows of the bedrooms encouraged cross-ventilation, and the house's white-colored exterior walls deflected heat. The screened porch, which was often used for nighttime sleeping, could catch cooling breezes from the lake and keep out high-flying mosquitoes.

Vertical louvers were later added to the screen's west side to shade its interior from the sun.

To help ventilate the house, William and his brother Jacques installed an attic fan in the plenum (insulation) space between the ceiling and the roof of the central hall. Attic fans were not commercially available at the time, and their fan, which was constructed from an electric motor and an airplane blade, apparently did not work particularly well because it sucked out air too vigorously and was very noisy.[8] The air was expelled through a pipe, which added a nautical touch to the lakeside house. The four-foot high insulation space, particularly noticeable over the entrance where it extends to form a canopy, became a developed feature in later houses, taking on an aesthetic as well as a functional role.

Unlike the exterior and contrary to ideas about modern houses being entirely white inside and out—an assumption based on the black-and-white photographs published in journals—the interior was colorful. Sam had seen that modernist houses incorporated color at the Bauhaus and the Schroder House. William's son, Bill Wiener Jr., who spent his childhood summers at the house (Bill's grandparents spent the entire summer here because the lake made it cooler than their house in Shreveport), recalled that the living-dining room was painted light green, the hall in the center a creamy white, the bedrooms peachy-cream, the kitchen bright blue with a black door, and the trim throughout the house was a neutral color; the bathrooms, however, were white. Curtains were in a bold checkered pattern. The floors were pine, and the living-dining room's fireplace surround was slate. Lighting was recessed with incandescent bulbs. Because the modern furniture the architects wanted to complement the house was mostly unavailable, they built cabinets and chairs as well as the kitchen fixtures, and some of these were painted in the primary colors of red and blue.[9]

The Cross Lake house was sleek, taut, and planar. Seen from a distance against the lake and the sky it followed Le Corbusier's ideal of the sharp, pure line that a flat-roofed building cuts across a sky. The house was demolished in the 1980s.

I. EDWARD AND JESSAMINE THALHEIMER WILE HOUSE

As Shreveport's population increased, fashionable new residential neighborhoods were laid out south of downtown. Real-estate developers A. C. Steere and Elias Goldstein developed South Highlands and Broadmoor, which were annexed to the city of Shreveport in 1927. By 1930, the city's population had increased to 76,655, and as it continued to multiply to 98,167 by 1940, suburban growth expanded with it. It was in these neighborhoods that Sam and William designed several houses for family and friends. Among them was a young couple, Ed Wile, cousin of Sam and William, and his wife Jessamine (Jeppy). Wile was the owner of the Big Chain Grocery Company, for whom Sam had already designed the Fairfield Big Chain store.

In 1933, Ed Wile acquired a 100-by-150-foot lot in the Glenwood Park subdivision of South Highlands for his family's new home. Wile purchased the property from Colonel Alfred Wilder, who owned several acres of land bounded by Wilder Place and Line, Elmwood, and Creswell avenues. Wilder had built his house in the development in the late 1920s and subdivided the remaining land into residential lots for sale; the houses constructed there were in one of the popular period revival styles of the time. Wilder lived at 701 Wilder Place at the intersection of Dillingham and Wilder Place, and within sight of the lot he sold to Wile at 626 Wilder Place. Wile's daughter Mimi recalled that Wilder told her father that, had he known what kind of house Wile was going to build, he wouldn't have sold him the lot.[10]

Sam completed the drawings for the Wiles' house, which is credited in *Architectural Record* to Jones, Roessle, Olschner and Wiener.[11] The L-shaped house's roof is flat, its smooth upper walls are painted white, and there is no ornamentation. Horizontal windows wrap around the corners of the house, dissolving these corners and making ambiguous commonly understood ideas about structure and support. A column of industrial steel piping rather than a traditional classical column marks the entrance porch and gives the house a machinelike quality. The house makes few external references to what were then commonly shared ideas about what a house should look like. Even such a traditional feature as a front door was now tucked into a corner of the house, not the focus of the facade (see Plate 3).

This was the first modern house in the city of Shreveport, and it was under construction the same year as Chicago's Century of Progress Fair. There, several experimental houses were open for the public to explore, and apparently Shreveport's public assumed—or wanted to believe—that the Wile House too was a model or prototype for a "house of the future." Consequently people felt free to walk in and inspect it. The Wile family hired a policeman to protect their property from intruders and, according to the family, to prevent the sightseers leaving handprints on the white stuccoed walls.[12]

The facade of the first story is faced in dark red brick, but the upper floor is of wood stud construction with wood sheathing and white-painted stucco on metal lath. To prevent cracking, the stucco is divided into comparatively small panels by strips of sheet metal secured to the sheathing to form expansion joints, as at the Cross Lake house. A combination of materials—here, brick, stucco, and steel—is characteristic of Sam's work. His early work of the 1920s shows his imaginative manipulation of contrasts in texture and color, and he never lost his fondness for the expressive qualities of brick. No gutters disturb the line of the house's flat roof, and instead a cornice flashing protects its edge and two downspouts carry rain to the ground. Originally the cornice was painted bright red and the steel-casement window sashes were black. The windows are set in wood frames and project beyond the plane of the walls to give a more waterproof construction. The house appears to be composed of shifting volumes and planes through the projection of the dining room at the front and the breakfast room at the rear away from the main mass of the house and by the smooth white walls. In the photograph published in *Architectural Record* in 1934 (the photographer is not identified) the windows are open, enhancing the effect of hovering planes and emphasizing the house's lightweight, almost floating, qualities. Photographed when the sun is at an angle, the window frames form a geometric play of shadows on the walls. This image

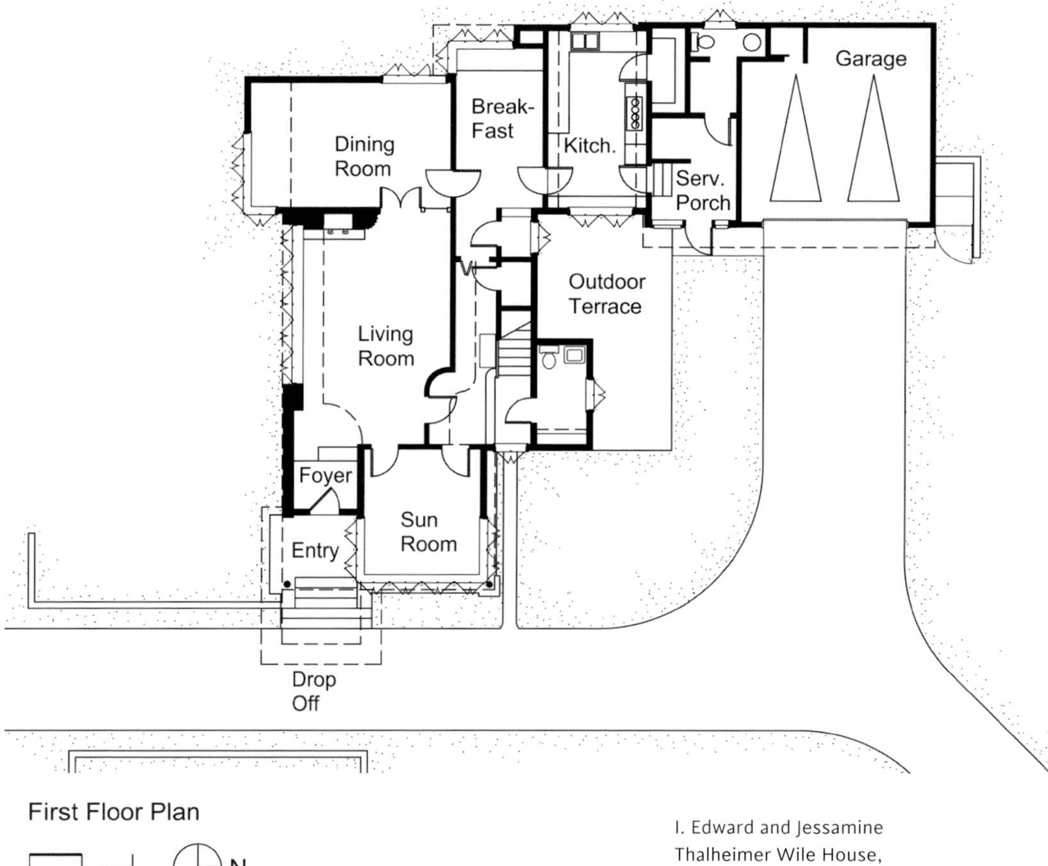

I. Edward and Jessamine Thalheimer Wile House, first-floor plan.

Drawing by Guy W. Carwile.

I. Edward and Jessamine Thalheimer Wile House.
Courtesy of LSU-Shreveport Archives and Special Collections.

of the house with open windows and transparent surfaces recalls a widely published photograph of the Schroder House with its windows opened to form a similar abstract composition. The Wile House reveals how much Sam had absorbed of the geometry of modernism.

Entrance to the house is cut into the southeast corner past a steel column that supports an extended sheltering canopy. Inside, a small foyer is merely a brief transition for space that bursts open into the large south-facing living room. The living room and, beyond it, the dining room fill the ground floor front, and above them are three bedrooms. The stair hall runs laterally to the rear of the living room. The southwest corner of the house that encloses the dining room projects slightly from the plane of the facade. Not only does it seem to anchor that front corner of house, but it allows corner windows for cross-breezes. A breakfast room, kitchen, and service area on the first floor and bathrooms on the second fill the rear wing of this essentially L-shaped house. The sunroom behind the entrance looks out to a garden.

The large living room focuses on the end of the room where a fireplace surround of limestone is streamlined with vertical fluting as it curves back to the wall and finishes with a black Carrara Glass (structural glass) top.

Curved forms are a recurring motif, linking the living room to the stair hall, in the double curve of the staircase banister, and in the lowered sections (furr or fur downs) of the ceilings; the curved furr down in the stair hall was added in the 1950s for heating and cooling ductwork. The living and dining rooms were painted in two shades of dull orange, the trim was white, and the carpet was olive green. Color application intensified the house's surface qualities, stopping and starting at an interior corner, and with a ceiling matching the color of a room's walls. A horizontal mirror over the living room's fireplace reflected the garden from the adjacent window, which created an integration of exterior with interior and the effect of a continuous panorama. At the same time, this mirror also increased interior light in this room, reducing the sense of enclosure. The use of Venetian blinds instead of curtains in the living room added to the impression of this interior as a composition of geometric planes and lines. The house was heated with radiators. When the house was air-conditioned in the 1950s, William renovated the kitchen and one of the upstairs bathrooms, and replaced the foyer's cement flooring with cork. The other floors in the house were wood.

Sam designed the garden to complement the house. The landscaping echoes the curved forms of the interior and serves as a foil for the angularity of the house. At the front a low hedge curves around and encloses the southwest corner, and at the rear a semicircular terrace fits in the reentrant angle of the L-shaped plan. Behind the garage, flower beds were organized in the form of an open-ended rectangle. Sam and William created landscape schemes for many of their projects.

Regional Adaptations

The Cross Lake and the Wile houses were the first in a series of modern houses constructed in Shreveport in the 1930s. In formal terms, each house was boldly modern and each attempted to shape the radical new forms of Europe to American domestic needs and to the specifics of the region's climate. The houses were smooth and streamlined, had no extraneous ornament, and were finished with flat roofs. Windows placed for cross-ventilation and screened porches for sitting or sleeping were just two of the ways that William and Sam adapted modernist forms to local considerations. In the houses that followed, the architects resolved issues of heat, sun, and ventilation that these two early houses with their flat roofs finishing at the walls failed to address. The European modernists were working primarily in northern Europe where shelter from intense heat and sun was not a consideration and, instead, sun and light were encouraged to enter the interior. The Wieners extended roofs to provide deep overhangs to protect interiors from the sun, and they began to use the extensions as part of the compositional aesthetic. Similarly, exterior staircases and roof ventilators were not seen as mere functional add-ons, but were integral to the overall design and to be clearly expressed. These adaptations were the first and crucial steps in formulating a modernism that responded to regional needs and made their designs so distinctive.

JOHN S. AND GLADYS PRESTON HOUSE

John S. Preston commissioned William in 1934 to design a small one-story house for him and his wife, Gladys, at 222 Jordan Street.[13] The basically square-plan house is unusual in that its exterior is of pine, horizontal V-groove (tongue and groove) siding, not smooth stucco, though the house was painted two shades of light neutral colors to reduce heat retention. The screened porch of copper mesh is a prominent feature, and here it is placed at the front of the house at the opposite corner to the entrance. The porch opened to both the living room and to the house's one bedroom at the rear. A tall air space between the ceil-

John S. and Gladys Preston House. *Courtesy of Christopher Coe.*

ing and roof gives a strong visual finish, giving the impression of a massive entablature, as implied at the Cross Lake Weekend House, also designed by William. The house has wraparound casement windows that project from the wall surface. A garage and storeroom are set well back from the front of the house to allow more windows along the sides. The Prestons' house reveals William's preference for allowing the interior functions of a house to be read more easily from the exterior. At the same time, his sophisticated eye, playing with the geometry of vertical and horizontal line and of solid and void, is added to by the horizontal wood strips on the lower part of the screened porch.

DAVID J. AND FLORENCE FLESH HOUSE

In the house for petroleum geologist David and Florence Flesh at 415 Sherwood Road, William further resolved some of the problems of sun and heat, and in doing so he created one of his boldest designs. The roof extends five feet beyond the walls to help screen the house from the sun, and the upper-story windows are pushed up under the eaves to give them maximum shade. In plan, the house has two setbacks at the front. The entrance is inserted into the setbacks and shaded by a projecting canopy that echoes the plane of the roof. The entire effect is a play of doubled horizontals balancing the height of the

building and the single narrow vertical window illuminating the stairwell. This geometry is intensified by the grid of the casement windows. Because the windows project from the wall, wrap at the corners, and the trim was dark (as were the fascias and soffits), the stuccoed walls appear as a weightless skin, an effect emphasized by making the structural steel columns visible inside the corners of the upper windows. A one-story screened porch at the rear of the house also carries a deep extension of its roof. The roof extension and high-placed windows recall the early twentieth-century work of Frank Lloyd Wright, yet the architects never claimed such influence and the rather boxy massing of the house is more reminiscent of the teachers' houses at the Bauhaus.

In plan the rooms are staggered, which allows all of them on both floors to have effective ventilation, and most of them have cross-ventilation. On the upper floor the rooms pinwheel from the central core. The master bedroom has its own small sleeping extension above the larger sitting porch on the first floor. An attic fan for venting heat from the house was incorporated into the design, and its enclosure rises from the roof to form its own miniature dwelling. Heating was probably by radiators. Lois Ann Flesh Rosenfield, who spent part of her childhood in the house before her parents moved from Shreveport, felt that the living-room fireplace, which was near the sitting porch, was strangely located and did not recall it being used.[14] It was flueless, like that of the Wile House, and used gas logs. Lois's parents did not like the openness between the living and dining rooms and installed drapery to separate the two. In the 1930s living and dining rooms usually were individually defined spaces, especially if they were large rooms, as were these, and the continuity of the two here was atypical. William specified furniture for the family, and the Herman Miller–designed dining room furniture—table, chairs, sideboard, and china cabinet—was as modern as William's design for the house. William also designed the martini service piece that was the same as the one he created for the Cross Lake Weekend House. Linoleum in a geometric pattern originally covered the foyer floor; all other floors were wood. The small bedroom was used by Lois's father for his study.

Lois described the garden as heavily planted with a fruit orchard and a sunken garden of roses, hyacinths, and dahlias (see Plate 4). A large greenhouse with servant quarters was also located in the garden. The greenhouse was re-

left

David J. and Florence Flesh House.
Photo by Guy W. Carwile.

right

David J. and Florence Flesh House.
Courtesy of Lois Flesh Rosenfield.

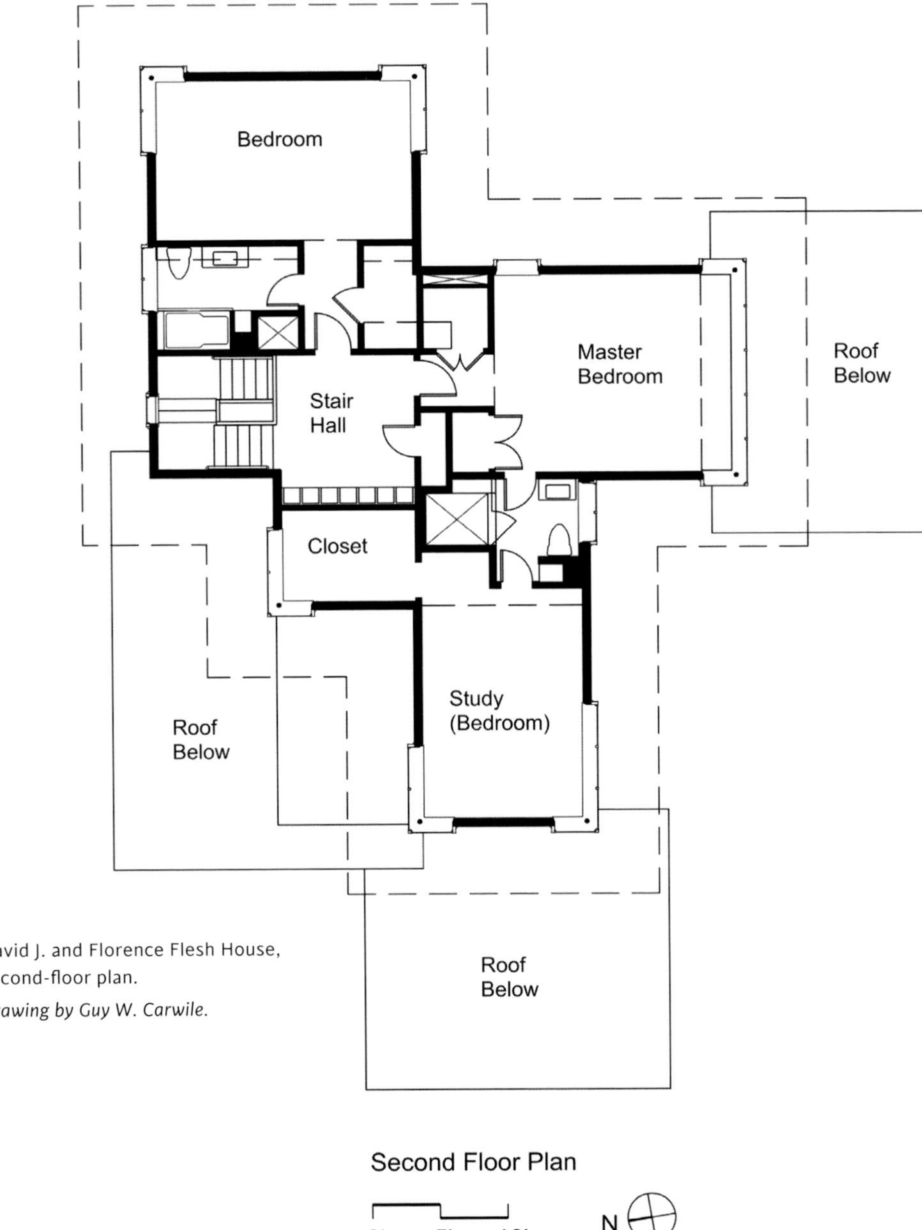

David J. and Florence Flesh House, second-floor plan.

Drawing by Guy W. Carwile.

placed by a storage structure and servant area designed by William in 1947 for the next owners, the Walker family.

Comfort, Convenience, and Pleasant Surroundings

In 1951 Sam was asked to give a talk in Memphis, Tennessee, at a regional meeting of the American Institute of Architects on the topic of the effect of modern architecture on the community. His talk, which was published in *Southern Building,* deviated somewhat from the topic, but is illuminating in understanding his lifelong approach to design.[15] Much of his presentation focused on residential design, and the views he expressed are central to understanding the houses he created from the 1930s and, later, his many designs for schools. Sam held to the principle that the provision of "comfort, convenience and pleasant surroundings" were of primary importance. Noting the discomforts of southern summers, he recommended, "We should start with a thorough study of the climatic conditions of the region and the particular site," and enumerated the various methods to alleviate sun and heat. He spoke of advances in construction, air-conditioning, and lighting, and the obligation of an architect to respond to a changing world.

In discussing the formal qualities of a building, Sam explained that historic styles, such as Colonial or classical, required that the internal plan and the placement of windows and doors conform to the design of the exterior. He enumerated such inconveniences to modern life as "a main entrance on the front center with no relation to the driveway, or recognition of the use of automobiles. Single windows had to be separated to allow space for the imitation blinds attached in an open and fixed position on the exterior walls. . . . It was soon apparent that is was necessary to decide whether to continue to plan and design in the accepted styles or to strive for results that we considered essential. That was more than twenty years ago." The opinion that a house, or any kind of building, should work from the plan out in response to the needs and comfort of its users was central to Sam's body of work.

SAMUEL G. AND MARION PFEIFER WIENER HOUSE

In the spring of 1937, Sam designed a house for himself, his wife Marion, and two sons in a new subdivision within the South Highlands area of Shreveport between Line Avenue and Gilbert Drive. The subdivision, called Pine Park due to the large number of loblolly and longleaf pine trees covering the site, was designed and recorded in January 1937 by Sam, William, and their brother, attorney Jacques L. Wiener, who provided legal counsel. The development was envisioned as a romantic park-like landscape that was to be primarily pedestrian, accessed by automobile only from the rear. The city's zoning regulations prohibited such an approach and compelled the Wieners to add vehicular access through the middle of the site, running east-west. The initial configuration of the road, which they named Longleaf Road, was rejected by the planning and zoning department because it was too narrow. Closer to a meandering path than a roadway, which was conceptually appealing to the Wieners, they resubmitted the layout with additional pavement added only at corners and intersections instead of uniformly along the length, contrary to the intent of city officials, but which was approved. As developers, each of the three brothers selected a site on which to construct a house, and the remaining sites were sold for profit. Sam built his house on Longleaf Road in the 1930s and Jacques in 1940, but William waited until 1951 to construct his house on a small lane that led from the road.

Sam initially selected lot number 54, located along the outside edge of a sweeping curve on the road. Of the eighty lots in the subdivision, this was one of the more visually conspicuous and was ideal for the bold approach to be undertaken by Sam later that year. He quickly determined that the one lot was not sufficiently large and added lot number 53 to the rear to accommodate a more elaborate garden and a tennis court, although the tennis court was never constructed. This house on Longleaf was going to serve as his magnum opus, showcasing his skill as a modern architect of note following his earlier experimentations in modernism—the Wile House of 1934 and his probable involvement on William's Weekend House (1933) on Cross Lake. Sam designed his two-story house with the traditional arrangement of public spaces on the first floor

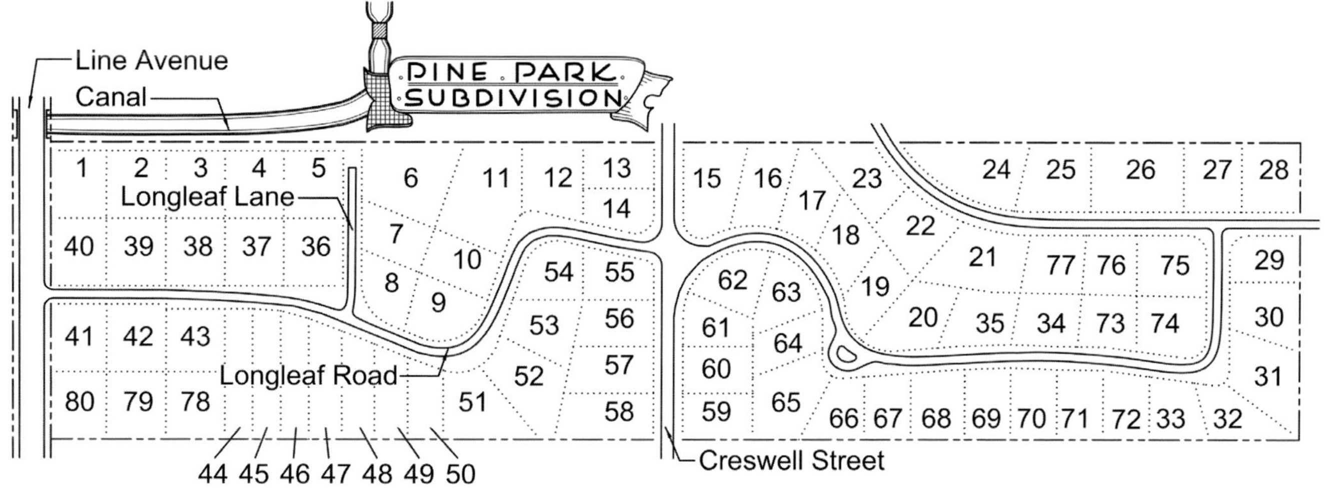

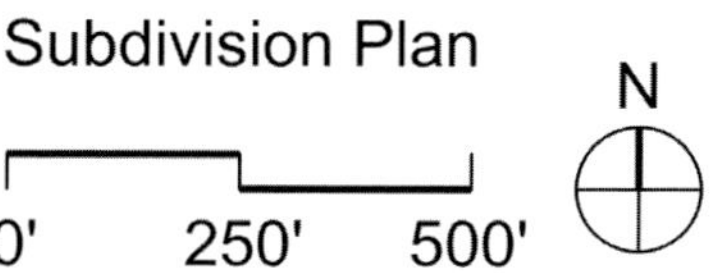

Subdivision plan of Pine Park. *Drawing by Guy W. Carwile.*

Samuel G. and Marion Pfeifer Wiener House, first-floor plan. *Drawing by Guy W. Carwile.*

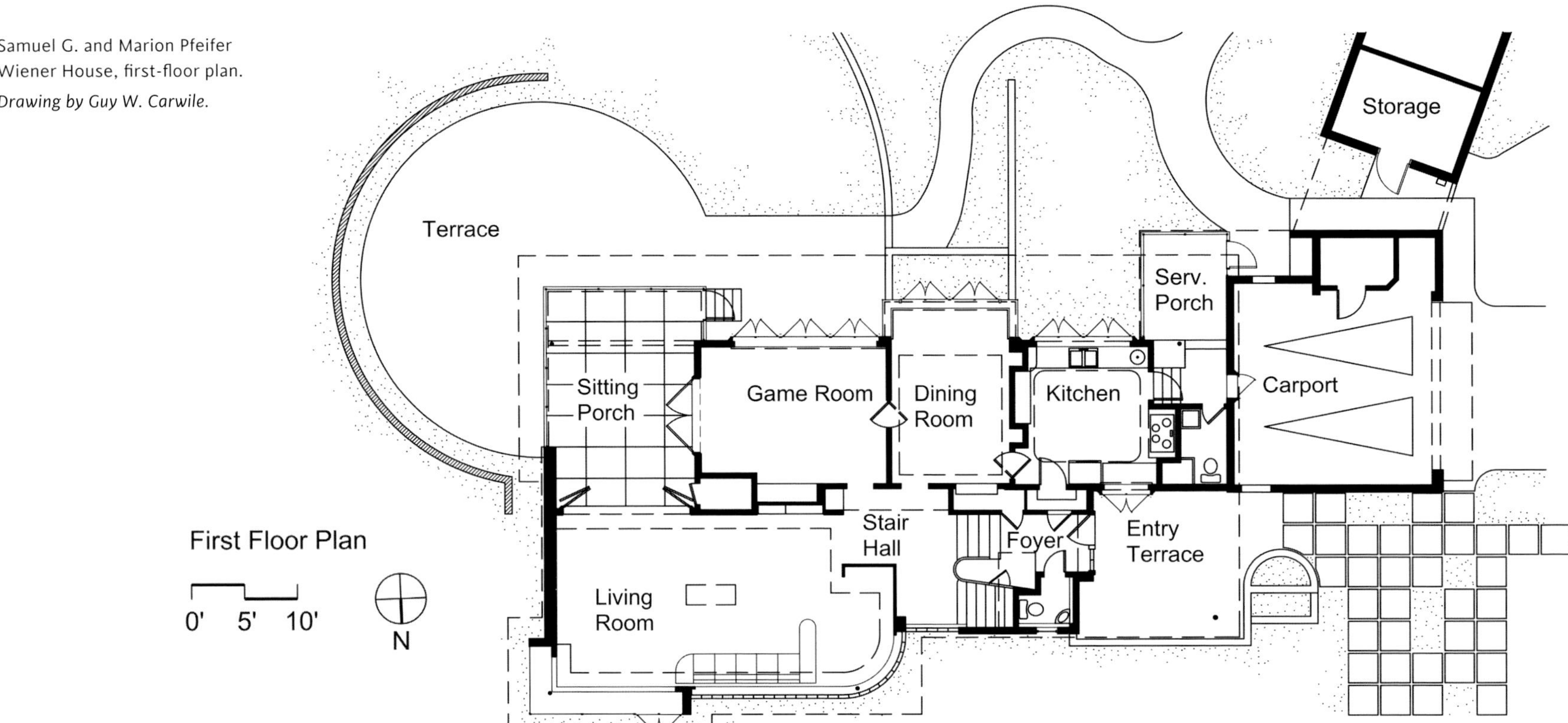

and private on the second (see Plate 11). The long dimensions of the house face north and south with the stepped main body of the structure fitting neatly within a rectangle of roughly 1:2 proportions. The orientation and proportions are ideal for a structure in the hot humid climate of Louisiana. In plan, the house is organized as a series of spaces that shear past one another, allowing entrances at or near the corners. Capping the house is a four-foot-high attic zone finished with a flat roof edged with an aluminum coping. This attic space extends seven and a half feet at the rear to shade the southern wall and windows. *Architectural Forum* noted, when it featured the house in its February 1939 issue, "The emphatic use of overhangs on much residential work in the South is one feature which gives these houses a definitely local character."[16]

The house, set on a reinforced concrete slab, is of balloon frame construction augmented by steel columns. Red brick is used on a portion of the facade at the ground story, and white cement plaster (stucco) covers the wood sheathing of the second. The stucco is divided into panels, usually less than six feet in either direction, set between reveal-less steel control strips. Sam and William preferred using reveal-less control joints to prevent the plaster from cracking, which gave the impression that the surface of the plaster was continuous. Windows are industrial steel casement, which are painted red and project beyond the surface of the cement plaster to limit the amount of condensation running down the face of the plaster. The projection of the windows reduces the sense of thickness and therefore the mass and weight of the wall, suggesting that the facade is a curtain wall as opposed to a traditional bearing wall.

At diagonally opposite corners of the house, space is hollowed out to create an entrance portico at the front and a two-story screened porch on the rear east end. The two-story-high entrance porch is carried on a single column of industrial steel that was painted bright red and forms a monumental entrance to the house. The slender column emphasizes that the house is a product of modern architecture and simultaneously references in an abstract way Louisiana's columnar Greek Revival houses, many of which have columns two stories in height. The screened porch at the rear provided an outdoor sitting area (also used for plants) as an extension of the living and game rooms. On the second floor the porch provided a space for summer sleeping. *Architectural Forum* recognized the importance of this feature, noting that it was "a climatic necessity" and further remarking, "the screens, it will be noted, have been treated not as an afterthought, but as the main element in the design."[17] This two-story porch appeared colossal because the screen's framing stands forward from the structural frame of the house. The framing was a series of lightly colored, projecting horizontal bands and receding darker verticals that blended with the screen material. In the late 1990s, the screened porches were enclosed to increase the heated livable area of the house, although the sitting porch contains a fireplace so that this room that mediates between interior and garden could be used in cool times of the year. Sadly, most of the sleeping porches the Wieners included in their residential designs have been enclosed for the same reason, reducing the passive environmental effectiveness.

Air entered the house through the numerous operable steel-casement windows on the perimeter walls and through the stacked screened porches. On the first floor, air was drawn to the open stairwell and vented to the exterior through a hopper window at the top of the well. For the heavily fenestrated second floor, air was drawn to the exterior by an attic fan positioned in a roof-mounted fan house in the circulation area between the boys' bedroom and the guest bedroom. The fan exhausted air directly to the exterior in an easterly direction and was protected by a curved-roofed fan house. The four-foot-high attic zone served as an insulation barrier separating the interior spaces from the sun-soaked roof surface.

The principal entrance to the house (there is a service door at the rear) opens to a small foyer dominated

Samuel G. and Marion Pfeifer Wiener House, stair hall. *Photo by Guy W. Carwile.*

Samuel G. and Marion Pfeifer Wiener House, boys' bedroom. *Courtesy of LSU-Shreveport Archives and Special Collections.*

by a staircase appearing to float in the open stairwell as it curves upward, which reinforces its monumentality. Glass block surrounding the door and the wood-framed glazed window over it bathes the foyer and stair with light. The staircase's guardrail (or banister) is a closed continuous surface constructed of two-inch-thick plaster and capped with Monel metal, the precursor of stainless steel.

Color played an important role in this house, more so than in those he designed for his clients. Interior colors and their placement were employed to emphasize the abstract forms and planar qualities of the house. The entrance hall was painted cream with a green wall opposite the stairs as it turned the corner into the living room, which had pale green walls, a green carpet, and a white ceiling. The game room was blue; the dining room was yellow with a white ceiling; and the kitchen had white walls, a red ceiling, apple-green trim, a terrazzo floor, built-in wood cabinets, and stainless-steel countertops and sink drain boards. A bluish-green color was employed for the walls of the principal bedroom, but the children's rooms were much brighter in primary colors of red, blue, and yellow; ceilings in the bedrooms were white. Sam finished the master bathroom with a combination of black and white tiles and a one-inch-wide red ceramic tile border to accentuate the geometric and planar design elements, and a red ceiling. The sons' bathroom was a much simpler design with white tiles on the tub fascia, base, and floor and cobalt blue tiles on the walls surrounding the tub. Following World War II, Sam removed the floor tiles and installed a wall-to-wall ceramic mosaic-tile mural of the principal north elevation of the house. Originally, the living room and master bedroom had wall-to-wall carpet, the other rooms had wood floors, and coral-colored terrazzo was used for the foyer, the stair hall, and the screened sitting porch. Terrazzo became Sam and William's preferred flooring material for houses and commercial buildings after World War II.

The flow of space from one room to another was primary, and Sam accomplished it here, as he did in his other designs, by lowering part of the ceiling (furr downs) along one wall in a room and continued it into an adjoining room. This spatial linkage was emphasized by painting the lowered ceiling element the same color in both rooms. In the 1950s, when the heating system and ductwork were modified to install air-conditioning, it was accommodated in the existing space, allowing the appearance of the interior to remain almost unchanged.

Marion Wiener decided two features of the house.[18] One was the cantilevered flower window in the corner of the living room. And it is here that the separation of structure from wall can be seen most clearly in the steel support standing freely inside the house. The shelf on which the plants rest is covered with sea-foam-green ceramic tile with drainage holes so that any water spilled while feeding the plants would be ushered to the exterior. Marion's other request was that the window in the breakfast-dining room be extended to form a rectangular bay so that it would receive more interior light and provide a better view across the garden. Marion appreciated the amount of light that the design allowed into the house.

Sam's site plan for the house and landscaping reveals that in the placement and shape of walls, terraces, and trees and plants, the garden was conceived as an extension of and complement to the house. When in Europe, Sam and Marion would have seen how the relationship of a building to its site and landscaping was integral to the designs of the architects they admired. The European modernists' use of low walls, curving terraces (a favorite of Erich Mendelsohn), trellises, and plant borders were part of their overall composition, unifying building and site, interior and exterior. Other than the curve of the living-room bay wall and the fan house on the roof, the Wiener House is composed of rectilinear forms. By contrast, curved forms dominate the garden plan. Formal access to the house, situated at a bend in the road, follows a path set at a counter-curve to the street, thus acknowledging the layout of the Pine Park subdivision. At the entrance portico there is a small paved terrace and a semicircular low brick wall enclosing some azaleas and guiding passage to the front door. The wall that outlines the living room is also curved, and this was emphasized by a line of ligustrum. An acacia tree and a bed of nandina marked the building's corner.

The extra lot they acquired for their property allowed a large garden at the front and at the rear of the house, and it is in the latter that the play of angle and curve, shape and height, and texture and color is fully exploited. By coincidence Walter Gropius's house at Dessau stood among pine trees, and the Wieners' site was dotted with pines. Sam kept several of the large pines on the site, where they form vertical counterpoints to the horizontality of the house, and the feathery texture of the pine needles contrasts with the smooth-surfaced, crisp, stuccoed walls. An undulating line of trees extending from behind the kitchen to the rear of the site veils the service yard behind the garage from the dining-room window and carries the eye through the garden. As well as two pines, the trees included, in sequence, persimmon, fig, red-bud, flowering peach and almond, pears, holly, and yaupon holly, all plants that are attuned to Shreveport's climate. To the rear of the sunroom is a semicircular paved terrace outlined by a low brick wall that is echoed just beyond by another and larger arcing brick wall bordered by a continuous row of rose bushes. From there the garden reaches back across a lawn past a couple of pine trees to a planned but unbuilt tennis court and finally to a row of pampas grass framing the property's boundary. As in the house, the flow of movement and connection was repeated in the garden, here by the use of plants and walls, and it is the essence of modernism. Sam's asymmetrical and dynamic garden design had drawn on what he saw in Europe and predates those of the California School of landscape architects, whose influence—notably that of Garrett Eckbo—informed garden design throughout the United States from the mid-1940s. Sam and William's scheme of 1954 for the Muslow House (discussed in detail in chapter 7), however, does reflect aspects of Eckbo's designs. The garden layout at the Wiener house today is similar to the original scheme.

The Sam and Marion Wiener House is one of the best preserved and least altered modern buildings in Louisiana. Here Sam most successfully resolved his experiments with materials and construction methods, climatic concerns, spatial organization, and comfort in relation to the aesthetics of modernism.

CHARLES AND LETTIE MAYER HOUSE

In 1938, attorney Charles Mayer and his wife, Lettie, asked his friend William to design a house for them with a comfortable plan. Mayer later recalled that at one point in the process he asked William about the exterior, to which William reportedly replied "We don't worry about that—we just put walls around it afterwards."[19] In many ways

Charles and Lettie Mayer House.
Courtesy of LSU-Shreveport Archives and Special Collections.

this was true of the way both Sam and William conceived a building, designing from the inside out to create rooms that worked as efficiently and comfortably as possible for their users. That a building had to function well for its occupant was a principle the European modernists held as essential to architectural design. The external characteristics of modernism gave the freedom to work from the interior out, as Sam had noted in his talk and essay of 1951.[20] At the Mayers' house the exterior reflects that more clearly than in William's previous designs.

Like the Preston House of 1934, the two-story Mayer residence has wood siding but, unlike the other boxy-shaped house, this one has a linear plan. The house is situated on a cut-off of the Red River at 907 River Road, has its entrance at one corner of the long side, and is sheltered by the overhang of the second floor. At the other end of the house, the voluminous two-story porch is screened on three sides and plays a major role in the design, which is emphasized by the massive airspace between the ceiling and the roof that extends to shade it. In Sam's house the two-story screened porch was discreetly placed at the rear of the house. William was far more willing to make it a highly visible component of the design, as he had at the Cross Lake and the Preston houses. The stair hall also is clearly expressed by the vertical window, also seen at the Sam Wiener and Flesh houses, that wraps its corner placement, as is the upper hall by a bank of four windows and its projection over the ground floor below. Windows throughout the house are grouped in banks, revealing the spaces within. The window frames, the horizontal bars on the screened porch, the prominent roof ventilator with its own flat roof, and the projections and recessions of the house's body set up an especially lively geometry. The local Booth Furniture and Carpet Company furnished the house in Danish modern light-colored wood, and the store ran notices announcing that in the local newspaper. The house has since suffered alterations.

Yandell and Frances Boatner House.

Photo by Guy W. Carwile.

HOUSES OF THE LATE 1930s

Described as an "interesting experiment" by *Architectural Forum,* William's design of a combination garage and apartment for Mrs. Robbie Ramsey was sited at the rear of a duplex apartment her son and his wife owned.[21] The two-story building with a three-bay garage on the ground level rises on brick piers, and the upper floor, which is cantilevered over the garage, is sheathed in wood siding. A freestanding staircase at one corner of the facade rises to her upper-story apartment. At the opposite end of the facade is the screened porch that is accessed from both the living room and bedroom. From the Weekend House on Cross Lake to these late-1930s residences, William increasingly makes explicit the function of each element that composes a house.

Sam and William also designed houses for several clients who were not as adventuresome as the Wile, Flesh, and Mayer families, but two of them—the Boatner and Jacques Wiener houses—are quite beautiful. Sam remodeled an early twentieth-century Colonial Revival house at 1040 Delaware Street for attorney Yandell Boatner and his wife Frances in 1935.[22] The two-story house was given a stucco finish over its wood frame and an extension made to one side that encloses a sitting room and screened porch with a bedroom and sleeping porch above. On the upper floors of the main body of the house and the addition the vertical windows are grouped in continuous bands. Tucked up under the eaves, these are reminiscent of Frank Lloyd Wright's residential designs of the early twentieth century in the Chicago suburbs. The low-hipped roof with a deep extension and a prominent chimney adds to that impression, but the house seems lighter and airier than Wright's houses. Unfortunately, Boatner did not long enjoy the changes for he died shortly after the renovations were complete.

The house for the architects' brother Jacques and his wife, Betty, at 622 Longleaf is similar to the Boatner House with its grouping of windows under the eaves, though here the emphasis is strongly horizontal. Sam and William designed the house together in 1941. The house is constructed of vertical wood siding with high relief and has a canopy over the entrance porch. As with the Boatner

Jacques L. and Betty E. Wiener House.
Photo by Guy W. Carwile.

House the windows here are a prominent feature, which gives the house a sense of lightness. In 1946 a swimming pool (among the first in Shreveport) was built in the back garden. Perhaps Yandell Boatner and Jacques Wiener, both of them attorneys, opted for a more conservative approach to modernism in order not to deter more traditionally minded clients.

Two other houses share characteristics of the Boatner and Jacques Wiener houses, though both have been altered. The one at 721 Longleaf Road was built around 1938 for Hyman B. and Mary T. Wile Badt. Mary was a cousin of Sam and William, and Hyman was a manager for the Big Chain grocery stores. The original windows have been replaced and shutters added. The other at 722 Unadilla Street, and dating to 1939, was for dentist Len Udes and his wife, Doris, who were friends of the Wieners. Other than the deep corner porch and cantilevered second floor, the house is now almost unrecognizable as a Wiener design. Vinyl siding covers the house and, like the Badt House, the windows are replacements and are flanked by decorative shutters.

Suitable for the Modern World

In the 1930s the Wiener brothers developed an architectural expression that they believed was appropriate to and epitomized the twentieth century. They saw what they were after in the architecture that had emerged in Europe, and particularly in Germany, Holland, and France, immediately after World War I when architects and designers set out to create buildings, furniture, and objects of everyday use "suitable for the modern world." The Wieners wanted to make their buildings fit modern modes of living and their designs to clearly state by their rational and functional forms that society had entered a new age. Their house designs were fundamentally different from what was being built in the United States at the time, and many of their houses incorporated elements that would have been considered impure according to the tenets of the International Style espoused by Hitchcock and Johnson. While clearly their buildings show European influences, the Wieners were not designing in Europe but in the Deep South, and their residential designs were a deliberate and thoughtful response to local conditions. Still, they could not have achieved their goals without clients willing to share their ideals. As the 1930s drew to a close, the Wieners were about to embark on a new phase that involved the design of new building types that included schools and commercial and institutional buildings needed for a postwar society.

4

BUILDING COMMUNITY 1930s TO 1940

On July 13, 1931, Shreveport celebrated the opening of the Municipal Airport (Downtown Airport) and the inauguration of service by American Airlines. The airport was replaced in 1953 by a larger facility designed by Samuel G. Wiener, E. M. Freeman Architects and Engineers. Sam, who had spent part of 1931 in Europe, returned to Shreveport to Jones, Roessle, Olschner and Wiener. His first project, a clubhouse on the shore of Cross Lake for the El Karubah Shriners, was a rare commission in the immediate aftermath of the Crash of 1929. Other than the residential commissions, which were the focus of William's practice, the architects' energy in the 1930s also went into securing other kinds of commissions, including those funded by the Public Works Administration (PWA). One of them, the Municipal Incinerator, gave Sam and his firm international recognition. At the end of the decade, commercial buildings became a major focus.

Shreveport, the Great Depression, and Federal Programs

Shreveport and its surrounding area did not experience the effects of the Great Depression as severely as did much of the nation. The oil and gas industry remained robust, Caddo Parish's fields continued to prosper, and oil and gas fields in east Texas (Rusk County and Rodessa), both of which opened in 1930, helped Shreveport in the Great Depression. In addition, the establishment in 1933 of an Army Air Corps base (later renamed Barksdale Air Force Base) in Bossier City helped lessen the impact. A pilot-training program established there in 1939 also boosted the region's economy, but by then the nation was coming out of the Depression and about to gear up with manufacturing for World War II. Nevertheless, while the 1930s was less disastrous in Shreveport than elsewhere, architectural commissions were few and often for small buildings that yielded little income. Sam and William were fortunate to get as many projects as they did, but in large part this was due to their relationships in the community.

Nationwide it was estimated that, in 1934, 80 percent of workers associated with the building industry, from carpenters to electricians and architects, were unemployed.[1] The federal government stepped in by funding construction programs to help relieve the problem, and these federally funded projects resulted in a significant upgrading of the nation's infrastructure. The two programs that had the most impact on Louisiana were the Public Works Administration (PWA) and the Works Progress Administration (WPA), and architectural firms competed vigorously for the few commissions. Among the funded projects in Shreveport and the surrounding region were schools, school additions and auditoriums, street improvements, and in Bossier Parish, a number of one- and two-room rural schools for African American students.

In September 1931, the firm of Jones, Roessle, Olschner and Wiener was actively seeking PWA projects in Louisiana, Mississippi, and Texas, but none were available. In a letter of September 14, 1931, to Olschner and Sam, Jones, who was based in New Orleans, was devising strategies to get more work, including preparing a portfolio of their designs to present to various officials and, where possible, to establish political contacts. Jones wrote, "we are very friendly with the Jahnke's and I am quite sure we can arrange to have the influence of Ernest Lee [Jahnke], the Assistant Secretary of the Navy."[2] Ernest Lee Jahnke was a member of the family who owned the Jahnke Shipbuilding Corporation in Madisonville that had built ships for the Navy in World War I. On September 30, 1931, Sam wrote to Perry K. Heath, assistant secretary of the U.S. Treasury, offering the firm's services for the design of the federal post office in Morgan City, listing the members of the firm and their qualifications, noting some of the buildings they had designed, and including some photographs of their work.[3] In a reply of October 19, 1931, assistant secretary of the U. S. Treasury Seymour Lowman informed the architects that all projects for Louisiana were taken.[4] Finally, the architects made a connection with Jahnke, and Olschner visited him, but nothing came of it and Jahnke was still trying hard to identify projects for them in 1932.[5] Eventually, the firm was funded for a few PWA projects, mostly gymnasium/auditoriums for schools, but significantly a municipal incinerator for Shreveport and a high school for Bossier City (discussed in chapter 8). The incinerator became one of the most acclaimed Modern buildings in the nation after it was completed in 1937, and the Bossier City school received its share of accolades.

MUNICIPAL INCINERATOR

Although credited to Jones, Roessle, Olschner and Wiener, and specifically to Olschner on the PWA documentation, the Municipal Incinerator was a project of Olschner and Sam, as was invariably the case for the firm's buildings in northern Louisiana. Unusually for an industrial building, the firm was responsible for the entire scheme, serving as engineers as well as design architects. Olschner planned and engineered the structure, and Sam fashioned the exterior. Designed in 1935, the incinerator began operations on January 1, 1937. The building, located at 1731 Kings Highway, was demolished in 1974.

The city of Shreveport had applied for PWA funds to construct the incinerator in order to deal with the problem of people "depositing garbage and rubbish on dumping grounds," which was creating "a serious menace to health."[6] Dumping, apparently, also contributed to a general decline in property values in the areas where it occurred. In order to understand the most effective and modern systems of waste incineration, Olschner visited and inspected incinerators in several cities. Following his investigation, he wrote a fascinating and detailed account of how incinerators work and the innovative features he incorporated into Shreveport's building.[7] Sam's outer shell, into which all the equipment and operations were to fit, is an icon of modernism. In a letter to Sam that includes reminiscences of their joint projects, Olschner acknowledges the design, writing "your incinerator design, *great!*"[8]

The operation of the incinerator—it had a 150-ton capacity every twenty-four hours—began with trucks delivering the garbage at ground level and dumping it into below-grade-level concrete bins where it was stored (dry and wet garbage separated). From there, cranes lifted the garbage in grab buckets and moved it laterally to hoppers on the third floor, where it was released into the furnaces on the second floor. No fuel was used in the furnaces, which worked on the principle that, if a sufficiently intense fire was maintained and the garbage was loaded in small quantities, the garbage itself acted as fuel. To avoid releasing odors, a combustion chamber insured the complete burning of the gases before they passed out of the chimney. Ashes from the furnaces dropped to the ground level directly into trucks or ash disposal pits. Olschner introduced various refinements to the Shreveport incinerator that made it more technologically advanced than its contemporaries elsewhere; a great improvement for the workers inside was the addition of windows that afforded direct ventilation and light to the stoking room. The building included truck-storage space at ground level.

As for the incinerator's aesthetics, the reinforced-concrete-frame building rose in a series of rectangular units faced in cream-colored glazed brick. Sam treated the windows that illuminated the stoking room as a horizontal band across the center of the incinerator, and he repeated that line with similar windows at the building's top and base. The bands of windows were intermittently interrupted where columns of the building's structural frame rose between groups of panes, and these were accentuated by dark red brick, a formal detail he would use in the 1940s in some of his school projects. The upper and lower rows of windows were visually extended in a band around the building in the same dark red brick, and he repeated that linearity with five rows of red brick circling the top of the chimney. A glistening strip of stainless steel formed the incinerator's fascia, adding to the building's dynamic horizontality, which was the epitome of European modernism.

The incinerator drew critical acclaim nationally and internationally. It projected exactly the austere, streamlined forms admired by Europeans and increasingly by American architects as well. Photographs of the building give it a monumental image. The first photograph appeared in *Manufacturers Record* in August 1935, followed by those accompanying Olschner's article of October 1935 in *The American City*. But the seven pages devoted to the building in the November 1935 issue of *Architectural Forum*, which included an almost full-page photograph of the exterior, and an additional seven photographs, along with floor plans and sections, attracted the attention of architects and critics. *Forum*'s text was laudatory: "The Shreveport incinerator is a strikingly clean piece of design. Its unfamiliar appearance arises from the fact that the plan is a radical departure from customary practice, and a plan without precedent has quite logically resulted in a building as new as it is sound. Both the plan and fine architectural quality of the exterior are cogent reasons why competent architects need not ban themselves from industrial work where their collaboration has not hitherto been considered essential."[9]

Municipal Incinerator.
Courtesy of LSU-Shreveport Archives and Special Collections.

A flood of invitations followed for photographs of the incinerator for display in exhibitions and museums. Images were included in the United States Pavilion at the International Exposition of 1937 in Paris and was the only building specifically named in a review of the section on architecture and urbanism in *La Revue Moderne.* The preliminary invitation letter of May 4, 1937, came from Swiss-born, New York City–based architect William Lescaze, one of the organizers of the exhibition. Lescaze, with his partner George Howe, had designed the modernist Philadelphia Savings Fund Society skyscraper of 1931 that was featured in Hitchcock and Johnson's book *The International Style.* In 1938 New York City's Museum of Modern Art requested a photograph for an exhibition it was mounting in Paris on industrial architecture.[10]

Praise for the incinerator came from quarters other than architectural journals. Renowned author and critic Lewis Mumford wrote a review for the *New Yorker* magazine on the New York Architectural League's 1938 photographic exhibition in which the incinerator was included. In a sharp appraisal, he declared, "the fact comes out pretty plainly that the vigorous and positive work in architecture is being done in the Northwest and the Deep South."[11] Mumford selected the incinerator from all the other buildings exhibited as worthy of special praise, stating: "If I had any gold medals to distribute, I would quickly pin one on Jones, Roessle, Olschner & Wiener for their municipal incinerator at Shreveport, Louisiana. This is one of the best examples of the rational use of the ribbon window and the overhanging building, with the ground floor accessible to vehicles that I have come across—an excellent design, with no vulgar attempts at prettifying a form that needs no additions."[12] In part, it was because the Municipal Incinerator was an industrial building that the critics could shower it with accolades for its bold form, praise they might not have bestowed on a more common or traditional building type. Despite this recognition and perhaps because it was an industrial building, it did not increase visibility for the Wieners' many other designs.

The incinerator was included again in a New York Architectural League exhibition, this time in 1940 where two schools of architecture—modern and traditional—were displayed on two separate floors of the league's building. The Architectural League was established in 1881 by architect Cass Gilbert as an organization and venue where young architects could get their work critiqued by more seasoned practitioners, and it had expanded over the years to become an organization sponsoring exhibitions and lectures. The invitation to display photographs of the incinerator came from architect and artist Hugh Ferris, whose dramatic sketches and drawings of American skyscrapers had a considerable influence on American and European architects. Ferris described the incinerator as a "distinguished example of modern architecture."[13]

Photographs of the incinerator appeared in the Art Division's section of the 1939 Golden Gate International Exposition in San Francisco as one of the "25 Best [contemporary] Buildings East of the Rocky Mountains." Designer George Nelson invited Olschner and Wiener, acting on behalf of *Architectural Forum* and describing the structure as "one of the twenty-five best contemporary buildings east of the Rockies." Nelson requested four to six of the "most dramatic photographs" along with the plans.[14] Altogether, the incinerator was featured in five international journals, a book, an encyclopedia, and five exhibitions.

After his work on the incinerator was completed and with no more PWA-funded projects then available in Shreveport, Olschner left the city for a position as an engineering inspector for federal programs in Fort Worth, Texas. Sam established his own firm, and William, too, worked independently, though sometimes the brothers collaborated on a project. While much of their work in the 1930s was residential, Sam already had an established reputation, which enabled him to get some commercial projects. Nevertheless, their commissions, whether residential or commercial, came primarily through family, friends, and acquaintances. Sam was also a partner in a real estate venture (Martin and Wiener) during this period, which helped stabilize his cash flow.

Clients

Among the most significant clients in these years was Sam and William's cousin Ed Wile. He hired Sam to design buildings for his string of grocery stores, Big Chain, and to design his house. Other family clients included their brother Jacques and their cousin Mary T. Wile, who was married to Hyman B. Badt, a manager at Big Chain. Cousins William B. and Julian Wiener, both physicians in Jackson, Mississippi, commissioned houses in the 1950s. Most of their clients, like Sam and William, were part of Shreveport's fairly extensive Jewish community.

Jews were among the area's first settlers and, by 1848, twelve families lived in Shreveport, just twelve years after the town was founded. The first Jewish congregation was organized in 1857, and they met at the home of a member of the group until a temple was built in 1870 on Fannin Street. Jews, both Reform and Orthodox, seem to have assimilated relatively easily in Shreveport and by the beginning of the twentieth century had established important businesses, were property owners and developers, became prominent in the medical and legal fields, and were active in civic and cultural affairs.[15] In 1915 the Fannin Street synagogue was replaced by the grand Beaux-Arts classical temple, B'nai Zion, at Cotton and Common streets, designed by Edward F. Neild and Clarence Olschner. The Reform congregation moved in 1956 to a new synagogue designed by Seymour Van Os and Theodore Flaxman in consultation with Sam (discussed in chapter 9). Among B'nai Zion's members were the Wiener families and their cousin Ed Wile's family, as well as those of Hyman B. Badt, William G. Fellman, Sylvian W. Gamm, Simon Herold, Louie Levy, James Muslow, and Len Udes, all of whom had houses or businesses designed by Sam or William. Philip Lieber, another member of the congregation, hired Van Os to design his house and later called on Flaxman to design an addition. Jan Madison, the daughter of Charles and Lettie Mayer, was an interior decorator, and her husband worked in Jacques Wiener's law firm. Thus, family and business connections brought commissions, fostering the development of modernism in the city.

Shreveport in the 1930s had an unusual convergence of a cultural group and modernism, and the Jewish community—architects and patrons—were instrumental in introducing modern architecture to the city, to Louisiana, and to the Deep South. This raises the question of why this occurred, why modern buildings proved particularly attractive to Shreveport's Jews. Bill Wiener Jr., William's son, suggested that, because the Jewish community was culturally and religiously independent of the region's heritage and they did not have a southern plantation tradition, they could more easily embrace new ideas.[16] Journalist Richard Baudouin, who in the early 1980s was editor of *Upstate Newsweekly* and regularly wrote articles on Shreveport's architecture for this now defunct regional newspaper, asked Bill if his father's and uncle's Jewish heritage affected their designs and about the willingness of the city's Jewish community to experiment with a new architecture. According to Bill, "the Jews had no architectural heritage to fall back on. They wanted to be modern."[17] Baudouin also interviewed Marion Wiener, asking why she and others in the Jewish community rejected the traditional styling of the buildings they inhabited as children and were so receptive to the new architecture. She gave a response similar to Bill's, saying that, while Shreveport Jews were part of southern culture, "they weren't steeped in it" and added, "they were willing to try new things, new ways of life."[18] For the architects, and presumably for the clients, the traditional forms or styles seemed both out-

Orthopedic Clinic.
Courtesy of LSU-Shreveport Archives and Special Collections.

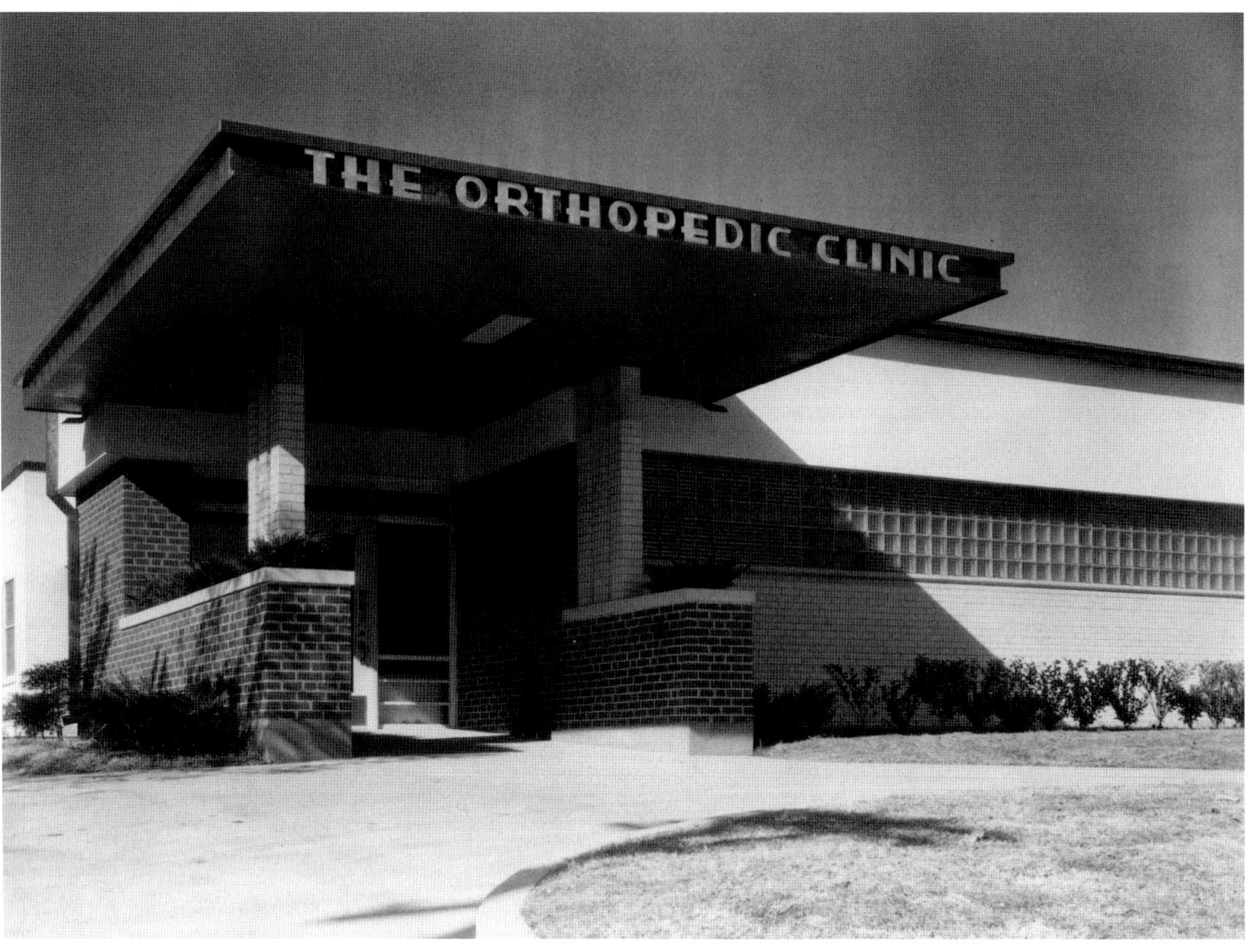

dated and inappropriate, and possibly represented aspects of a southern tradition with which they were not ideologically in tune. Another dimension of cultural identity and style might lie in the fact that many of the European architects the Wieners met and whose works they saw were Jewish and that their work represented a culture or heritage that Sam or William wanted to grasp.

This then suggests that forms or styles might represent or signify a cultural or social intention. Sam addressed the question of a Jewish style relative to the design of synagogues in a short piece he wrote, "No American Jewish Architectural Style," published in the section on Synagogue and School Management in *The National Jewish Post and Opinion.* His essay can perhaps be understood as applying more broadly to architecture than to synagogues alone and, given his and William's extraordinary buildings, it is likely that he addressed this question of Jewish style more than once. He wrote, "I presume that the question assumes the meaning of style in architecture as the character inherent in buildings that permits them to be recognizable as belonging to a group such as different cultures have produced at various times in their history. Thus a true style belongs to a people and to an age."[19] Sam explained that synagogues took on new functions in the twentieth century, that they were no longer built in the densest area of a city as in previous centuries, and that inevitably their exterior appearance would respond to the needs of their time and place. He does not reject the notion that certain historic qualities of planning, construction, and appearance might be repeated in the future and "result in what can truly be called a Jewish Temple style."[20] However, Sam's observation near the beginning of the essay that "New requirements and new building techniques demanded new forms" may be read as his acceptance that an architect should always design for the age.[21] His and William's careers are an affirmation of this view.

ORTHOPEDIC CLINIC

It was a friend of the Wieners, physician Guy A. Caldwell, who commissioned Sam and William in 1936 to design an orthopedic clinic (demolished in the 1970s) for his practice.[22] In 1922, Caldwell had established a clinic for crippled children on Crockett Street. In August 1938, after pediatricians Lucas, Webb, and Wolfe acquired the building, they made some minor alterations, including air-conditioning, and renamed it the Children's Clinic. The L-shaped building had a projecting corner entrance that was sheltered by a deep overhang and led into the waiting room. The medical consultation, examination, operating, X-ray, and physiotherapy rooms were spaced along the length of the building on two sides of a central corridor. Consultation and examination spaces faced the street and were illuminated by a continuous horizontal window of glass-block, placed high on the wall to assure interior privacy. In the ell to the rear of the waiting room were workshops for fabricating orthopedic equipment. The clinic was streamlined, efficient, and clean in appearance, a necessary image for a medical facility. Yet because the simplicity of the building imparted a degree of anonymity, the clinic's name was emblazoned across the edge of the entrance canopy to make clear its purpose. The clinic's demolition reflected the changes taking place in medical care as well as in the area it was located, on Line Avenue at Margaret Place just south of downtown, which had lost much of its residential character to commercial development.

After World War II, Sam and William designed a similar one-story brick-faced clinic at 2515 Line Avenue for physician William Fellman to accommodate an eye specialist, a dentist, and two lab technicians.[23] This L-shaped clinic, which opened in 1951, has since been added to and altered. Its entrance portico was tucked into a corner of the building, and the sheltering roof extension carried on a single metal column. While reminiscent of the portico on Sam's house, here the low-scale space was more intimate than monumental and reflected the self-effacing trend of postwar entrances. The clinic stretched back on its lot with dental offices and laboratories facing north to gain continuous light, and the optometry offices faced south, enclosed by windowless brick walls. Interior finishes included terrazzo floors as well as walls that varied from painted surfaces to mahogany plywood and exposed brick. The waiting room had a calming view out to the pine-wooded site.

Commerce and the 1930s

In the 1930s civic leaders throughout America were promoting a "modernize mainstreet" movement, principally through persuading merchants to make fashionable improvements to their shops and stores, especially to the facades.[24] The hope was that such improvements would bring customers back downtown, as well as give employment to out-of-work architects and builders. The movement was relatively successful. In Shreveport one of William's acquaintances in the Jewish community hired William to modernize his men's clothing and accessories store, Rosenblaths, at 403 Texas Street. William clad the upper half of the facade with a "screen" that extended two feet over the sidewalk.[25] Spread across the full width of the new facade, the building's name was spelled out in large angular modernist letters of stainless steel that were halo-illuminated from behind with neon tubing. Above the store's name, and providing compositional balance to the facade, was the "Hart Schaffner & Marx Clothes" logo with the identifying lettering orbiting the circular emblem. The facade's new composition of angles and curves was the height of commercial fashion. Adding to the glamor, the bulkheads (the lower walls of exterior display windows) were finished in stainless steel with plate-glass display windows that angled in to the entrance door to draw customers inside. Red terrazzo with aluminum strips formed the floor of the vestibule. The interior was also remodeled in the latest mode. A broad straight aisle flanked by show cases ran through the center of the shop's deep narrow space. Single longitudinal lighting fixtures emphasized and illuminated a lingering passage past display counters of birchwood with stainless-steel trim.

BIG CHAIN STORE, BROADMOOR

The term "supermarket" is generally understood to mean a self-service store that sells a wide variety of foods. In 1940, the Bureau of the Census issued a report on data it gathered in 1939 on retail operations. The bureau's figures showed that 88 percent of supermarkets were chain operated, a growth that had accelerated in the previous two years.[26] Among the dominant chains were A&P (Great Atlantic and Pacific Tea Company), Piggly Wiggly, and Kroger. In Shreveport, Ed Wile was the most influential figure in this shift to a one-stop shopping expedition. Following on his success with the Fairfield Big Chain store, he opened a new and much larger supermarket at the corner of Youree and Ockley drives. He celebrated the opening of a new Big Chain store on April 15, 1941, with a two-day fair promoting food demonstrations and sale prices.[27] According to one local newspaper, the new building was "truly a commercial palace worthy of being listed as one of the show-places of Shreveport."[28] Sam and William jointly designed the store, one of several projects they worked on together. Though they were the architects of record, the input of Ed Wile on the final product cannot be overstated.

In 1940, Wile had begun planning a flagship Big Chain Store for the growing automobile suburb of Broadmoor. As he had done successfully at the Fairfield store, Wile again conveyed the image of progressive merchandising by incorporating the most innovative retailing features. He decided that the store would have no display windows, the sales area would be mostly column-free to maximize fixture layout, the building would have year-round climate control, and the store would be surrounded by parking. Within those conditions, Wile gave the architects a free hand in the design.

Big Chain was the centerpiece of four clusters of stores at the intersection of two major arteries, Youree and Ockley drives. Because various sections of the site were under different ownership and came under varying zoning restrictions, the center was divided into four groups of stores. But all were visually linked in design and signage. The Broadmoor Drug store was first on the site in 1936. It was followed by Big Chain in 1940 and, attached to it were three smaller spaces that were leased between 1940 and 1941 to a variety store, a dry-cleaner, and a beauty shop. This group was the largest cluster and included the biggest building and the focus—the Big Chain grocery store. To the south was a small block of three shops arranged in a curve and known as the Quarter Round Shops; these included a jewelry store and a shoe repair shop. Stretching behind the Big Chain group was a row of shops in a sawtooth arrangement, known as the Zigzag Shops. These were de-

Big Chain Store, Broadmoor.
Courtesy of LSU-Shreveport Archives and Special Collections.

signed and added in phases, beginning in 1947 and completed by 1958. William B. Wiener with associates Jesse O. Morgan Jr., P. Murff O'Neal Jr., and draftsman Jack L. Roeger designed these stores. They were leased to merchants selling such goods as floor coverings and fabrics, and to a laundry. To the north across Ockley Drive and also facing Youree was another cluster that included a cinema and six small shops, most of which sold women's clothing or accessories. Begun in 1945, they were demolished in 2001. On a separate "island" was a filling station completed in 1941 and sold to Conoco (Continental Oil Company). Wile had created a planned retail development with a well-balanced group of stores that formed a one-stop shopping trip aimed primarily at women. The shops were harmonized in design and materials and included ample parking space.

The design of Big Chain, a streamlined unadorned curve of brick wall with no exterior display windows, was unique. Because the store was designed for customers primarily arriving by automobile, there was little value in display windows. Pedestrian window-shoppers would be few, and a solid wall could be used more effectively on the interior for shelving and display space. The walls of buff-colored brick rose from a two-foot base of red brick to a five-foot-tall clerestory window of five rows of glass block that wrapped the entire building. The glass block admitted muted natural light into the store during daylight hours and at night allowed artificial light from the interior

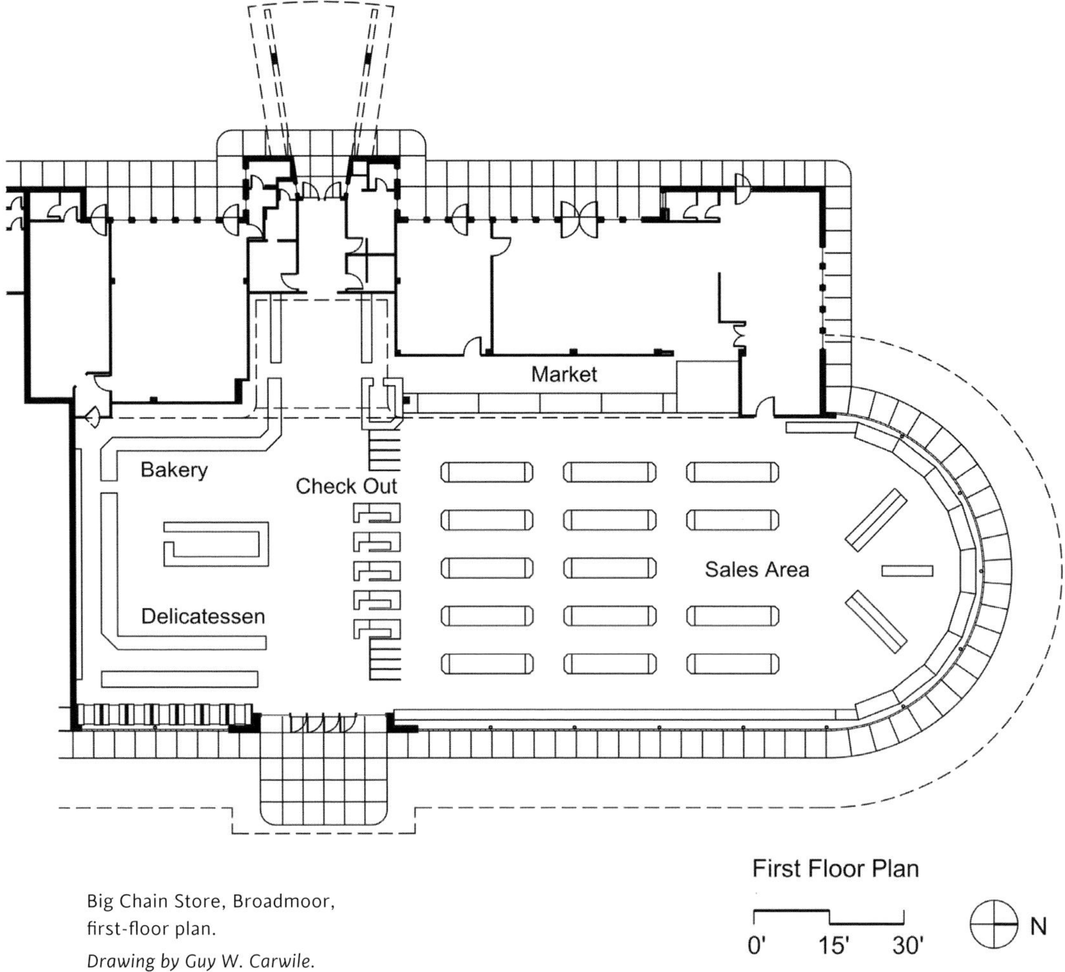

Big Chain Store, Broadmoor, first-floor plan.
Drawing by Guy W. Carwile.

to partially illuminate the exterior. The nighttime ribbon of light also provided a dramatic horizontal beacon to attract customers from the street and across the parking lot. Two colored neon tubes running behind the glass block added color to the building's face. Big Chain concluded with a prominent cantilevered canopy, painted red on its outer edge, echoing in color the brick base and the brick framing the principal entrance doors for shoppers.

A fifteen-foot-deep canopy facing Youree Drive (there was also an entrance at the rear for access from the larger parking lot) provided a strong cap to the building, shaded the windows from the sun, and protected customers from sun and rain as they approached the store. The canopy marked a continuation of the interior ceiling line, unbroken from inside to out. From the exterior the canopy could have appeared visually overbearing, but by tapering from around five feet in height at the building's wall to approximately one foot at its outer edge, the impression of weight was diluted. To emphasize the store's entrance, the canopy extended a further five feet above the door and was topped with the store's name, Big Chain, in 3.65-foot tall, red neon-illuminated letters. Situated well above pedestrian eye-level, the store's name was intended to be visible primarily from afar and to motorists. Aesthetically, the building's sweeping curve and horizontal lines derived from the dynamic expressionist buildings designed in the 1920s by Erich Mendelsohn that Sam had seen in Germany, notably the Universum Cinema of 1928 in Berlin and Erwin Gutkind's Children's Home on the Sonnenhof housing estate (1927) in Berlin-Lichtenberg, the latter a glass building with a rounded end and a flat roof that extends as a canopy to shade the window wall. Within Shreveport, the store with its streamlined shape, extended canopy, ribbon window, and red signage and fascia edging stood out because it was so distinctive, just as Wile wanted.

Big Chain and its adjacent shops did not sit at the street edge but instead were set back seventy feet from Youree Drive in order to provide easily accessible parking space in front of the store, and the street itself was widened sixteen feet to allow a strip of head-on parking. While the building was oriented to the street, which was important, such an extensive setback meant that the store had to be readily visible at a distance and at automobile speed. Thus, the bold colorful signage and distinctive simplified lettering were essential. The clean lines of the building's curve, the glass block, and the canopy signified modernity, and they echoed the horizontality of the road, movement, speed, and the efficiency of contemporary life. Wile and his architects had established a signature look for the store, and most of these features became identifiers for the stores that followed. If the complex intricate ornament of Fair-

Big Chain Store, Broadmoor.

Courtesy of LSU-Shreveport Archives and Special Collections.

field Big Chain made the store conspicuous and could be appreciated at close range, a decade later when the Broadmoor Big Chain was constructed, buildings needed to respond to different priorities. This Big Chain provided its customers with parking spaces for a total of 150 cars at the front, sides, and rear, and all on a concrete-paved surface.

The interior of the store was equally innovative and impressive. At almost twenty-five thousand square feet, it was the biggest grocery store in Shreveport. There were no interior support columns, and the sixty-foot steel trusses formed one of the largest single-span grocery interiors anywhere. Clear-span structures for supermarkets had been built in the early 1930s in Los Angeles, but Broadmoor Big Chain's free span dwarfed the West Coast antecedents. The clear span allowed for the utmost flexibility in the organization of the interior and the placement of display spaces. It is said to have had a mile of display shelves. The absence of display windows allowed the walls to accommodate self-service shelving, hanging fluorescent light fixtures were laid out parallel to the perimeter walls and perpendicular to the shelving, and the walls had a smooth plaster finish to serve as a neutral backdrop to the merchandise. To the left of the entrance was a luncheonette, a new department for Big Chain, and the store included two large kitchens, one for the luncheonette and delicatessen and one for the bakery goods. There were five checkout stands. For the comfort of shoppers the store had year-round air-conditioning, and the acoustical tile ceiling muffled noise.

Big Chain was so innovative that ten years after it opened Geoffrey Baker and Bruno Funaro included it their book, *Shopping Centers: Design and Operation,* published in 1951, as a leader in efficient design.[29] The trade journals *Chain Store Age* and *Super Market Merchandising* featured articles on the store, praising it as exemplary.[30] Big Chain was an early harbinger of things to come, for it was not until the late 1940s that supermarkets dominated food shopping, replacing small specialized markets, and self-service stores were commonplace.

By 1958, Big Chain had opened five more stores, but this Broadmoor market remained the biggest in size and importance. The store changed hands in 1963, becoming the Broadmoor Supermarket, and was later occupied by a sequence of discount stores until it was destroyed in 2003 by a fire of electrical origin in the attic.

Shreveport on the Rise

The success of Caddo Parish's oil and gas industry had set off a construction boom in the 1920s that included public institutions, commercial buildings, and exclusive suburbs. In downtown Shreveport, Edward F. Neild and Dewey Somdal produced Caddo Parish's magnificent and massive courthouse that at eight stories could almost be described as a high-rise. A true high-rise, however, had been constructed in 1910 at 509 Market Street for the Commercial National Bank. This ten-story steel-framed building designed by the distinguished firm of Mann and Stern of Little Rock, Arkansas, is considered Shreveport's first modern skyscraper. When the bank decided in 1939 that it needed a new building it again looked beyond Louisiana for an architect, this time to the New York City firm of McKim, Mead and White. Although by then all three of that firm's original architects had died, the partnership's name carried such prestige that it had been retained. To a large extent, though, the building is Sam's design for he acted as associate architect for the project. The bank is the only high-rise building that Sam created.

COMMERCIAL NATIONAL BANK

The Commercial National Bank (CNB) was organized in Shreveport in 1886, specializing in oil, cotton, and lumber financing, and the buildings it occupied successively became too small for its business. This new building at the corner of Texas and Edwards streets in the heart of downtown replaced its Mann and Stern–designed former headquarters of 1911 at Texas and Market streets. Jones, Roessle, Olschner and Wiener had made some interior modifications to that building in 1930.[31] It is interesting to speculate whether Sam's father, Sam Jr., who was a director of the bank, had anything to do with the choice of architect.

The new steel-framed building of 1940 is a tall narrow camel-shaped structure, six bays wide and seventeen stories tall facing Texas Street, and sixteen bays wide and thirteen in height along most of its length on Edwards Street. At the front portion facing Texas Street, it concludes with two pronounced setbacks, the first at the fourteenth story and the next at the sixteenth. The setbacks put the building in line with contemporary skyscrapers in New York City. One of Sam's preliminary sketches for the bank, however, depicts a structure simpler in outline and

left

Commercial National Bank.

Courtesy of LSU-Shreveport Archives and Special Collections.

right

Commercial National Bank, sketch.

Courtesy of LSU-Shreveport Archives and Special Collections.

with a much greater emphasis on verticality. That design soars with strongly emphasized piers that rise unstopped to the top, but a more subdued scheme with setbacks won. In part the building's design was a result of cost. When bids were first received, it was determined that the building could not be built within the allowed budget.[32] Consequently, the architects along with the engineers from the James Stewart Construction Company revised and simplified the design and changed the materials from face-brick to Indiana limestone, all of which brought down the cost.

Despite the differences, the completed design does give an impression of height, mostly because it is tall and narrow on the Texas Street front and there is some emphasis from piers between the windows that rise without interruption to the building's summit. However, because the piers project only slightly from the wall surface, vertical movement is subdued and from a distance the exterior appearance resembles a grid. The setbacks, from six bays to four on each face, a row of medallions and a fluted cornice around the top of the fifteenth floor, and a row of ornate windows on the uppermost setback, bring verticality to a fussy stop. Additional ornamentation consists primarily of sculpted eagle motifs rendered in the stylized manner of Art Deco flanking the entrance, which is enriched by fluted column-like jambs that curve in to make a gentle transition from exterior to the inset entrance door. Inside

Commercial National Bank.
Photo by Guy W. Carwile.

the lobby are Texas artist James Buchanan "Buck" Winn Jr.'s murals, painted on Belgian linen, depicting scenes of the area's history.

As well as being the tallest building in Shreveport at the time, the bank also boasted structural advances. It was early in using cellular floors (known as Q-floors), which were speedier to construct than other systems and provided six-inch-deep spaces within the floor structure for easy access to electrical wiring. The bank was featured in double-page spreads in advertisements promoting the system in three contemporary architecture journals.[33] Completed in late 1940, the building was occupied in February 1941, and apparently all the spaces were filled. A bigger, taller, and shinier CNB opened in 1987 next to the 1940 building.

Concluding the 1930s

Despite the multiple problems caused by the Great Depression, Sam and William had sufficient commissions to realize their ambitious designs. In large part this was due to their connections in the community and to clients who were eager, or at least inclined, to live or work in the most modern of architectural creations. Shamefully, two of Sam's greatest pioneering works, one in the mid-1930s and the other at the start of the following decade, both lauded in magazines and books as state-of-the-art in their respective type, are gone. The Municipal Incinerator was demolished in 1974, and Big Chain, Broadmoor, burned in March 2003.

On the basis of its streamlined Moderne design, another commercial establishment has often been attributed to Sam, though there is no documentary evidence to support this.[34] The Hotel Palomar Courts of 1937–38 are composed of two parallel rows of free-standing white cement-plaster (stucco) clad cottages, with low-pitched hipped roofs, three front steps between curved railings, and wraparound steel-casement corner windows. It is probable that the owner, local businessman Charles Rinaudo, wanted his establishment to convey the most up-to-date and modern appearance, of the kind repre-

Hotel Palomar Courts.

Courtesy of the Library of Congress, Prints and Photographs Division, HABS, Reproduction number: HABS 1308-30. Photo by Guy W. Carwile.

sented by the Wieners' house designs. Rinaudo also owned a Moderne building, a drive-in hamburger stand, named Famous Subway Hamburgers, that was razed to make way for the interstate.

As the decade came to a close, Sam got his first commission to design a school, Bossier City High School. This was the beginning of a new design trajectory that became increasingly important in the post–World War II era. It also set him and William on a new path of discovery and investigations into the art and structure of building.

I. Edward and Jessamine Thalheimer Wile House.
Photo by Guy W. Carwile.

5

MODERN METHODS

Following the European trip of 1931, Sam and William's work took a new direction that was not just formal and spatial but clearly tied to progressive construction methods and materials. At the same time, their work became increasingly sensitive to climatic conditions. Their investigations with structural systems and materials did not stop as the 1930s came to an end but continued after World War II, when new technologies and building systems became available. And, like most modernist architectural firms, both before and after the war, though not all their commissions could equally satisfy the brothers' desire for formal purity, their work shows the contemporary marriage of method and art.

Practice

Although Sam and William maintained independent architectural practices throughout their professional lives, they often collaborated, particularly for clients who were family members. Their buildings, whether they worked together or independently, are similar in appearance, materials, and structure. Even their approach to detailing is analogous, which adds to the difficulty in pinpointing who was primarily responsible for any given project.

Sam's office during the years he was a partner in the firm of Jones, Roessle, Olschner and Wiener was in Suite 413 of the Ardis Building. Clarence E. Olschner worked with Sam from this office, while Ernest W. Jones and Rudolph B. Roessle were based in New Orleans. After the firm dissolved during the Great Depression, Sam maintained the office in the Ardis Building. He relocated to Suite 820 in the Commercial National Bank Building, the skyscraper he had helped design, shortly after its completion in 1941. Little is known about the architects or draftsmen Sam employed, though there must have been several over the years, especially for the large commercial and institutional projects. Theodore Flaxman worked with Sam in the Jones, Roessle, Olschner and Wiener firm, as did Frederick V. von Osthoff from 1922 to 1929.

William also worked with Sam in the Jones, Roessle, Olschner and Wiener practice from 1930 to 1932, then joined a firm in Dallas for a year before returning to Shreveport and establishing his own office in 1933 in the Slattery Building. By the early 1950s he had relocated to Suite 622 in the Commercial National Bank Building. Paul Murff O'Neal Jr. (1921–2011) was hired by William's firm in 1946 as a draftsman, and in 1950 Jesse O. Morgan Jr. (1922–2014) joined the practice. In 1958 the firm became Wiener, Morgan and O'Neal.

In the years Sam was with Jones, Roessle, Olschner and Wiener, the firm appears to have been responsible for engineering their designs, and in their application for PWA projects, two engineers are named—L. H. Roeger and consulting mechanical engineer R. F. Taylor of Dallas.[1] Clarence Olschner, however, took primary responsibility for the Municipal Incinerator, one of the firm's most complex buildings. Later, when Sam had his own architectural practice, he frequently associated with structural engineer E. M. Freeman, as did William. Freeman worked on the Shreveport Municipal Airport and on J. S. Clark Junior High and Woodlawn High schools for William B. Wiener, Morgan and O'Neal.

Sam and William worked with many different contractors and builders over the years, including the Ashton Glassel Co. (for the Municipal Auditorium); W. A. McMichael Construction Co. (Fellman Clinic and Woodlawn High School); Southern Builders (J. S. Clark Junior High School); and Werner Co. (Fairfield Building, Big Chain Uptown Center, and East Building of the Physicians and Surgeons Hospital).

Structure

To build anywhere, an architect must have an intimate knowledge of the composition of local soils and how they are affected by heat and cold and the amount of water they contain. Shreveport's clay soils shrink and swell dramatically depending on the amount of groundwater, which fluctuates throughout the year, and this cyclic condition can play havoc on buildings that have not been designed to accommodate the accompanying movement. To form a stable foundation for a building, Sam and William used closely spaced drilled concrete pilings, rather than driven pilings, that extended down to a stable stratum. They employed the same system for residential and small commercial projects. For larger buildings like the Municipal Auditorium, they used traditional driven piles under reinforced concrete-pile caps. For residential buildings, the pilings supported either a floor structure of wood joists spanning above-grade cast-in-place concrete beams capped with wood sheathing, which formed a crawl space beneath the building, or below-grade earthen-formed grade beams. After World War II, they continued to employ concrete pilings in their residential projects, but crawl spaces were no longer used, principally because postwar buildings employed slab-on-grade construction, not wood-floor framing. The earth was used to insulate the building from underneath, which was beneficial for houses built when heating, ventilation, and air-conditioning systems (HVAC) were becoming a common feature of houses.

For large or medium-sized institutional or commercial buildings, the Wieners supported the building on a reinforced-concrete frame. The Municipal Auditorium, the Municipal Incinerator, and Bossier and Haughton high schools all have reinforced-concrete frames. Sam employed steel frames for some of the post–World War II schools, notably Caddo Heights Elementary School, which served as a prototype for the Caddo Parish school system. The frames, whether concrete or steel, were not made visible but sheathed in brick and glass.

An exception was William and Sam's design for the now-demolished Weekend House on Cross Lake, where the principal floor level was elevated on pilotis. The house was inspired by French architect Le Corbusier's Villa Savoie of 1929 in Poissy on the southwest outskirts of Paris, which, among other things, was a prototype for an efficient structural system of concrete framing. Both the Villa and the Cross Lake House used monolithic one-way concrete floor slabs carried on continuous beams tying together the pilotis. At both houses the beams were exposed on the exterior, though only under the overhang of the Villa, not on the exterior wall surface, whereas the brothers celebrated structure by making the floor slab beams visible on the Cross Lake house. Displaying the floor slab's outer edge communicated its inherent planar quality, something most architects did not embrace until after the war. The effect of displaying the beams and slabs suggests they were making a clear distinction between exterior and interior, between the world of structure (strong, revealed) and that of the inside (covered, concealed). Also unlike the Villa Savoie, at the Cross Lake house the floor slab was tapered at its cantilevered lakeside end, which gave the house a dynamic forward-thrusting movement.

The raised principal living floor allowed breezes from the lake to help cool the interior. This house was the only one that adopted this solution, but it showed that, from the beginning, the brothers were finding solutions to problems posed by the regional climate. In their subsequent projects, air circulation was achieved by careful positioning of windows for cross-ventilation.

For their residential work, however, Sam and William used typical balloon framing in wood, which was standard throughout the nation for house construction until World War II. After the war, balloon framing was mostly replaced with western platform framing, which allowed for the use of wood from smaller trees, particularly convenient for the one-story houses typical of the postwar period. Balloon framing uses continuous vertical wall studs over two floors, with the horizontal floor joists firmly secured to the studs. This creates a rigid structure on top of which is placed a traditional pitched roof and attic. When structuring a house with a flat roof, the Wieners took the rigid balloon frame one step further by extending the studs upward so that both the top and bottom of the roof's supporting trusses could be tied to the wall studs, making the house's wood structure act as a rigid frame. This system parallels that of flat-roofed industrial buildings. When the Wieners used a pitched roof, which typically was to satisfy a client's request, the balloon frame was used in the normal fashion.

Several of the Wieners' projects incorporated steel columns and beams to assist in structuring wide openings for casement windows or where casement windows wrap an outside corner. In some cases, the steel columns were revealed as a visual element, as at Sam's own house and at the Wile House, where a steel support supports the porch; at Sam's house, another is visible inside the corner plant window of the living room. In a few houses of the 1940s and 1950s William and Sam revealed the steel columns on the interior, notably at William's house, where they are above the cabinet separating the living and dining areas, though the columns were sheathed in aluminum.

Walls and Veneer

In many of their 1930s houses the Wieners used a cement plaster (stucco) wall surface. Examples are the Weekend House on Cross Lake, the Wile and Flesh houses, and Sam's own residence. Occasionally they used stucco in conjunction with some exposed red brick for contrast, as at Sam's house and the Wile House. Stucco provided a clean, taut surface that could be easily applied and, without extraneous ornamental detail, was the ideal surface for a modern building, where the expression of plane and weightlessness was paramount.

The Wieners' method for applying the stucco was to attach it and its supporting metal lath to regularly po-

Stucco on the Samuel G. and Marion Pfeifer Wiener House. *Photo by Guy W. Carwile.*

sitioned four-by-four-inch spacer blocks on top of felt-covered sheathing of shiplap wood siding (typically one by six inches) that was laid on the diagonal for lateral bracing. By attaching the lath with its stucco surface to the spacer blocks instead of directly to the felt-covered wood sheathing, the stucco did not directly adhere to the wall. This made it more watertight and kept structural movement from migrating to the outer surface of the plaster. If the cement plaster adhered to the sheathing, any movement in the plane of the sheathing would telegraph directly out to the finished surface of the stucco and cause cracking.

There are two negative characteristics of stucco: it cracks easily with movement of the substrata, and it stains easily from the mold and mildew that abound in hot and humid Louisiana. Cracking in the relatively thin plane of stucco, which is usually one inch thick or less, was controlled by subdividing the stucco into relatively small panels (less than six feet in any direction) and connecting them with metal control-joint strips. These strips prevented cracking in areas where it was likely to occur by accommodating a certain amount of expansion and contraction of the stucco. In most cases the W-shaped strips are placed with the reveal (or recess) facing the exterior. Sam and William preferred using L- or T-shaped divider-strip joints that adhere to the sheathing through which the moisture barrier did not show. This allowed the plane of stucco to appear continuous and uninterrupted except under certain lighting conditions. The wisdom of their method speaks for itself when one sees how well the buildings have weathered over time. The air space behind the stucco helped the plaster dry out more completely and thus hindered the growth of mold and mildew.

The Wieners, Sam in particular, also used brick. Sam's buildings of the 1920s show he fully exploited the decorative and textural potential of the material. In the 1930s his application of a deep-red brick for the ground story at the Wile House and his own house effectively defined and emphasized the contrast between the ground floor and the smooth and planar stuccoed second story. For the Municipal Incinerator, the brick walls were laid to create an almost seamless surface, as they were at Big Chain Broadmoor. In the 1940s both architects employed brick for their Caddo Parish schools. Stone, a building material not native to Louisiana, was rarely used. The Muslow House, where the stone was imported from Colorado and the flagstone slate flooring from Vermont, is an exception.

Sam used vertically oriented, highly articulated dimensional siding at, for example, the Jacques Wiener House. The "ins and outs" of the siding create shadow patterns that give the facade a lot of visual interest. William used horizontal V-groove siding, which differed from the typical vertical installation of the siding in that it allowed rainwater to slide down the facade. William's decision to orient the siding horizontally was apparently economic in that the horizontal boards could be adhered directly to the studs without the need for a layer of sheathing between the siding and the studs. However, the lack of a sheathing layer led to premature failure of the buildings where he used this method of installation. At the Preston House, William had celebrated the horizontality of the wood sid-

Stone on the James and Jean R. Muslow House.
Photo by Guy W. Carwile.

ing by eliminating the vertical corner boards and mitering the sidings outside corners. This detail, although attractive, apparently failed fairly early in the building's life, which forced him later to add corner boards and to include them at the Ramsey garage/apartment and the Mayer House. The problem of premature failing associated with the horizontal siding at the Ramsey and Mayer residences was so substantial the respective owners covered the wood with asbestos-shingled siding, probably in the 1940s.

Siding on the Charles and Lettie Mayer House.
Courtesy of LSU-Shreveport Archives and Special Collections.

Roofs

When a building design called for a flat roof, the Wieners used parallel-chord trusses that were constructed inexpensively on-site from pieces of standard-sized 2 x 6 or 2 x 4 lumber. Trusses were more efficient and lighter than structurally comparable solid wood (2 x 12 inches) because the pattern of openness can accommodate ductwork and the greater depth provides dead air insulation. In most cases the truss depths were between 3.5 and 4.0 feet, with the notable exception at the Flesh House where the trusses were only 1.67 feet deep. The depth of the trusses appears to be less a function of span or load than to accommodate an attic of sufficient depth to allow hot air to stratify. The top chord of the trusses was sloped for effective drainage. In most cases, water ran off the roof surface to conductor heads and downspouts. Roof surfaces were of shiplap wood or lightweight concrete, as at the William Wiener House.

The intersection of the wall and the roof was handled in a variety of ways: a metal gravel guard that was more or less flush with the wall surface below, or a fascia with three continuous projecting horizontal fins as at Big Chain Broadmoor, or a coping that overhung the wall by a few inches. In each case the exposed metal provided contrast with the wall through material or color variation. Roof drainage at the flat-roofed Flesh House and the Cross Lake Weekend House was handled with an internal roof drain so as to overcome difficulties with applying downspouts at the large overhang.

Windows

While traveling in Europe, Sam and William became aware of the widespread use of industrialized components in both commercial and residential architecture. The most readily available industrialized components for architectural use in the United States in the 1930s were the steel-casement window and frame, which although more expensive than their wooden counterparts were reasonably affordable. Coincidentally, the wood-framed casement was the window of choice in Louisiana during the eighteenth and early nineteenth centuries, which makes an interesting link between the modernist Wiener brothers and the vernacular traditions of the Deep South. A casement window allows 90 percent of its opening to serve ventilation, and the window itself could be positioned to capture directional breezes. The steel casements used by the brothers were outfitted with screened panels that were held in place by friction and accessed from the building's interior in order to make them easily removable for cleaning and maintenance. Because frames and sashes made of steel are much smaller in dimension than their wooden counterparts, they give a facade or wall less visual weight. When budgets allowed, the brothers used steel-casement windows throughout a residence. The Preston House's limited budget, however, only permitted steel-casement windows on the street facade, and the remaining windows were double-hung with wooden frames. At the Ramsey garage/apartment, all of the windows were wooden double-hung.

One of the most interesting facets of Sam and William's early houses was their preference for projecting the steel-casement windows from the exterior wall surface. This proved particularly beneficial for stucco-finished walls because it limited the amount of condensation running down the face of the stucco and staining its surface. Stucco veneer is the least forgiving surface with regard to staining. Moreover, projection of the windows from the wall suggested that the wall was merely a skin, not load-bearing, a visual objective of modernist architects. The genesis of this detail appears to date to 1933 or 1934 with the design of the Weekend House and the Wile and Preston houses. However, the original phase of the Weekend House was designed for wood-framed double-hung windows. The window type was changed to steel-casement windows prior to commencement of construction. They were placed within the thickness of the wall, and only when the house was expanded shortly after with an addition to the land side did William and Sam employ projecting steel-framed windows.

In the 1930s and early 1940s the Wieners occasionally used hollow glass block for windows. The principal advantage of glass block, besides its decorative and textural qualities, is that it admits soft natural light to an interior while preventing sun glare. The clerestory window at Big Chain Broadmoor is glass block, as is the window that frames the entrance door of Sam Wiener's house. At the house the glass blocks provided privacy as well as illuminating the foyer. The glass block (twelve inches square and four inches thick) was manufactured by the Insulux Products Division of the Owens-Illinois Glass Company (400 Series) and has vertical convex ribs on both its exterior faces and horizontal convex ribs on the interior faces. Sam used Glass Block Design Pattern No. 2, which was manufactured for only a brief period before being discontinued shortly before the United States entered World War II in 1941. The process of pressing a pattern into the interior and exterior faces of both surfaces of the block was too labor-intensive when American factories were turning to the war effort.

Sun and Shade

In Louisiana's hot and humid climate, interior shading and cooling are invariably essential from May to October. Sam and William successfully resolved this challenge in two principal ways. Wherever possible they oriented buildings to face north and south in order to avoid morning and afternoon sun and the consequent heat build-up. To counter the summer sun and heat of the southern exposure, they added deep roof overhangs to their buildings. Sam's house, for example, had a 7.5-foot-deep roof extension shading the south wall and a shallower overhang on the north. In winter when the sun is low on the horizon it helped warm the interior. The asymmetry of the differently sized overhangs at Sam's house proved felicitous for it added to the abstract geometry of its composition. At the Flesh House, William provided a five-foot-deep overhang that tapered to a shallow six-inch fascia, which added a sense of energy to the design, as did the tapering of the roof extension at the Big Chain Broadmoor store. Similar shading strategies for exterior walls were continued in the Wieners' postwar buildings.

Screened Porches

One of the signature features of the Wieners' 1930s houses was the integration of a traditional southern screened porch into the design. Historically, porches provided additional living area in a house and, during summer months, were used for sleeping. Before the introduction of mesh screens, porches were fitted with hooks from which to hang curtains in order to provide privacy and deter mosquitoes. In houses without porches, typically one was added after the initial construction. The Wieners, by contrast, embraced the screen porch and conceived it as a formal enhancement.

Their first project to include a screened porch was not for a house, but instead at the El Karubah Club House on Cross Lake. After that almost all of their prewar houses included a screened porch, two stories in height at the Mayer and Sam Wiener houses and single story at the Weekend House on Cross Lake and the Ramsey, Boatner, Flesh, Preston, Levy, and Jacques Wiener residences. The design of the horizontal and vertical framing varied from project to project, and in all cases the proportions were matched to the overall design of the house. The two-story screened porch at the Mayer and Sam Wiener houses had a monumental appearance because the interstitial zone between floors did not interrupt the framing for the screen. The frequency of the screen's horizontal members was greater

Screen porch at the David J. and Florence Flesh House.
Photo by Guy W. Carwile.

near the floor level, giving the illusion of a guardrail and of stability to the screen. In all documented examples of the Wieners' screened porches, the top horizontal members were sloped in order to shed water and extended beyond the vertical supports to give them increased prominence. The mesh was usually bronze or copper to avoid the rusting that would occur on a steel screen, and the mesh's darker color adjacent to pale stuccoed walls enhanced the play of light and shade and solid and void in a building's composition.

Inside, large openings between the porch and the house maximized flow-through ventilation. Later, when air-conditioning became available, the Wieners no longer incorporated screened porches or other passive cooling methods in their projects. With the exception of the Flesh House, all the porches have been enclosed.

Mechanical Ventilation

The Wieners began to include forced-air ventilation in the houses they designed shortly after completion of the Weekend House on Cross Lake, which at first relied on cross-ventilation through casement windows in parallel walls. The house's four-foot-tall attic space helped insulate the living areas below and allowed the hot air to stratify and be expelled to the exterior through simple sheet-metal gravity vents. Sam and William knew that the interior comfort level could be increased if natural ventilation was enhanced. To accomplish this they fabricated an attic fan from an electric motor and an aircraft propeller and placed it vertically in the attic space. The fan drew air from the casement windows up through vents in the ceiling into the attic and out through the mounted gravity vents at the roof, thus assisting both interior and attic ventilation, three years before attic fans were commercially available. The diminutive Preston House also had a vertically positioned attic fan that ventilated in similar fashion through the attic space.

In 1934, during construction of the Wile House, the brothers began employing roof-mounted fan houses for all their residential designs. The fan was placed vertically inside this roof projection and drew air from the interior directly up and out to the exterior without dispersing through the attic. The fan house was given its own flat roof with an overhang to protect the fan and the interior from wind-blown rain. A baffle, manipulated by a sash cord, blocked outside air from entering the fan house in the closed position and was held underneath the overhang when in the open position. Pulling on a sash cord hanging from the ceiling grille opened the baffle during periods of warm weather when ventilation was desired, and releasing the cord closed the baffle during the winter. The automatic louver mechanism associated with mid-century attic fans was not patented and available until 1946. The Wile House was not originally designed with a fan house, but one was added during or shortly after completion of the initial construction phase. It was removed during a subsequent reroofing project. Exterior fan houses as a regular part of the Wieners' residential designs began with the Flesh House and Sam Wiener's own house and were incorporated in most house projects designed before the war. In all cases the boxy-shaped fan houses with their own roof overhangs echoed on a diminutive scale the geometry of the houses of which they were a part.

Interiors

In the early houses, rooms were knit together through the use of plaster furr downs (lowered sections of the ceiling) that housed the forced-air heating distribution and gave spatial definition to the interconnecting rooms. Later at, for example, the Sam Wiener and Jacques Wiener houses, the furr downs were easily modified to house the ductwork for air-conditioning systems. The Wieners often painted the furr downs in a color complementary to the walls and one that might be used for the walls of an adjacent room. In this way they achieved an effect of one space merging into another. To further enhance a flow of space and continuity of surface, they recessed site-built custom light fixtures into room ceilings. Yet, other than these fixtures and the furr downs, much of their approach to the interiors in the prewar residential work was fairly typical for the day.

In his own house Sam had used terrazzo as a floor finish for the downstairs screened sitting porch and the entrance hall to give a sense of linkage. In their residential work built after the war Sam and William used terrazzo frequently when the building foundations were on grade, pouring it before interior partition walls were installed. This practice began with William's house of 1950. The continuity of floor surface corresponded with the then-new trend of blending the living room with the dining area and the interior with the exterior through large plate-glass windows. Terrazzo has many advantages, among them durability and ease of maintenance, but the Wieners also must have appreciated terrazzo's capacity to add color to an interior through the choice of the marble chips. And the material's polished reflective surface, which dissolved the impression of solid weight, could be enhanced by the placement of area rugs in contrasting matt textures and colors to increase the abstract qualities of their interior spaces.

The Influence of Books and Magazines

Sam maintained an extensive library of architecture books and architectural journals. Although there is no complete record of the contents of his collection, a significant number of titles are known from a donation Sam made in 1966 to the library of Louisiana State University in Baton Rouge. The journals filled in gaps in LSU's collections, and there is no record of what they were, but LSU did keep a record of the books, which were integrated into the main collection. Sam's books ranged from studies of historic and early twentieth-century European architecture to a 1914 monograph on Austrian architect Otto Wagner and Oliver Reagan's three-volume edition of *American Architecture of the Twentieth Century,* which was published in 1927. The donation also included such useful trade publications as Maurice M. Sloan's *The Concrete House and Its Construction* (Association of American Portland Cement Manufacturers, 1912); *Color and Style in Bathroom Furnishings and Decoration* (Pittsburgh: Standard Sanitary Manufacturing Co. 1929); *Architectural Terra Cotta* (New York: National Terra Cotta Society, 1914); and an undated catalog of *The Northwestern Terra Cotta Co. of Chicago.*[2]

The Shreveporter Highway Hotel.

Courtesy of LSU-Shreveport Archives and Special Collections.

6

SHREVEPORT'S GROWTH AND MODERNIZATION, 1940 TO THE 1950s

Sustained by the wealth generated from nearby oil and gas fields, Shreveport survived the Great Depression less disastrously than other American cities and, as the war effort surged in the first years of the 1940s, so did the city's economy. Barksdale Air Base was expanded, aided by its role as a center for training pilots from 1939 on, and the construction of an ordnance plant east of Shreveport and various defense contracts brought new jobs. With six rail lines serving the city and four federal highways, including US 80, a transcontinental route from Savannah to San Diego, and US 59 to Houston, Shreveport affirmed its position as a commercial and transportation center for the region.

Although improvements to Shreveport's infrastructure had been made during the 1930s, most notably the Municipal Incinerator, many others had been delayed and private building had slowed. At the conclusion of World War II, these problems came to the fore, made more urgent by the leap in Shreveport's population from 76,655 in 1930 to 115,000 in 1946. It continued to increase during the remainder of the 1940s to reach 127,206 in 1950. Housing shortages, overcrowded schools with the anticipation of worse to come as families reestablished so-called normal life, and outdated and insufficient medical facilities marked the postwar era. In 1946, Shreveport's mayor, Clyde Fant, issued a report to the City Planning Commission emphasizing the necessity of new construction and improvements to streets, sewerage, and electric power.[1] Bond issues put before voters in 1946 and 1947 to fund the improvements were overwhelmingly approved, and the 1947 issue of *Shreveport Magazine* could trumpet the city's growth and modernization, featuring news on planning issues, residential and commercial development, road construction, and the expansion of educational and medical facilities. From the late 1940s, the magazine regularly published reports on building contracts issued and information on housing developments and new subdivisions. In this context of vigorous growth, one project in particular summed up the city's aspirations to confirm its place as a major regional center. This was the new airport, and for Sam and William it was one of the many buildings that formed their greatly expanded architectural practice in the postwar years.

SHREVEPORT MUNICIPAL AIRPORT

In 1947, Shreveport's citizens approved a bond issue to fund and construct an entirely new airport, rather than attempt to enlarge the existing downtown airport of 1931 designed by Jones, Roessle, Olschner and Wiener. The decision was based on the conclusions of a study by the renowned Detroit architectural and engineering firm of Smith, Hinchman and Grylls, hired by the city to prepare an *Airport Survey and Suggested Program of Development.* Completed in November 1948, the report recommended that, although the downtown airport had the advantage of being within just one mile of the city's downtown and business center, its location on a concave bend of the Red River made any runway extension necessary for larger planes and increased flight traffic, especially the anticipated leisure travel, virtually impossible. Additionally, the old airport's proximity to Barksdale Air Force Base—a mere three miles—had considerable potential for danger. The report advised the city to locate the airport approximately ten miles from Barksdale, approved the city's proposed site in the Hollywood area southwest of downtown, and suggested that the terminal be capable of handling 450 to 500 passengers during peak hours of operation.[2]

The airport, built under the authority of the city's Department of Public Works, was financed in part by a voter-approved bond and from a grant from the Civil Aeronautics Administration. The contract for design and construction was awarded to Samuel G. Wiener, E. M. Freeman and Associates, Architects and Engineers, a joint architect-engineer collaboration. Sam already had experience with some of the complexities of an airport project for he had worked on the downtown airport of 1931 that this new complex was supplanting. Sam's partner for the project, Freeman, a civil engineer with a practice in Shreveport, had collaborated on projects with Edward F. Neild for two years before setting up his own firm in 1930. William was also a member of the design team for the airport. In an interview in 1972 he observed that of all the projects he had worked on, the airport best exemplified his approach to architecture because a successful outcome depended on the resolution of planning and circulation.[3]

The airport site was sixteen acres of partially wooded and cultivated land to the southwest of downtown, which already had direct access from Hollywood Boulevard and Monkhouse Drive. Site preparation consisted of clearing trees and leveling the slightly hilly ground, and the rerouting of West Seventieth Street to the south to circumvent the runways. (This explains the U-shaped curve on what is otherwise a perfectly straight road.) In addition to the terminal building, Sam and his associates designed structures for maintenance, gasoline fueling, and other essential facilities, and two concrete runways, with the main and longer runway running east-west and the secondary north-south.

Today the airport, which has been supplanted by the adjacent terminal of 1971 (with later additions), has suffered alterations to serve its current office-and-storage use. Its control tower has been decapitated, an exterior observation deck that overlooked the landing field was removed, and much of its interior space is now divided up and obscured. Yet enough of Sam's design survives to give an idea of the airport's original comfort and convenience, and the sophisticated glamor that characterized air travel in the 1950s.

In response to the rapid expansion of commercial air travel in the 1940s, the U.S. Civil Aeronautics Administration (CAA) began to publish guidelines focused on airport planning and design. Periodically updated, these handbooks outlined factors in site selection, airport layout, runway lengths for different sizes of airports and types of aircraft, runway orientation in relation to prevailing winds, runway surface material, the proximity of other airports and residential neighborhoods, and provision for the servicing of airplanes and equipment. The CAA's publication of 1949, for example, also addressed the necessity of providing rapid exchange between air and ground transportation through accessibility to public parking areas, and it stressed the importance of making the airport a civic asset with landscaping, driveways, plantings, and shade trees.[4] Looking to the future, the guide recommended that an airport and its terminal should be designed with the thought

of enlargement or alteration. But even the CAA in 1949 could not anticipate the enormous increase in passenger and freight travel that would occur over the next decades and the impact of jet travel. That growth has resulted in the demolition or major alteration of many beautifully designed airports of the 1950s and 1960s. Fortunately such masterpieces as Eero Saarinen's TWA Terminal at John F. Kennedy Airport (initially known as Idlewild) and Dulles Airport terminal outside of Washington, D.C., both completed in 1962 (though the lengthening of Dulles has

Shreveport Municipal Airport.
Courtesy of LSU-Shreveport Archives and Special Collections.

Shreveport Municipal Airport.
Courtesy of Guy W. Carwile.

spoiled its proportions), have been recognized and maintained. As for Shreveport's terminal, although replaced by the 1971 building, enough survives to convey its original sophisticated plan and aesthetics.

Along with the CAA handbooks, architectural journals in the early 1950s embraced the topic of airport design. While much of the journals' advice and recommendations were drawn from the CAA guidelines, their focus was primarily on the design of a terminal building in relation to passenger use, circulation, services offered, weather protection for passengers as they walked out to the apron to board a plane, and airport furniture. Interestingly, one article proposed that issues of circulation and services that an architect faced in designing an airport were comparable to those of a modern shopping center, a building type that also was a favorite topic in the journals of the 1940s and 1950s.[5]

Drawings for the new airport were finalized in 1950. Conceived as a showplace for the city, the airport's design, materials, and interior fittings fully demonstrated that goal. The terminal building has a reinforced concrete frame, and steel was used for the framing of the observation decks. Faced in light-colored beige brick, the terminal was divided into two sections, one for the public and the other for such administrative and operational facilities as the control tower, radar room, weather bureau, post office, and various offices. Although separated by a breezeway, the roof continued the same line across both units to give the appearance of a single building. All public spaces and offices were air-conditioned.

To achieve a pleasing and coherent appearance from the air as well as from ground level, the architects made a model of the building in order to study and understand its appearance from the perspective of passengers observing it while landing or taking off. Seen from ground level, whether approached from Monkhouse Drive or Hollywood Boulevard, both of which were less built up than today, the terminal had a monumental presence in the open spaces of its airfield. Although the building's massing was primarily horizontal, the pronounced verticals of the control tower at one end and the tall rectangular entrance portal balancing it near the other acted as strong markers of place.

Of the terminal's public section, the main entrance and lobby survive in almost their original state. The entrance is framed by a deep monumental rectangular portal, which on a grand scale repeats the portal Sam designed for Caddo Heights Elementary School (1949) and later employed for other buildings in the 1950s. This portico opened into a double-height lobby, an airy and light space illuminated by clerestory windows at each end. Along the length of the lobby's ceiling were three large circular coves for concealed incandescent lights. Now containing pendant light fixtures, the coves would have appeared like glowing disks, perhaps alluding to the global reach of the airport.

To the left of the lobby were the restaurant and kitchen, and to the right a large space that incorporated a row of ticket-counters and the waiting room. This was the grandest of all the spaces, with walls clad in glistening pinkish-brown veined marble, and a terrazzo floor, lit by clere-

Shreveport Municipal Airport.
Courtesy of LSU-Shreveport Archives and Special Collections.

story windows, one over the ticket counters and the other illuminating the waiting area. The ticket-counter area was delineated from the waiting room by evenly spaced angled supports (called bents and which rigidly tie the beams), also clad in the pinkish-brown marble, which carried the gently single-pitched ceiling. The space conveyed the shiny smoothness of modern beauty. Architect-designer James R. Lamantia of New Orleans designed the furniture for the waiting room—inch-square wrought-iron-framed chairs with seat cushions and floating backs and small side tables, sturdy but light in appearance and through which space flowed as freely as between the ticket and waiting areas. The clear contrast between the tough iron frame and the soft cushions emphasized their different function, a modernist distinction that was always present in Lamantia's designs. As *Architectural Record* described the chairs, they are "not for the man intent on hours-long lounging," but "they serve visually as crisp, angular shapes wandering lightly and rhythmically around the expansive, wealthily marble-walled and terrazzo-floored waiting room."[6] Although this entire area is now closed off and subdivided for office and storage space, the marble facing and the terrazzo floors survive.

Access to the airplanes, in a pattern typical of the time and recommended by the journals, was along a covered "finger" walkway. Here it extended 350 feet into the airfield apron, which had parking spaces for six planes, nose-in and positioned at a diagonal. The walkway was enclosed only by a low steel guardrail painted bright red.

The airport offered another feature no longer found in today's airports. A two-hundred-foot-long outdoor observation deck on the runway side of the terminal allowed visitors to stand and view airplanes and passengers arriving and departing. The deck was accessed from a flight of stairs at the rear of the lobby or by an exterior spiral staircase, and the railings of the stairs and deck were painted red to match the walkway's guardrail. A color illustration of the deck on the cover of the February 1953 edition of *Architectural Record* presented a glamorous and progressive image of travel. Air transportation was still relatively novel for most passengers, and the spectacle of airplanes taking off and landing was thrilling, for adults as well as children, though in the last few years airport designers have been reincorporating areas to view the runways, always glass-walled. Three months after the airport opened on July 5, 1952, the deck served as a speaker's stand for President Dwight D. Eisenhower, who addressed an audience of more than twenty thousand gathered on the airfield below on October 16, 1952, during a campaign tour.

Both the site and the buildings were designed for future growth, and while the site proved sufficiently large for runway extension, the terminal was replaced in response to vastly increased traffic and evolving federal safety regulations.

From Downtown to the Suburbs

The airport was built on the edge of Shreveport in an area with few buildings, although now the city's growth has reached it. Closer to downtown, outward growth, which had begun in earnest in the 1920s, accelerated after World War II. To counter the drift from center city to the suburbs, there was a sustained effort to revive downtown commerce. In a program similar to the "modernize mainstreet" initiative of the 1930s, old stores were glamorized with new facades and the shopping experience enhanced with new facilities. Sears, which now owned Feibleman's, added air-conditioning, remodeled the store's interior, and built a parking garage. Sam and William gave the Palais Royal, a fashionable women's clothing store at the northwest corner of Milam and McNeil, a facelift in 1948 by encasing the building with stucco panels, which transformed it into an unadorned box with a rounded corner, interrupted only narrowly by three horizontal bands of windows. Founded in Shreveport by Isadore Erlich in 1921, the Palais Royal, a chain with stores in Texas and other neighboring states, and as far north as Washington D.C., sold out to Alexandria-based Wellan's in 1985.

The Shreveport firm of Neild and Somdal renovated Jordan and Booth in 1949, and Selber Brothers, a Jewish-owned company that had grown rapidly from a one-person operation established in 1900, commissioned Neild and Somdal to design an entirely new air-conditioned clothing store. Completed in 1955 at the southwest corner of Milam and McNeil, the five-story brick-faced store was linked at mezzanine level to a parking garage that allowed customers to enter the store without exposure to the weather. Increased traffic and minimal curbside parking had forced commercial businesses to build or rent parking garages in order to encourage shoppers to come downtown. Nevertheless, in the 1960s, improved highways to suburban shopping malls, especially the new enclosed and air-conditioned malls, with their unlimited free parking on surface lots, cost downtowns their customers, and Selber's closed in the 1980s. Similar changes were taking place in cities throughout the nation.

Simultaneously, progress saw other business ventures spread their tentacles from downtown to construct high-rise office and institutional buildings in nearby residential districts. Within a few years the character of the Highland neighborhood immediately south of downtown was transformed from a middle-class, early twentieth-century residential enclave to a mixed-use area. The impact was especially profound in the Fairfield neighborhood and along its principal thoroughfare, Fairfield Avenue, and its adjacent streets. Fairfield Avenue curves and extends from downtown to the Cedar Grove neighborhood.

THE FAIRFIELD BUILDING

On a site one block south of the Fairfield Big Chain store of 1928, the Commercial National Bank commissioned Samuel G. Wiener and Associates in 1948 to design a four-story building to accommodate a branch of their bank on the first floor with rental space above. A parking lot large enough for the bank's clients and the building's employees was an essential part of the project. Completed in 1949, the structure was named the Fairfield Building for its location on that avenue.

The building, which sits at the corner of Jacobs Street, forms a remarkable contrast with the Big Chain store, demonstrating not just changing architectural fashions but the preferences of the clients. Certainly the Fairfield Building fit much more with Sam's architectural taste. Nevertheless, both buildings are visually appropriate for their function. Where the grocery store was richly embellished and tactile with its brick and shiny terra-cotta detailing, this building is restrained in its smooth-surfaced austerity, celebrating the era's aesthetics and seriousness of purpose in its form, materials, and technology.

Bands of windows continue uninterrupted around the building's corners to suggest that the walls are merely a skin, as indeed they are over the steel frame. The light-colored beige brick, later painted white, for the building's outer skin and the metal-framed windows flush with the walls enhance the weightless quality. This was a feature that Sam and William had made central to their buildings of the 1930s, but which only gained popular acceptance in the postwar period in America. At roof level a steel track placed to carry the maintenance and window-washing cart forms a wide curve as it negotiates the building's corner. The visual impact of this curved line is all the more intense in its contrast with the building's insistent angularity and complete lack of traditional ornamentation. The gentle curve of the cantilevered metal-edged marquee over the off-center entrance is the sole echo of the maintenance track's arc. And vertical window mullions are the

Fairfield Building.
Courtesy of LSU-Shreveport Archives and Special Collections.

only counter to the building's emphatic horizontal expression. The lower walls are clad in polished black granite. Inside, the interior walls were non-load-bearing partitions allowing for flexible room layouts, a planning feature that became ubiquitous nationwide in postwar office buildings.

The small two-story brick structure on the Fairfield Building's south side predates it. Also designed by Samuel G. Wiener and Associates, the building served as offices for the Southern Production Company. The Commercial National Bank later moved out of the Fairfield Building, but by then the area was undergoing another transition. To a large extent this was the result of the construction of Interstate 20 just to the west, which sliced the Fairfield area from downtown.

Transitions

Several large institutional buildings in the Fairfield area denote the local changes that were taking place in the 1940s and 1950s. Opposite the Fairfield Building is the former eight-story office structure of 1940 designed by Neild and Somdal for the United Gas Corporation. The oil business that had boomed with the war in Europe did not slacken afterward and, with the increased use of automobiles and other oil-hungry machines, it flourished. United Gas built a twelve-story addition to the original building's rear in 1952. Subsequently, demonstrating the rapidity of change in the ownership of oil corporations, Houston-based Pennzoil acquired United Gas in 1965 and moved its headquarters to that city. This was an event not specific to Shreveport, but part of a general pattern of oil-related business shifting from Louisiana to Houston and other Texas cities. The building closed, and the state purchased it in 1975.

In 1950, when the Fairfield area was still experiencing its immediate postwar building boom, Sam and William designed the three-story former East Building of the Physicians and Surgeons (P&S) Hospital that occupies the corner of Jordan Street and Line Avenue, a few blocks east of the Fairfield Building. Originally only six bays wide on Jordan Street, the building later received additions, not by Sam or William. The Wiener-designed section is still recognizable by the cantilevered canopy shading the ground floor, the upper-story windows that are so closely spaced that from a distance they seem to form two parallel horizontal bands, and the continuous louvered canopy that extends to filter sun and light to the interior. A short distance to the southwest at Kings Highway and Linwood Avenue stood the Confederate Memorial Medical Center. Sam was a member of the hospital's design team with the firms of Neild and Somdal, and of Van Os and Flaxman. Completed in 1953, the hospital was physically absorbed into the LSU Medical Center Hospital, which now spreads across and beyond its original site. A drawing of the hospital featured in the June 1953 edition of *Shreveport Magazine* shows the building composed of a rising sequence of rectangular blocks to reach ten stories, with an adjoining five-story School of Nursing. Aerial photographs of the time reveal that it dominated in size and height what was then its low-scaled still primarily residential district.

Transitions were also occurring in the way people shopped for everyday needs and the places where they shopped. From the late 1940s, urban decentralization and new residential subdivisions accelerated the development of new shopping centers. In a nationwide pattern, these centers increasingly consisted of a group of stores planned, developed, and maintained as a unit with ample off-street parking provided on the premises. It is estimated that eighteen hundred such centers were built nationwide between 1950 and 1955. Ed Wile had established this formula successfully in 1940 at Big Chain Broadmoor, making the supermarket the dominant presence or anchor of a cluster of smaller shops. In many ways that center was a pioneer in the development of the type, yet it belonged to a tradition of locating the stores in separate clusters at all four corners of an intersection, recalling historic downtown or small-town configurations. This pattern was soon to change.

BIG CHAIN, LAKESHORE, AND BIG CHAIN UPTOWN CENTER

Opened in 1947, Big Chain on the southwest corner of Lakeshore Drive and Jewella Avenue followed a similar scheme with an attachment of several smaller stores that wrapped the corner. Sam and William reinforced the chain's brand image with the same features and iconography as that of Big Chain Broadmoor—exterior canopy, red letters, and red detailing, clerestory window, and interior organization. As at Broadmoor, the block is set back from the sidewalk to provide a row of parking in front so that customers could drive directly into the lot from either of the two streets it dominates. With greater size and

Big Chain Store, Lakeshore.
Courtesy of LSU-Shreveport Archives and Special Collections.

height than the companion shops clinging to the store's side walls, bands of glass block clerestory windows were inserted just below Big Chain's roof to illuminate the interior. The roofs of the supermarket and those of the accompanying shops projected to create a shaded walkway in front. This roof canopy also formed a horizontal line linking the individual parts into a unified complex. But Big Chain dominated, and to emphasize its entrance the roof thrusts further forward as a canopy and the store's name in huge red letters marched across the edge of its confident upward tilt. The name, the color, and the familiar design gave reassurance of the store's reputation. Although altered and no longer occupied by Big Chain, the center retains its essential massing.

Historic photographs of the store reveal a spacious and well-lit interior, with strips of fluorescent light running parallel to the shelving units. The location of various foodstuffs was announced in large letters in a clean angular font similar to the store's sign on the wall area between the display shelves and clerestory window. The store had five checkout stands, and a lunch counter and a seated dining area occupied the cafeteria, which was placed conveniently in the corner opposite the entrance.

The site and plan of the Big Chain Uptown Center designed by Samuel G. and William B. Wiener and Associates and begun in 1955 represented the next generation of shopping centers, where vast surface parking lots foreground the stores. Occupying nearly two blocks at the corner of Line Avenue and Pierremont Road, Uptown Big Chain followed a scheme that became synonymous with the strip mall. Although the Big Chain store is now occupied by another chain, the other shops have found new occupants, some additions were made to the end of the strip, and the individual shop fronts have been altered and united with a postmodern facade, the center still conveys the concept behind the original scheme. It was a continuous single-story strip of shops set to the rear of the site and preceded by an enormous concrete-paved parking lot that could hold more than seven hundred automobiles.

Twice the size of any shopping center in metropolitan Shreveport when built and three times the size of the Broadmoor complex, this center included retail stores, service establishments, and easy access directly into the parking area from Line Avenue. Big Chain anchored one end of the strip, with a cafeteria to its side that could seat 250. Among the shops were a beauty salon, a barber, a pharmacy, two women's ready-to-wear shops, a shoe-repair shop, a laundry service, as well as jewelry, men's, children's, variety, and hardware stores. A service station occupied the corner of Line and Pierremont. As at the Broadmoor complex, the center focused primarily on the shopping responsibilities or preferences of women. Although the center's continuous row of shops is reminiscent of a nineteenth-century main street, this was a new form of commercial urbanism, providing one-stop shopping with sufficient and dedicated parking.

Three towering pylons carrying lights to illuminate the parking lot are substitutes for the originals, and the original tall sign at the lot's edge announcing the center has been replaced. When commercial buildings were fronted by vast surface parking areas as here, a means of indicating their presence was essential and free-standing pylon signage raised high above their surroundings served that purpose. In their 1951 study of shopping-center design and operation, Baker and Funaro recommended, "Signs must be large enough to be read at 40 m.p.h. . . . [and] should be set at an angle to the traffic flow."[7] Hotels, motels, restaurants, and gas stations strung along America's highways had already begun to add similar features.

The strip scheme proved such a success that it became ubiquitous nationwide. In Shreveport, the Big Chain Uptown scheme was followed, more or less, in the Wieners' subsequent designs for Big Chain stores in Bossier City in 1954 and Shreve City Regional Shopping Center in 1961 on Shreveport-Barksdale Highway. Yet shopping strips and malls and supermarkets sometimes have relatively short lives. Often it is because their physical location makes them no longer commercially sustainable, especially when their customer base disappears or a supermarket might be bought out by another hungry chain. Big Chains Fairfield and Broadmoor went out of business because their customer catchment areas changed. The creep of institutional and commercial buildings into the Fairfield store's formerly residential neighborhoods doomed it, and Big Chain Broadmoor was displaced as Shreveport expanded to the south and larger shopping centers on a single site were preferred to those that spread across an intersection. At Big Chain Uptown the site's continued viability was made possible by its residential neighborhood, which has changed little over the years. As for the Big Chain company, Wile sold his share of the stores in 1957, but Louie Levy remained as vice-president, though he had also joined the Uptown Development Corporation, which was one of the developers of the Uptown Shopping Center. Big Chain stores remained in operation for several years until bought out by Kroger. Supermarkets, so dependent on location, share many parallels with hotels and motels constructed in the 1950s and 1960s along highways that have lost the necessary traffic with the expansion of the interstate highway system.

THE SHREVEPORTER HIGHWAY HOTEL

When he selected a four-hundred-foot-wide site on Greenwood Road (US 80) at Broadway, A. Jack Tullos was anticipating that future growth in the hotel business lay along such cross-country routes. The site was on the same road as the state fairgrounds, just two miles from the recently opened Municipal Airport and a mere four miles from downtown. The hotel would thus appeal to business people, tourists and vacationers, and those on route elsewhere. Tullos, the principal stockholder in the group of shareholders who developed the hotel, had served from 1929 to 1952 as manager of the now-demolished Washington-Youree Hotel at Texas and Market streets. Sam with Jones, Roessle, Olschner and Wiener had

The Shreveporter Highway Hotel. *Courtesy of LSU-Shreveport Archives and Special Collections.*

worked on alterations and additions to the hotel in the 1920s. It is probably no coincidence that Sam Wiener Jr.'s office was on the first floor of the building.

Designed by Sam and William, with Jesse O. Morgan and Aubrey E. Butler as associates, The Shreveporter Highway Hotel was begun in 1953 and opened in 1955. Every aspect of the hotel was architect designed, from the building to the landscaping, interior decoration, menus, and stationary.[8] The reception building comprised the front portion of the hotel and included a lounge, a dining room, and the kitchen (see Plate 5). A small unit of guest rooms was attached to its side. Behind this portion was a spacious courtyard with a dining terrace and a swimming pool, and beyond these were two single-story V-shaped blocks of guest rooms. Instead of the rows of separate cottages common before World War II (and as still evident at the Palomar Hotel located on US 80 only several hundred feet to the west of the Shreveporter), in the 1950s linear blocks of attached rooms became standard for motor hotels and motels. This format allowed for the much more economical system of center-core construction with rooms arranged back to back along a utility core and the bathrooms of every four units grouped at the intersecting corners; a single row of rooms would have the bathrooms attached to the adjoining walls. At the Shreveporter, both systems were employed.

The V-shape of the guest-room blocks gave each room an orientation less than twenty degrees off the Wieners' ideal north-south orientation. Rooms varied in size, and those facing the swimming pool were larger and more deluxe and intended for families and leisure travelers. These rooms had sliding glass doors that opened to individual patios shaded by a deep extension of the flat roof and fins (wing walls) between the units for privacy and blocking of noise. Parking for automobiles was at the entrance to each room and at the rear of the units that faced the main courtyard. The swimming pool, an irregularly shaped rectangle, was surrounded by a paved terrace and grassy areas, with clusters of plants in planter boxes, including ornamental banana trees. The dining-room terrace was partially bordered by low bushes. Inside, each guest room was decorated with an unpainted wall of exposed brick, a newly fashionable interior feature but one that also reduced the maintenance costs that a smooth-painted surface would require. An abstract painting by Sam's son, artist Samuel Wiener Jr., decorated each room. The rooms included individual control of air-conditioning.

Set well back from the road behind a semicircular driveway and grass-covered forecourt, which shielded it from the noise of highway traffic, the hotel needed bold signage to be seen at a distance and at automobile speed. At the street edge, a tall freestanding triangular-shaped steel pylon carried three monumental placards to herald the hotel. The pylon's summit carried "The Shreveporter" spelled out in white letters on a blue background, with the letter "S" in a dynamic zigzag shape. Underneath that panel was another that indicated that this was a "Highway Hotel," and below that an additional panel advertised that the hotel had a swimming pool and dining terrace. A row of flags representing various nations fluttered above the lobby's roofline to help draw attention to the hotel. The flags and the street sign, essential components of the design, were also a modern version of traditional ornament, but now simple, abstract, colorful, and graphic. Where the Wieners' ornament had followed the Bauhaus practice of eliminating applied decoration and instead resided in little more than a building's name spelled out on its wall or entrance canopy, here it had become an essential, if independent, component of the architectural composition. The street sign had an identity of its own yet was in a relationship with its building that, much like a marriage, emphasized the importance of the space between as well as the bond. Later, when the Shreveporter became a Sheraton Motor Inn, the hotel chain retained and used the pylon for its logo (though substituting its own signature letter "S") and kept the flags along the lobby's roof.

Plate 1.
Kings Highway Christian Church.
Photo by Guy W. Carwile.

Plate 2.
Municipal Memorial Auditorium.
Photo by Guy W. Carwile.

Plate 3.
I. Edward and Jessamine Thalheimer Wile House.
Photo by Guy W. Carwile.

Plate 4.
David J. and Florence Flesh House.
Photo by Guy W. Carwile.

Plate 5.
The Shreveporter Highway Hotel.
Courtesy of Guy W. Carwile.

Plate 6.
B'nai Zion Temple.
Photo by Guy W. Carwile.

Plate 7.
William B. and Carolyn Wiener House, Jackson, Mississippi.
Photo by Guy W. Carwile.

Plate 8.
Marcus and Martine H. Ginsburg House, Fort Worth, Texas.
Photo by Trey Freeze.

Plate 9.
James and Jean R. Muslow House.
Photo by Guy W. Carwile.

Plate 10.
Haughton High School.
Photo by Guy W. Carwile.

Plate 11.
Samuel G. and Marion Pfeifer Wiener House.
Photo by Roy Parish.

Plate 12.
J. S. Clark Junior High School.
Photo by Guy W. Carwile.

Plate 13.
Woodlawn High School, classroom building.
Photo by Guy W. Carwile.

Plate 14.
Woodlawn High School,
atrium at cafeteria.
Photo by Guy W. Carwile.

Plate 15.
Masonic Temple.
Photo by Guy W. Carwile.

Plate 16.
James and Jean R. Muslow House.
Photo by Guy W. Carwile.

Jack Tullos, with Sam and William, created a hotel that had all the desired innovations and comforts of modern travel. Unfortunately its life was limited by events beyond its control. In 1965, Interstate 20 cut an east-west path just a mile and a half south of the hotel, drawing transient traffic from US 80, and although the hotel prospered for several years, the introduction of hotels at the interstate's access roads ultimately drew away too many patrons. It was demolished in the 1990s, and today only the concrete foundation slabs of the hotel's V-shaped room units and reception area survive. They are visible on satellite aerial views, as is the outline of the now filled-in swimming pool.

While the hotel was under construction in 1954, William designed a house for Tullos (discussed in chapter 9) a few blocks north of the hotel in a growing subdivision. Shreveport was growing to the west, encouraged in part by the location of the airport to the southwest. The city also continued its expansion south with streets of middle-class single houses set among trees and lawns, and modern schools for an expanding student population.

B'NAI ZION TEMPLE

It was in a residential neighborhood on the southernmost edge of Broadmoor that the B'nai Zion temple chose the location for a larger building that would accommodate worship, community activities, a school, and a library. Many of the congregants who attended the B'nai Zion temple on Cotton Street on the edge of Shreveport's downtown had already followed in the path of the southward residential developments. In 1956 the congregation moved from the Beaux-Arts classical building of 1914 designed by Edward F. Neild and Clarence Olschner to a new building on Southfield Road. The temple's design was a collaboration of equally distinguished architects—Seymour Van Os, Theodore Flaxman, and Sam. The Werner Construction Company was the contractor. B'nai Zion's appearance, however, was quite unlike the ornate classical temple of 1914; it was instead a long, low-key building of beige Roman brick with minimal exterior ornamentation, and in contrast to its former tight urban setting, the new building was surrounded by expansive lawns and trees (see Plate 6). The building, which incorporates an education wing with classrooms, offices, and a library, as well as an auditorium and a chapel, is a harmonious composition of advancing and receding, mostly rectangular, units. A signature feature of the building is the rectangular-framed deep entrance portal similar to the porticoes Sam designed for Caddo Heights Elementary School and the Municipal Airport. Its shadowy depths mediate between the bright sunlight outside and the muted light of a large lobby inside.

B'nai Zion Temple.

Courtesy of LSU-Shreveport Archives and Special Collections.

Although the interior has experienced some alterations, many of the original features survive, including sections of the black-and-white terrazzo floor in the corridor and of coral and buff in the auditorium (not unlike the terrazzo that Sam and William used for floor surfaces in their house designs of the 1950s). The wood-paneled auditorium has a stepped ceiling like that of William's solution for Linwood Junior High School (discussed in chapter 8). Other walls in the building were originally exposed Roman brick, though most of it has been painted. The chapel has been remodeled and, while the vertical wooden slats across the end have been retained, they have been placed in different configuration. Stained glass windows are replicas of those in the downtown building. Many buildings display the name of the architect inscribed on a cornerstone or on a plaque near the entrance, but the decision made here in 1955 stated that "it is intended that no individual names of committees, contractors, or architects be placed on the outside of the building."[9]

Change in Direction

During the 1950s, Sam and William moved their designs in a different direction. There was a greater emphasis on traditional materials, most particularly brick, and the way they treated it and the colors they chose were more subdued and serene than those of the 1920s and 1930s. Many of their commissions were for building types that were new to them and conceptually complex, which offered them novel challenges in developing plans and interiors that satisfied human needs. The houses and schools they designed in this period also reveal their sensitivity to changing client needs in a postwar world.

7

POSTWAR HOUSES

Following World War II, the number of Sam and William's architectural commissions quickly eclipsed prewar levels. While their projects were primarily commercial or institutional, both architects designed houses for affluent clients who were their relatives or members of the small but influential Jewish community in Shreveport, following the pattern of their commissions in the 1930s. Before the war, the brothers had looked to Europe for modern architectural inspiration, and in the postwar years their designs continued to reveal the impact of European modernism though now it was European forms translated for American culture and taste, and using newly available materials and technologies. In the 1930s, Walter Gropius, Marcel Breuer, Mies van der Rohe, and Erich Mendelsohn were among the European architects who immigrated to the United States to escape the rise of Nazism. Gropius, Breuer, and Mies, all of whom had taught at the Bauhaus, arrived in 1937. Gropius and Breuer were hired to teach in the new progressive curriculum that Joseph Hudnut established in 1936 at Harvard's Graduate School of Design (GSD). Mies taught at Chicago's Armour Institute, which became Illinois Institute of Technology and for which Mies designed the campus plan and many of its buildings. Mies came directly from Germany, but Breuer had fled that country in 1933 for England, as did Gropius in 1934 before coming to the East Coast. Mendelsohn also settled in England in 1933 before relocating to California in 1941. Under the tutelage of Gropius and Breuer at Harvard and Mies in Chicago, a new generation of American-born modernist architects emerged in the 1950s, extending the reach of modernism across the United States. Of the three, Breuer had the most profound impact on American single-family residential architecture. The houses he designed over more than two decades for clients in New England were widely published in journals and magazines, and Sam and William's work shows the impact of Breuer's ideas. The Wieners' houses also show parallels with those of Richard Neutra in California, more so after World War II than before, when all three architects employed wood and stone rather than smooth painted surfaces, and with the Case Study House program sponsored by *Arts and Architecture* magazine under the editorial guidance of John Entenza.

In the postwar decades, the brothers developed their architectural approaches, particularly in the realm of residential architecture, from primarily volumetric to planar. As well, Sam's experiments with modularity as a means of planning and ordering a building, as at Bossier (1938) and Haughton (1940) high schools, became a guiding principle in their residential designs, especially for William.

No project more clearly delineates this shift in approach than the house he designed in 1950 for himself, his wife Babette, son William (Bill Jr.), and daughter Karen (Kay). In this decade, too, Sam and William's work saw a greater geographical spread, as they designed houses for clients in Mississippi and Texas.

WILLIAM B. AND BABETTE WIENER HOUSE

Like Sam and Jacques before him, William selected two lots (numbered 5 and 36) for his house within the Pine Park subdivision, which he had helped design and develop in the 1930s. William's site was more secluded than those of his brothers and was well suited to the architecture he was contemplating.

The house is located at the dead end of Longleaf Lane and positioned to the rear (north) of the two-lot site to provide maximum distance from Longleaf Road. Privacy is accentuated by a large buffer zone of bamboo along Longleaf Road and a large garden on the south side of the house. In plan, the house is T-shaped with the body of the house forming the head of the "T" and a carport/service wing forming the leg. Oriented north-south, the body of the house draws on the concept of the binuclear (sometimes called binucleate) plan with private areas (bedrooms, bathrooms) grouped together and separated from public areas (living, dining, game room, kitchen). Here, the former are at the west end of the house and the latter are at the east. As described by the editors of *Architectural Record,* "living and sleeping areas are almost two distinct houses."[1]

Marcel Breuer had introduced the binuclear plan in the mid-1940s for his residential designs. In his published and famous design (1945) for the Geller House I in Lawrence, Long Island, Breuer divided the dwelling's public and private areas into two separate units but linked them by an entrance hall. He used a similar configuration for several subsequent houses, sometimes employing a courtyard as the separator and at other times a path. He saw this as a practical solution to the needs of American family life. This binuclear plan achieved considerable attention and was subsequently adopted in various configurations by forward-thinking clients and architects throughout the United States in the 1950s and 1960s. In two-story houses, the separation of public and private is clearly defined between downstairs and upstairs, but the single-story house that became the ideal in postwar suburban America needed a new solution for defining those zones. In reference to his unbuilt projects for the binuclear H-house (1943) and Bi-nuclear House III (1945), Breuer noted a particularly appealing feature of the plan for a family without domestic help when he stated, "Only the daytime wing needs to be kept up in a presentable condition."[2]

The Wieners' versions of the binuclear plan usually retained the house form as a single unit but separated public and private areas into two distinct zones by other means, most often by a family or service entrance from the carport, a hallway, and mechanical and utility rooms. When Sam and William incorporated an "open" space cut into the body of the house, such as the foyer at the Simon and Elaine L. Herold House and the atrium in the Julian and Kathryn Wiener House in Jackson, Mississippi, these spaces are within the public area surrounded by the living, play, dining, and breakfast rooms. In William's house, public and private areas are separated by a one-foot-thick brick fin wall that slices through the building approximately at its center and extends out to the north, marking the carport and service wing—the stem of the T. The wall effectively creates a physical and a visual division by defining public and private, and serving as a sound barrier and firewall between the two.

Breuer observed that the binuclear plan was "so flexible that differences in the slope of the land can be overcome in the link itself . . . while problems of orientation, view, and other site conditions can be solved by shifting the bi-nuclear elements in relation to each other."[3]

William B. and Babette Wiener House.

Courtesy of LSU-Shreveport Archives and Special Collections.

William's house responded to its gently sloping east-to-west site by a shift in levels between the bedroom wing, which is slightly higher, and the public areas.

The plan and the window wall system on the house's long north and south facades were organized on a four-foot module, and for the joints of the terrazzo floor, though he appeared to ignore the module to accommodate the needs of the site and define interior spaces. The public zone of the house is 52.50 feet in length and 28.67 feet in width; the private is wider at 32.67 feet by 54.82 feet, with the additional width on the south facade. The last structural bay at the bedroom end on the west side was reduced in size to accommodate the property width.

Unlike other residential projects undertaken by the brothers that were either constructed entirely of wood or of wood with a few steel elements such as porch columns,

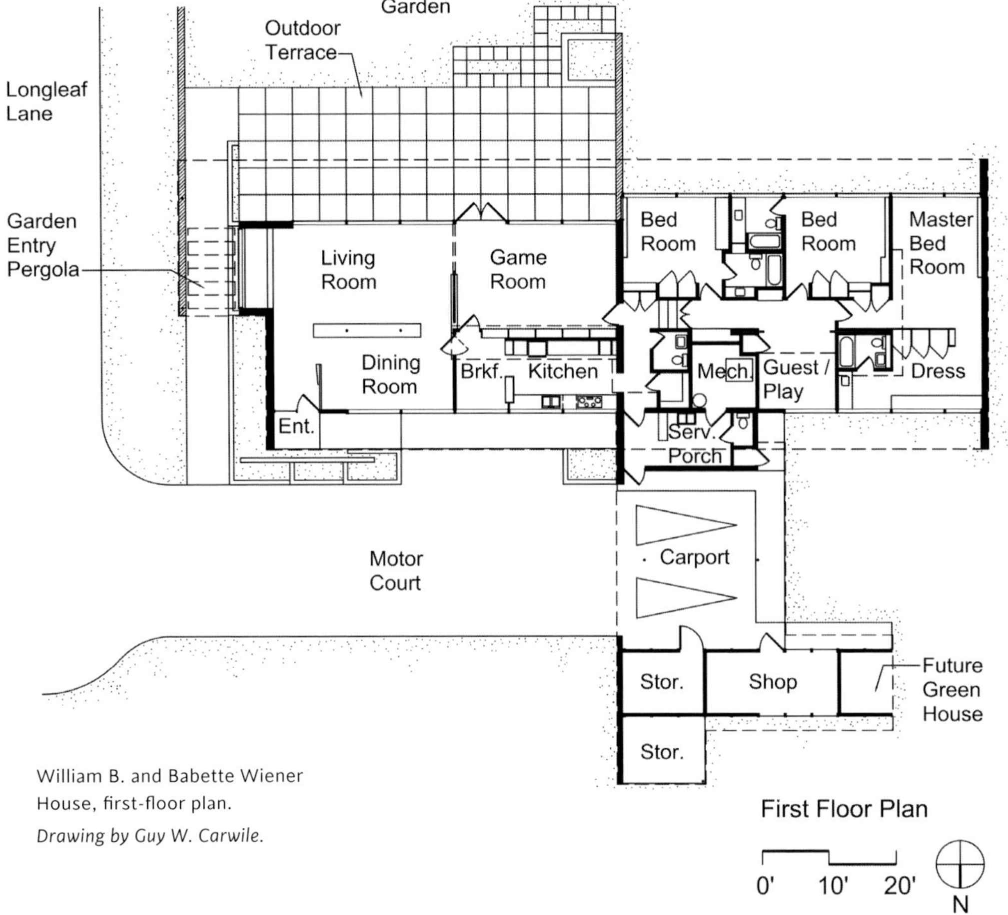

William B. and Babette Wiener House, first-floor plan.
Drawing by Guy W. Carwile.

William's house, with exception of the load-bearing brick walls, is steel-framed in its main portion. The columns at the window wall are three-by-three-inch square (called tube steel), and the central row of columns are three inches in diameter (called pipe columns). The structure of the T at the carport/service areas uses steel columns, but the roof was framed with standard wood joists. Rather than divorcing the structure from the wall and making it visible like some contemporary steel-framed houses of the era, notably the Farnsworth House designed by Mies van der Rohe in Plano, Illinois, and completed in 1951, William did not go to great lengths to celebrate structure. He did, though, celebrate the effects afforded by the same. The thin profile of the steel structural elements allowed William to keep the thickness of the roof overhang a mere one foot in height. Where the 1930s houses had a massive ventilation space and extension, which was sometimes visually exploited as a tall classically inspired entablature, William could now make it visually light and linear. With the addition of air-conditioning, he could reconceptualize the details of his house as well as its form.

To deemphasize the difference in width between the private and public zones and maintain the horizontality of the house's line, the edge of the flat roof continues uninterrupted for the entire length of the house, reaching out to form a five-foot overhang at the private end and a nine-foot overhang at the other, where the glass-walled living room is located. The house's long, low lines, which are emphasized by the roof canopy, are further underlined by the height of the garden's trees, particularly the pines. Yet, despite an emphasis on horizontality, the exterior was designed as a composition of discrete planes—the flat roof, the interior wall that separates public from private areas, the house's end walls, and the window walls facing north and south. All three brick walls extend as fins and are faced in Roman brick detailed with raked horizontal joints and flush head (vertical) joints as pioneered by Frank Lloyd Wright. Sam previously had treated some of the walls of Werner Park School's auditorium (discussed in chapter 8) in a similar fashion.

The house's roof is of poured lightweight insulating concrete. It is structured with eight-inch-deep beams running north-south and supported on columns. Three-inch-deep channels lie between the beams, and the concrete is poured over these. This would seem heavy, but insulating concrete weighs between 15 and 60 pounds per cubic foot whereas structural reinforced concrete weighs 150 pounds per cubic foot.

William's house has two entrances. The principal or formal entrance at the northwest corner of the house's public area opens to a small foyer, which leads to the living room. An entrance from the carport approximately midway along the north walls is reserved for the family and provides access to the bedroom wing. The formal entrance or front door becomes even less prominent than in their 1930s houses, and unemphasized it is just one more component in the total composition. The master bedroom, with its bath and dressing rooms at the west end of the house, forms the most secluded area within the private zone.

To give visual unity and formality to the interior, William established another succession of planes—the terrazzo floor, the uninterrupted ceiling, and the top of the cabinets and paneling, which match the height of the doors. In order to give the terrazzo floor a continuous and uniform appearance, it was poured after the three brick fin walls, the columns, and the roof were in place but before the interior non-load-bearing walls were installed. One row of steel columns is placed along the center of the house's length to reduce the span of the steel beams and consequently their depth. Those in the east-west direction are not aligned but instead shift to conform to walls and to form a support for cabinets and storage spaces. All the interior columns are hidden from view except for two visible above the low cabinet wall separating the living room from the dining room. The house was designed to include forced-air heating and air-conditioning, with separate units for the private and public areas. The equipment room is located at the intersection of the T and ductwork concealed above closets or cabinets, in furr downs, or underneath the floor slab and up into the freestanding cabinet wall between the dining and living rooms.

Interior walls are exposed brick, wood, and painted walls. The strong emphasis on warm tones and the expression of natural materials is new to the Wieners' work and parallels houses by Marcel Breuer, who tempered the severity of the International Style by incorporating stone and wood. Partial-height partitions separate the dining room from the formal entrance and the dining room from the living room; the latter had built-in cabinets for storage of dining service. The narrow galley kitchen corresponds to the ideal contemporary kitchen as perfected in Mies's Farnsworth House and those he included in his 1950s apartment buildings in Chicago and Detroit. While imply-

William B. and Babette Wiener House.

Courtesy of LSU-Shreveport Archives and Special Collections.

ing streamlined efficiency, in this house the galley kitchen allowed a continuous eye-level window with a view toward the driveway and carport.

In many ways the house focuses outward, not inward, especially after the game room's original wooden, hinged doors were replaced by glass sliding doors. They open to a terrace and garden. The integration of interior with exterior is also fundamental to the incorporation of the carport into the plan of the house, for it signals a modern relationship between home and of movement or freedom from it. A narrow passage beside the house's east-end wall leads from the driveway to the rear garden. It is bounded by a parallel brick wall that rises above eye-level and carries a pergola supported on two slender steel columns. This pergola continues the line of the house's roof and forms a counterpoint to the carport. The passage space is partially interrupted by a four-foot-deep rectangular bay projecting from the body of the house, which encompasses the living room's planter box; above the box is a large picture window. The planter box (which is similar in concept to the plant shelf in Sam and Marion's house) and window form a focal point in this room without a fireplace and provide yet another visual transition between interior and exterior.

The surviving plot plan draws only the broad strokes of the design and planting scheme. Most important was an undulating wall that reached deep into the site and was partially bordered by plants. Much of the sketch shows the site was covered in trees. A few years after the house's completion in 1950, a swimming pool was added.

Although the house has experienced other modifications, these have been relatively minor, and most of its conceptual purity remains intact. Bill Jr., the son of William and Babette, now owns the house.

SYLVIAN W. AND LEONA GAMM HOUSE

William's house is a larger and more elaborate version of the T-plan residence William and Sam designed in 1948

Sylvian W. and Leona Gamm House.
Courtesy of LSU-Shreveport Archives and Special Collections.

Sylvian W. and Leona Gamm House.

Courtesy of LSU-Shreveport Archives and Special Collections.

for attorney Sylvian Gamm and his wife, Leona, which occupies the Longleaf Lane lot opposite William's. The client suffered from arthritis and required a house that was simple and efficient in plan and the layout of its rooms. The one-story house has a north-south orientation, with the carport forming the stem of the T and a driveway forming an entrance court. This was the first T-plan house William and Sam designed. As well as the T-plan, the house also employed a modular system of six feet, which is perceptible in the window mullions and proportions of the rooms. The house width was originally designed to be twenty-five feet but was increased to twenty-seven feet to accommodate the furniture layout the Wieners designed. *Architectural Forum* described the house as having "an economical rectangular plan and an easy framing pattern, [that] was essential to balance the owner's space and cost requirements."[4]

The house is not divided into public and private areas so much as into service and served. The kitchen with a breakfast area, the bathrooms, a room for mechanical

David M. and Eleanor Davidson House.

Courtesy of LSU-Shreveport Archives and Special Collections.

equipment, and the entrances are spaced along the north wall, and the living-dining room, game room, and two bedrooms along the south. A hall separates the two zones, and there are no changes of level. One entrance opened from the carport, and the other, cut into the northwest corner of the house, leads into the living room. The house's south side with the living room is defined by a continuous wall of windows giving access to a patio bordered by flowers and views across the garden and its several trees, and is shaded by a six-foot roof overhang. The house is air-conditioned, but a later owner found the overhang sufficiently effective at shading the interior in summer that curtains were unnecessary. On winter days when the sun is lower and to the south it heats the glass to help warm the interior.

Constructed of brick and redwood siding, the house has a flat roof with a slight pitch. Insulating structural hollow-clay tile underlies the concrete slab floor, which also gave room for the soil to expand (when wet) without cracking the slab. Interior walls are a combination of exposed brick and painted plasterboard.

Designing Domestic Comfort and Convenience

In the Gamm and Wiener houses, William and Sam formulated their idea of a modern house appropriate for the particular circumstances and climate of their time and place. While the notion of intimacy and comfort, with spaces for various activities, is paramount, satisfying the need for independence and freedom from domesticity is crucial. They took the essence of the binuclear house, modified it with their innovative T-shaped plan and modular system, and adapted it for projects of various sizes and budgets. William's own house and the Gamm House were just two solutions.

The Wieners designed houses for the automobile age. Rather than a garage being an appendage to a house, either as a separate structure or an attachment, shelter for an automobile was integrated into the house by the extension of its roof, thus accentuating their inseparability. The incorporation of the automobile into the architectural composition had been stated as early as 1934, as evident in the photograph of the Cross Lake Weekend House published in *Architectural Forum,* which shows the family car parked under the house's raised portion.[5] Further emphasizing the automobile's significance to contemporary life, the carport also marked the family entrance in the 1950s houses, supplementing or even superseding the conventional porch or portico. It is interesting to see that in William's house the T-plan with entrance from the carport introduced a form of central hall and, although uncharacteristically narrow, gives the houses a feature that was traditionally southern. A truncated central hall separates the served and service areas of the Gamm House.

By developing a design based on a module, the Wieners

simplified construction and gave their houses an underlying rhythm and proportion which, while not overt, conveyed a sense of order and harmony. The houses also have a new spatial transparency with walls of glass to take advantage of or create views. The introduction of air-conditioning systems had a major impact on the design of residential architecture in the postwar era. Employed first in businesses, factories, and movie theaters (its use in theaters increased the popularity of movie-going in the steamy summer months), central air-conditioning became standard for architect-designed homes by the late 1950s. For the Wieners it meant that a house need not depend solely on a shading canopy to combat interior heat build-up.

HOUSES FROM 1949 TO 1955

In 1949 William designed a T-plan house in a version of the binuclear scheme for physician David M. Davidson and his wife, Eleanor, at 6336 Querbes Drive. Organized in a similar fashion to William's own house and designed for four people, it is close in size. It is built of Roman brick, vertical wood siding, and large expanses of glass walls. The public and private areas are grouped separately, with the T of the carport to the north and the combined living, dining, and gaming room facing south through glass walls opening to a free-form curved patio and shaded by an eight-foot overhang. The formal entrance is discreet and inset into the house's northeast corner. At William's house, each child had a bathroom connected to the bedroom, whereas at the Davidson House the bathrooms are across a hall. The Davidsons left Shreveport in 1950 and sold the house to C. H. and Marjorie Lyons in May of that year. William made some modifications to the house in 1957.

The house William created in 1950 for attorney Simon Herold and his wife, Elaine L. Herold, at 1050 Ontario Street diverges from the T-shape scheme in order to fit into its trapizoidal-shaped and sloping site. The site slopes down fourteen feet from east to west. Almost square in plan, the house has a single entrance adjacent to the carport that serves both family and guests; a small service entrance to the kitchen is on the house's east side. The principal entrance on the south opens into a small foyer that leads to an atrium, thus conforming more to Marcel Breuer's concept of the binuclear house. But rather than separating the private and public realms of the house, the atrium here forms a transition between the more formal public spaces (the combination living-dining room) and the more informal or service spaces (the game room, breakfast room, kitchen, and service porch). The breakfast room at the core of the house is unusually large and forms a pivot around which all rooms can be accessed (the game room by a short corridor). The three bedrooms are aligned along the north wall and are buffered from the public areas by their bathrooms. Unusually in this house, the living-dining room faces west, but it is illuminated by small vertical windows that are oriented to the north and

Simon and Elaine L. Herold House. *Photo by Guy W. Carwile.*

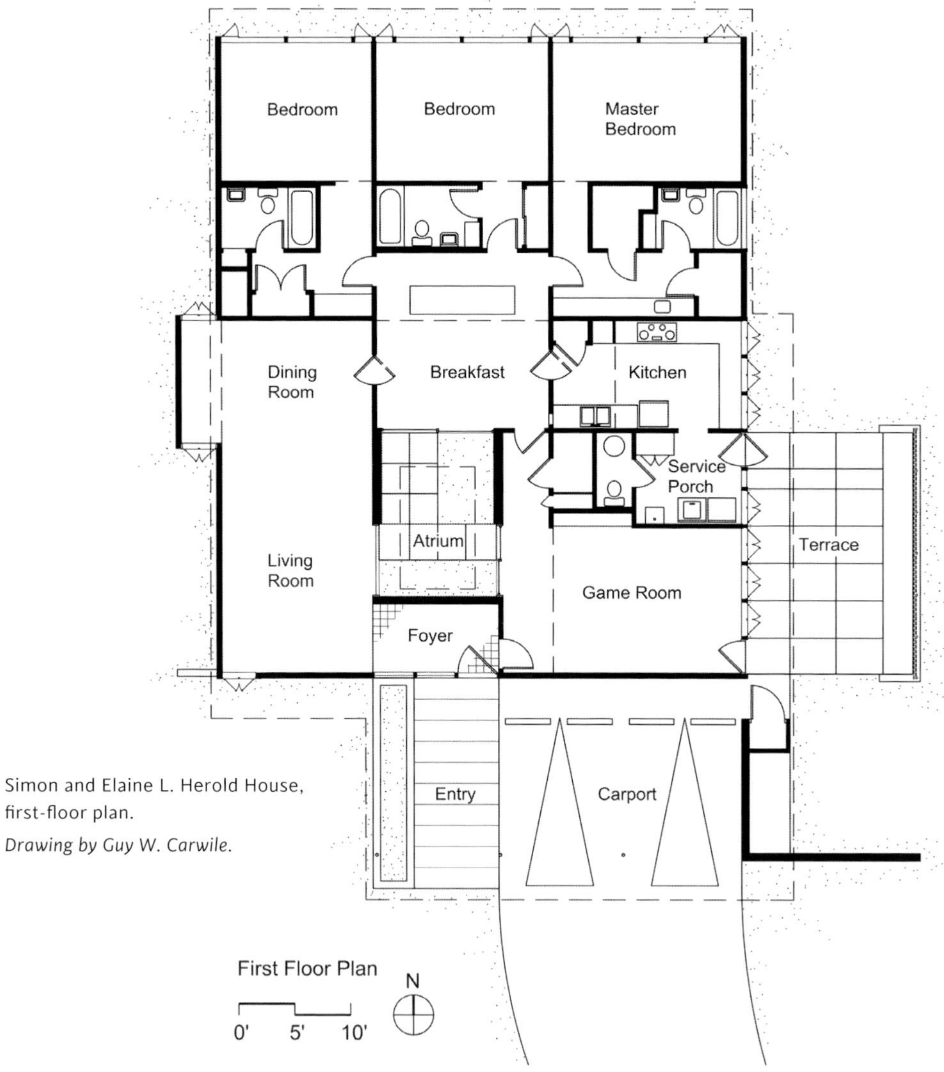

Simon and Elaine L. Herold House, first-floor plan.

Drawing by Guy W. Carwile.

south. The room is cozy rather than open. On the east side of the house the game room and kitchen have picture windows, and the former opens to a terrace. Although the breakfast room lacks windows, it affords a view into the atrium.

The house is constructed of vertical wood siding, stained an opaque dark brown, and the window trim, entrance door, and the edge of the gently pitched roof are painted bright blue. An extension of the house's roof covers the carport and, because the carport is adjacent to the principal entrance, emphasizes the status of the automobile.

In 1951 William designed a house for Elmer and Barbara Simon at 543 College Lane, one block north of Longleaf Road. Built with a limited budget, the single-story house has a rectangular plan with a double-pitched roof. The role of the automobile in family life is emphasized by the size and prominent position of the carport at the end of the facade, while the formal entrance to the house at the facade's center hides in shadow under the eaves. The house's garden side, facing south and sheltered under the roof extension, is almost entirely of glass. In 1955 Louie and Gertrude Levy and their family moved from their house at 835 Margaret Place, designed by Sam in 1938, to a new house by Sam at 3402 Madison Park, after their Fairfield neighborhood became more institutional and commercial. The Margaret Place house, expanded and renovated into a doctor's office in 1955, was altered so dramatically that it is barely recognizable. The horizontally organized and flat-roofed Madison Park house crowns its sloping site and, below it, the garage is wedged into the slope.

Beyond Louisiana: Houses in Mississippi and Texas

While most of the Wieners' commissions came from clients in Shreveport and its immediate vicinity, their architectural practices were not confined to the city. Sam had designed schools in Haughton and Winnfield, a store and apartment building in Natchitoches, a sanitarium in Many, Sabine Parish (the last two no longer exist), and a house in the Lake Vista neighborhood of New Orleans (demolished following Hurricane Katrina). In the 1950s and in 1960, the brothers carried out three residential commissions outside of Louisiana, two of which survive in nearly their original condition. Two houses are in Jackson, Mississippi, and one is in Fort Worth, Texas. These projects did not come through an advertising campaign but, like their Shreveport houses, through family, friends, or acquaintances.

WILLIAM B. AND CAROLYN WIENER HOUSE, JACKSON, MISSISSIPPI

Although both Sam and William's names are on the plans, it is thought that William designed the house (228 Ridge Drive) in Jackson for the brothers' cousin, physician William B. Wiener, his wife, Carolyn, and their two children. At this house, the long axis of the top of the T faces east-west due to the orientation of the lot. The house was constructed in 1950, and William designed an addition in 1957 after the couple had two more children. The addition extends from the rear of the house to the east and obscures the original T-plan. This house is the only one for which a perspective rendering is known. The drawing shows the house as approached from the south, a wall of buff brick, the carport supported on slender lally columns (steel outer shell filled with concrete in order to strengthen them) and the enclosing brick wall, the gentle pitch of the roof, the tree growing out of the patio, and the entrance to the right. The rendering captures the building's planar and horizontal qualities and immediate landscape, which remain almost identical to the drawing. The expression of family privacy is particularly strong at this house.

In plan, the public areas of the house occupy the southern half on the south, the bedrooms on the north, and the kitchen and service rooms form the stem of the T on the west. The formal entrance to the house is at the southwest corner, and it opens first into a small foyer and from there to the spacious combined living/game room. This room faces east with views through picture windows to a terrace and a garden. Running north from the foyer is a hallway, forming a spine through the length of the house to the bedrooms on the north. The living and game room (though apparently the game room was never used as such and instead became an informal sitting area or den) are separated only by a suspended cabinet. A single pitched roof rises as it spans the living room and extends over the patio to shade the picture windows. Two live oak trees in the garden were probably planted when the house was built.

Although the living and game room forms a single large space, punctuated only by a suspended cabinet, the plan is conventional in that the other rooms are closed boxes, unlike, for example, architect William's house, where space flows more freely. In this house the breakfast room has a window that overlooks an enclosed patio next to the carport, which was planted with a gingko tree, thus extending the interior to outside (see Plate 7). The floor throughout

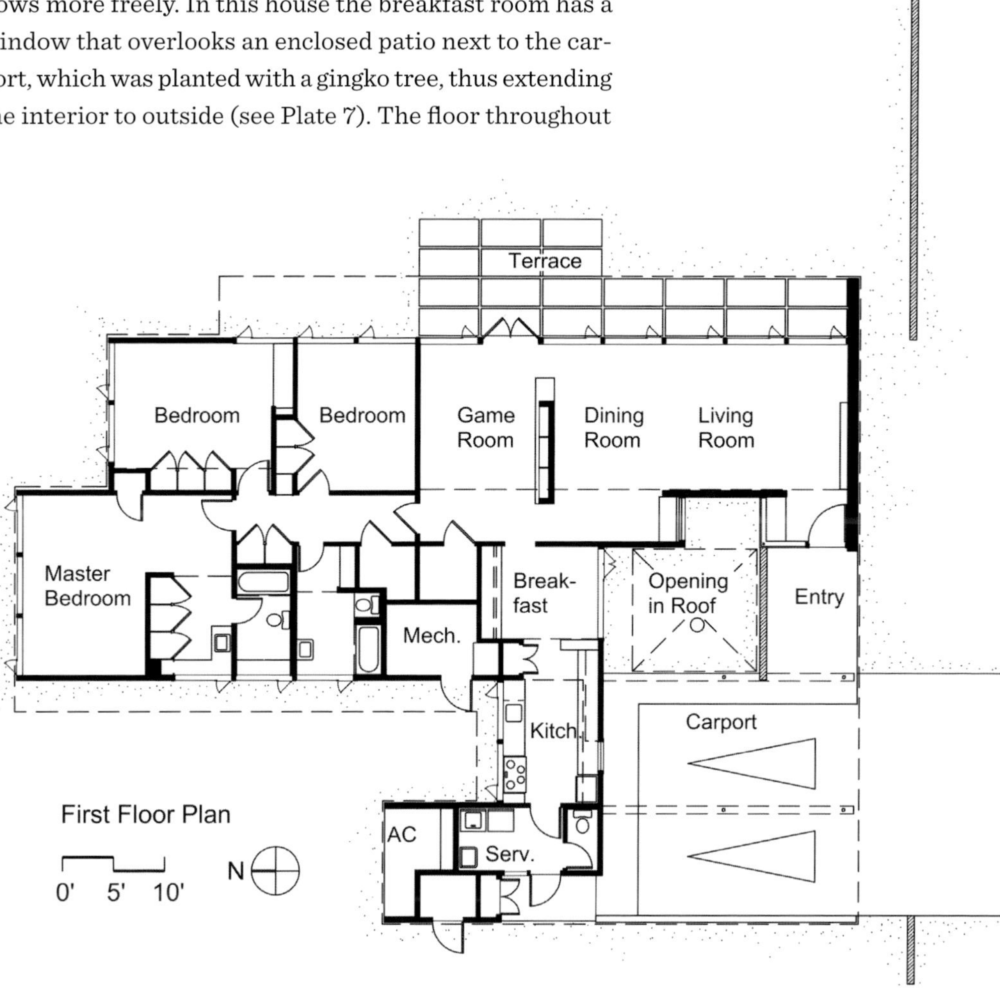

William B. and Carolyn Wiener House, Jackson, Mississippi, first-floor plan.
Drawing by Guy W. Carwile.

William B. and Carolyn Wiener House, Jackson, Mississippi. *Rendering by Jesse Morgan. Courtesy of Randall Ross.*

the house was terrazzo of Portland cement embedded with colored marble chips. Originally the ceiling of the living and game room was painted green and that of the kitchen was yellow. William designed a bedroom addition to the east of the original bedrooms in 1957.

MARCUS AND MARTINE H. GINSBURG HOUSE, FORT WORTH, TEXAS

A year after William B. and Carolyn Wiener's house was constructed in Jackson, Sam and William used a modified version of the T-plan for the residence of attorney Marcus and Martine Heilbron Ginsburg in Fort Worth, Texas. It is thought that the commission came their way through a friendship between the Ginsburgs and Sam and Marion. Because of the 190-mile distance from Shreveport, Fort Worth-based architect Paul T. Cahill (1888–1954) supervised construction of the house.

If the genesis of the plan is a T, the house is far more complex in its configuration. On the house's long west side, a carport and a courtyard form the stem of the T. From here, a recessed entrance opens to a foyer, but forward progression is halted by a freestanding wall containing a storage cabinet; on the reverse of the cabinet is a fireplace facing the living room. To reach the combination living-dining room requires movement around the cabinet wall. These spatial shifts give a sense of anticipation to passage into and through the body of the house (see Plate 8). Running south from the foyer is a hallway leading to a den (a space identified as a game room in the Wieners' earlier houses), equipment and storage rooms, and bedrooms. The north wing is narrower and includes a kitchen, beyond which are a service entrance and the living quarters for a servant. A new spatial complexity is introduced in this house, and the foyer, perpendicular to the entrance, presents unexpected circulation patterns. In 1962 Sam added a bedroom wing that extends east from the original bedrooms.

To emphasize transition and difference in how space is used, the house's terrazzo floor is a darker shade in the foyer than in the rooms, where it is mostly white with dark marble chips. The darker color also serves a practical function by disguising dirt tracked in from outside. Full-height picture windows flood the living room with light, and the room is in muted tones with a light-brown brick wall (brick is used for several rooms in the house) and a stained wood-slat ceiling that provided a subdued background for the brilliantly colored modern furniture by Charles and Ray Eames and Mies van der Rohe. From exterior to interior, the Ginsburgs fully embraced modernity in the creation of their house. The house was demolished in 2015 to make way for a larger residence.

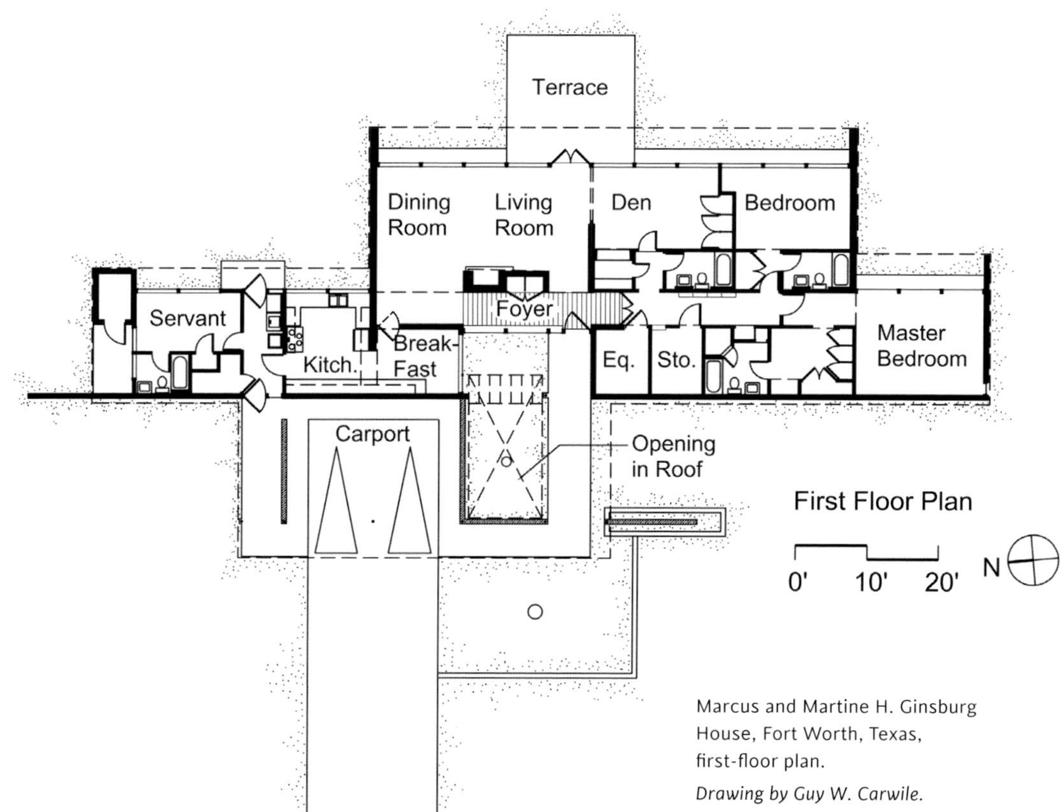

Marcus and Martine H. Ginsburg House, Fort Worth, Texas, first-floor plan.
Drawing by Guy W. Carwile.

JULIAN AND KATHRYN WIENER HOUSE, JACKSON, MISSISSIPPI

In 1959 when Samuel G. Wiener and Associates designed a house for his cousin physician Julian and his wife, Kathryn, the attributes of a modern house—single story, horizontal in the landscape, flat or gently pitched roof, picture windows—were no longer a rarity. In various forms, though usually with a pitched roof rather than a flat one, they had entered the mainstream and populated America's new suburban developments. This brick-and-glass house, however, had a feature architects seldom employed—a central atrium (identified as a court on the plan). William had used an atrium at the Herold House in 1950, but there the atrium had separated the formal and informal public zones. Here the living, dining, breakfast, and play rooms surround the atrium to form an almost square unit, and the private zone of four bedrooms and a study at the east end of the house is similar in outline. The atrium, open to the sky except where enclosed by an exposed grid of redwood beams, and landscaped as a tropical garden. This soon proved too hot and humid for comfort and was changed to an Asian-styled garden with pebbles and rocks. To replace its hoped-for fresh-air function, a porch was added to the side of the house for outdoor sitting, though with a garden vista of less exotic plants.

The house has two entrances, one from the carport and the principal entrance, which is cut into the adjacent corner of the house and provides passage from a foyer to the living room. Kathryn Wiener requested the wall of windows in the living room and, because it faces southwest, Sam extended the gently pitched roof to provide a sheltering canopy. The interior is rich in materials and textures—an exposed brick wall in the living room, wood paneling in the foyer, painted walls, and a terrazzo floor. Jay T. Liddle of Jackson was the associated supervising architect. From 1945 to 1948 Liddle had worked for Jackson-based modernist architect N. W. Overstreet.

Sam's son, Sam G. Wiener Jr. (familiarly known as Sam IV), designed the red-and-blue abstract-patterned "mosaic-style screen" at the front entrance. Sam IV intended to make the screen of large ceramic tiles on its street side and small mosaic tiles on the side facing the foyer. The screen's frame was constructed of structural steel angles and, although some thought otherwise, it could have supported the weight of the tiles; the decision to substitute plexiglass was probably to allow light through to spill into the foyer.

Back to Shreveport

These Mississippi and Texas houses that span a ten-year period extended the Wieners' opportunity to create houses that suited the needs and preferences of their clients and express the spirit of their era. But in the mid-1950s, before the second Mississippi house was commissioned, Sam and William designed two residences in Shreveport that garnered national recognition, though from quite dif-

Jack and Thelma Tullos House. *Courtesy of LSU-Shreveport Archives and Special Collections.*

ferent constituencies. The houses reveal that they could design equally as well for those of greater means as for those of less. One, the Tullos House, was published in *Popular Home,* and the other, for James and Jean R. Muslow, received more exclusive attention with an *Architectural Record* Award of Excellence for House Design in 1956, where it was described as one of the nation's most significant designs of the year.[6] It is one of the brothers' most sophisticated and fully realized houses in Louisiana.

JACK AND THELMA TULLOS HOUSE

At the same time Sam and William were designing the Shreveporter Highway Hotel for Jack Tullos, the firm of William B. Wiener and Associates, with Jesse O. Morgan Jr. and P. Murff O'Neal Jr., were working on a house for the hotel's owner and manager, Tullos, and his wife, Thelma. They moved into the house in 1955. Located at 3118 Country Club Drive, it was less than a mile from the hotel. Featured in 1956 in *Popular Home* magazine (distributed by United States Gypsum [USG] to provide families with ideas for renovations and new construction), the design was identified as Plan No. 13-7C and was accompanied by a floor plan, two color photographs, and a black-and-white photograph. The magazine informed its readers that blueprints for this affordable dwelling could be ordered from any prospective homeowner's "local lumber-dealer," who presumably, although it was not so stated, would provide the necessary lumber for the wooden residence and perhaps recommend a builder.[7] The house was named the "Bayou Beauty" model, which was somewhat misleading since bayou country is in south Louisiana, not the Shreveport area. But the name was evocative and doubtless was considered a selling point.

Tullos had spent thirty years in the hotel business and, with Thelma, much of his married life residing in hotel apartments. Now that they were building a single-family house, they wanted the compact planning of an apartment but with a view as well as easy access to their sloping and wooded lot. They also requested that their home have a contemporary appearance yet still be suited to traditional furniture. Photographs of the house shortly after it was completed reveal that "traditional" did not mean period furniture, but traditional within a mid-twentieth-century aesthetic. Jack and Thelma Tullos wanted the house built of materials that required little maintenance and an interior with space for entertaining. These requirements, all outlined in the *Popular Home* article, were intended to appeal to families of middle or modest income with aspirations to be fashionable and modern.

Jack and Thelma Tullos House. *Courtesy of LSU-Shreveport Archives and Special Collections.*

The house, set perpendicular to the street and sheltered under a softly pitched roof, has a T-shaped plan with the stem of the T forming the carport. It is constructed on a six-foot module and has board-and-batten walls except for the brick end walls, one of which faces the street. The house is bisected along its length by a corridor. One-half of the house is composed of a large living-dining room, a kitchen, a breakfast room, and a formal or public entrance, and the other half accommodates three bedrooms. To ensure that the Bayou Beauty model could be built on any site, anywhere, the plan in *Popular Home* gives no directional location, indicating its potential importance as a marketable design. The Tullos House, however, is oriented north-south, and the living-dining room faces south. The article emphasized that the house's high ceilings would help keep the house cool and lauded its built-in storage, which was an increasingly desired feature as people acquired more household goods in the boom period of the 1950s.

The published plan also depicts such possible landscaping features as the placement of trees and shrubbery along the length of the house's walls. This type of landscaping, known as foundation planting, became popular in shelter magazines and do-it-yourself garden books in the postwar period. Designed to repeat the horizontal lines of modern suburban ranch-style houses, the shrubbery invariably is larger at the house's ends to give a stronger conclusion, as in the *Popular Home* plan. The Tullos's carport could accommodate two automobiles.

James and Jean R. Muslow House, first-floor plan.
Drawing by Guy W. Carwile.

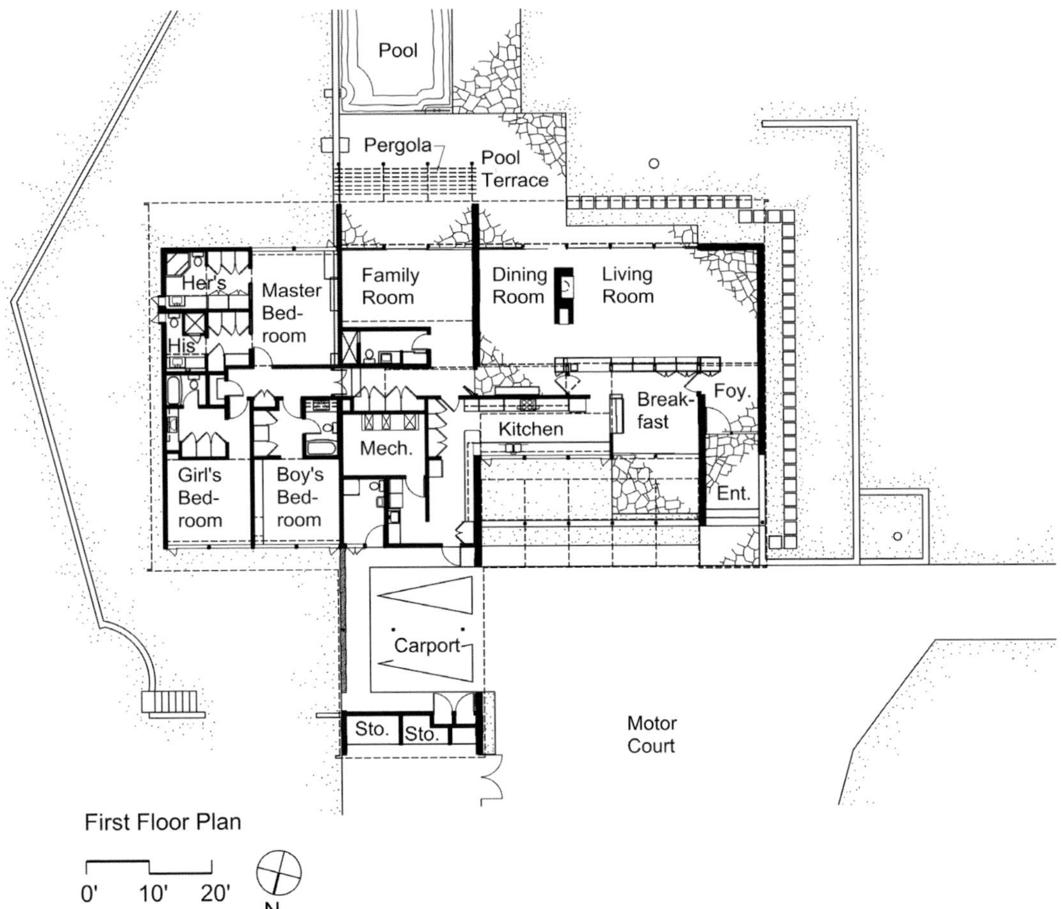

JAMES AND JEAN R. MUSLOW HOUSE

More upscale was the residence of James and Jean Muslow, designed in 1954. When the Muslows decided to build a new house, they asked Sam and William to be responsible for the entire project, including the landscaping and the selection of furniture. In several ways, the house for the Muslows and their two children highlights characteristics of Marcel Breuer's New England projects of the early 1950s, while retaining features that are identifiably those of the Wieners. Thus the T-plan and the modular scheme, here of seven feet, are accompanied by Breuer's typical collaging of stone and wood. The stone for the walls was specified as cherry-blend ledge stone from the Herman Schwartz quarry in Paris, Arkansas, but because it was not nearly as red as the client desired, the architects substituted stone from Colorado. Floors are randomly laid with gray-green slate from Vermont. The use of stone, slate, and wood sets up a luxurious contrast in texture and color for both the exterior and interior. While the materials satisfied the owners' desire for a "rustic" quality, they also add to the opulence.

Set deep into its slightly sloping lot, shrouded by pine trees and sited perpendicular to the street, the house presents a stone end wall to observers, thus further emphasiz-

James and Jean R. Muslow House. *Courtesy of LSU-Shreveport Archives and Special Collections.*

ing privacy. Oriented north-south, the house is rectangular with the T-shaped extension of the carport on the north balanced on the garden side by a swimming pool; consequently the house appears cross-shaped in plan. This house is the Wieners' version of a binuclear plan. The three bedrooms are grouped at the east end of the house and separated from the more public areas by a third zone composed of the entrance from the carport, utility and mechanical spaces, and the family room. Each of these three zones is marked by a stone or wood-paneled wall that emphasizes this tripartite scheme and extends beyond the house to carry the roof extension. Although there is no atrium-like space between the zones, a garden court is cut into the house's volume in front of the kitchen and breakfast room. The garden court, which is paved in gray-green Vermont slate, was intended to showcase an existing large thirty-inch-diameter tree, but because it was so close to the construction site, this was taken down for liability reasons and replaced with a row of dwarf yaupon holly and a parallel row of white camelia sasanqua (see Plate 9).

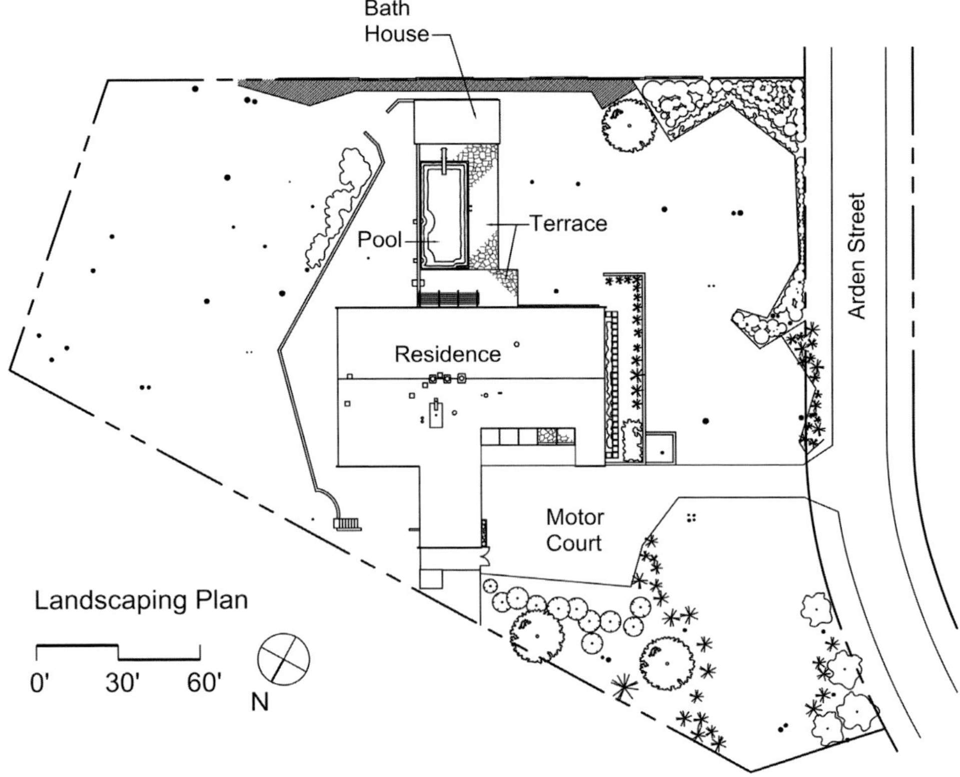

James and Jean R. Muslow House, landscaping plan.
Drawing by Guy W. Carwile.

As the Muslows requested, the house included ample space for entertaining. Only a freestanding fireplace of plastered brick marks the transition from dining to living space. This room and the family room next to it have glass walls overlooking a Vermont slate–paved terrace and the swimming pool, thus integrating exterior with interior, a hallmark of the Wieners' postwar work. William designed several pieces of furniture for the house and selected others crafted by Mies van der Rohe, Herman Miller, Eero Saarinen, Charles and Ray Eames, George Nelson, Hans Bellmann, and Warren Platner. The house employs an incredible series of spatial experiences—expansion, followed by compression, then back to expansion. Constraint and release are hallmarks, too, of the garden design.

Unlike the gardens for the Samuel and Marion Wiener House or the Wile House, where the trees and bushes almost seem to have grown naturally from their spot, here Sam and William replaced those undulating patterns of plants and lines in favor of sharply angled borders framing the strict rectangular forms of the house and swimming pool. In plan or seen from the air, the scheme brings to mind a modernist painting. As with their other garden designs, this one also is rich in textures and colors. The zigzag wall to the east of the house was formed of coursed Colorado cherry limestone, and the randomly angled retaining steel edge to the plants' borders at the west was four inches tall and painted green. A number of existing pine, oak, and gum trees were left on the site, and such trees and bushes as magnolia, holly, flowering crab apple, and forsythia that displayed color at different times of the year were added. Azaleas bordered the Colorado limestone low wall around the living room and the house's west wall, and espaliered pears and giant bamboo (one of William's favorite plants) closed the garden's southern boundary. James Muslow and William together went to nurseries to select the planting materials.[8] Today the garden differs only slightly from the original design.

In the postwar period, a swimming pool became an essential component of upper-middle-class houses in areas of the United States where weather permitted. Paddock Pools of California, the premier swimming-pool designer and contractor in the nation, which created most of the pools for the Hollywood elite, constructed the Muslows' pool. In 1956, William added a bath house to the south side of the pool for swimmers to shower and change before entering the house. The simple wooden structure is built over a steel frame and contained changing areas and showers covered by a translucent roof to allow natural illumination. To provide a shaded sitting area, the roof and supporting beams extend beyond the walls to form a canopy, which help give the entire structure the appearance of a Japanese pavilion.

Picturing Modernism

The photographs of the Muslow House published in *Architectural Record* in 1956 were taken by Frank Lotz Miller, who became the favored photographer for New Orleans modernist architects in the postwar era. Born in Shreveport, Miller moved as a child to New Orleans, where in 1953 he set up his own photography studio. Unlike many architectural photographers of his day, Miller preferred to shoot buildings in natural light rather than artificial, which gives his images a genuine sense of how natural light affects space and objects. He was not above manipulating his photographs to alter the background of an exterior shot, by removing or adding clouds or tree limbs to create a sense of place and time. Miller's architectural photographs were published in leading architectural journals and magazines.

The Wieners used several different photographers over the years, including Clarence John Laughlin, who was born in Lake Charles but moved with his parents to New Orleans while he was still a child. He is best known, though, for his misty, surrealist photographs of the South's plantation houses. Joseph W. Molitor's images of buildings by many of the nation's major architects made him one of the most sought-after photographers of his day. New York–based Molitor was trained as an architect, which undoubtedly gave him an eye for what was important about a building. He turned to architectural photography in the late 1940s. Dallas-based architect Ulric Meisel also photographed Wiener buildings in the 1950s. The architectural journals, particularly in the decade following World War II, often suggested or determined which photographer would be used in order to get the desired quality of print and the range of views of a building. As designs were changing, so was the photographic image—from the fully illuminated straight-on view that revealed every part of a building to a more dramatically lit image with strong contrasts of light and shade and maximum depth of field to emphasize form, structure, and texture. For their early buildings before this practice became standard, the Wieners occasionally employed local photographers Thurman Smith and H. O. Wiseman.

Until the 1960s and the development and affordability of color photography, images were published in black-and-white. Inevitably, for many years modern architecture and the International Style came to be seen by many as devoid of color. Yet, the importance of architectural photographers and photography in the reception and understanding of any building cannot be overstated. The photographs of European buildings that were published in *Architectural Forum* and the other journals compelled Sam, William, and Ted Flaxman to go to Germany, Holland, France, and elsewhere on the continent. Additionally, it is through the published photographs that we understand the form and structure of the Wieners' buildings soon after they were completed, and these are often the only record of the buildings that have been demolished.

Woodlawn High School, atrium at cafeteria.

Photo by Guy W. Carwile.

8

SCHOOL BUILDINGS

Between 1938 and 1940, Sam was responsible for the design of four schools in northern Louisiana, all with different requirewments and student numbers. This brief and intense focus proved an opportunity to figure out how to accommodate modern educational needs for a building type that after World War II became a prominent part of his practice.

The first school project Sam worked on was for the Bossier Parish school board, which hired him to design two high schools in Bossier City, one school for white students and the other for black students. The project is credited to Jones, Roessle, Olschner and Wiener even though, when the schools were finally built, the firm no longer existed as such. Funded in part by the Public Works Administration (PWA), these were 2 of 175 new school buildings in Louisiana financed by the federal agency and that varied in size from one-room rural structures to multiclassroom buildings in urban centers. The PWA financed more schools or additions than any other building type in Louisiana, and the agency was key to transforming facilities for public education.[1] In the lean years of the Great Depression, architects were keen to get these federal-funded projects, even for small rural schools, when private commissions were few.

In general the PWA schools built in the late 1930s followed the traditional H- or T-shaped plan, with symmetrical massing and an emphasized central entrance flanked by classroom wings. Classrooms and such communal spaces as an auditorium were maneuvered into this shell, and consequently their function was not apparent on the exterior. In style, Colonial Revival was popular for small elementary schools, which perhaps reflected (as it did elsewhere in the nation) a desire to evoke a more stable time before the Great Depression. Variations on Collegiate Gothic remained popular for multistory junior and high schools. Several of Louisiana's larger high schools projected a more progressive spirit in their Moderne or Art Deco styling. Two splendid PWA-funded examples are Port Allen High School (now Middle School) of 1938, designed by the Baton Rouge firm of Bodman and Murrell (Ralph Bodman and Richard C. Murrell) and Ruston High School completed in 1940 by J. W. Smith and Associates. Both of these schools emphasized symmetry for the classroom portion of the building by featuring a dominant tower over a central entrance and auditoriums at the end of the building, which were given emphasis by a separate entrance (interestingly, later additions to Ruston's school increased its appearance of symmetry). Port Allen's tower

Bossier City High School.
Photo by Guy W. Carwile.

enclosed a double staircase, and Ruston's tower accommodated a library. The tower-and-flanking-wings formula used at Port Allen may have had a special attraction in light of the similar formula employed by Weiss, Dreyfous and Seiferth for the recently completed State Capitol just across the Mississippi River in Baton Rouge. Yet while the outward appearance of these two schools was relatively up-to-date, Sam's design of 1938 for Bossier High School, by contrast, could be described as revolutionary. It broke with tradition in plan and exterior appearance, and its many innovative features had a profound influence on the region's schools built in the following decades.

BOSSIER CITY HIGH SCHOOL

In 1938, Jones, Roessle, Olschner and Wiener received the commission to design the two high schools for Bossier City. The schools served the city's rapidly growing population that resulted from the establishment in 1933 of Barksdale Army Air Field (renamed Barksdale Air Force Base in 1947), which became the largest single employer in the Shreveport metropolitan area. The schools were completed and opened in 1940. The larger and better-equipped school at Coleman and Mansfield streets was for white students; a much smaller school on Detroit Avenue was for black students. Jim Crow laws required that white and black students be educated in separate facilities.

Only one of the two schools received nationwide attention. Plans and photographs of the school for white students were widely published in contemporary architectural and educational journals for its inventive and progressive plan and design. The school for black students, about one-sixteenth the size of the white school, was not included in the publications. Little is known about it other than it was built of wood siding, was one story in height, had five classrooms, a small library, and rooms for sewing, cooking, and manual training. Drawings indicate it had indoor toilets, although it has been described as having outside toilets.[2] Following school desegregation, the school was demolished.

Bossier City High for white students was built on an eleven-acre site of a former cotton plantation and adjoined an athletic field and the city park. As described by Sam in an article published in *American School Board Journal* in 1941, he was given "the general requirements, a list of the spaces needed, and an explanation of the teaching and the administrative system. Within these limits the architect was given complete authority in decisions relating to the location, planning, style, and construction" of the schools.[3] His solution for the white school was a group of buildings of different uses, "a five-building-in-one structure, ultramodern, practical, and efficient, it is oriented to the southern climate."[4]

The school is composed of five distinct but related units: a three-story linear classroom block, a gymnasium, an auditorium, a cafeteria, and a manual-training shop. The gymnasium is located at the western end of the classroom wing, and the auditorium projects to the rear to form a grouping that approximates an L-shaped plan. The remaining two of the five units were the cafeteria and the manual-training shop. These were single-story freestanding buildings to the rear of the classroom block (canopies were later added to cover the walkways linking the buildings), the cafeteria to isolate delivery of food and improve ventilation and the shop at the northeast corner of the school to muffle noise. Bossier High School was the first school in northwest Louisiana with individual units for the different functions. Traditionally, auditoriums were incorporated into the body of the school, often in the center since they did not require natural light, or tacked on one end of a symmetrical design as at Port Allen.

Although situating an auditorium or gymnasium at the end of the classroom block was not new when Sam designed Bossier in 1938, it was relatively rare, and his clustering of the two components to form an L-shaped composition was more unusual in Louisiana. While all three units are accessed from the main lobby, each is autonomous and can be accessed without passing through one or the other. As well, the classroom wing could be closed off. This simplified circulation pattern allowed the gymnasium and auditorium to serve such non-school uses as community meetings or events, an increasingly significant function from the 1930s on when school buildings were conceived as being a center for and the center of their neighborhood. The design also allowed for future growth through straight-line extension of the classroom unit's unencumbered end, if necessary.

Each of the school's five units physically expresses its function: bands of windows illuminate the row of classrooms, the gymnasium's box-like shape has only a narrow clerestory window, and the wedge-shaped auditorium has side walls stepping down toward the stage. The classroom block, 250 feet in length, was laid out with rooms on both

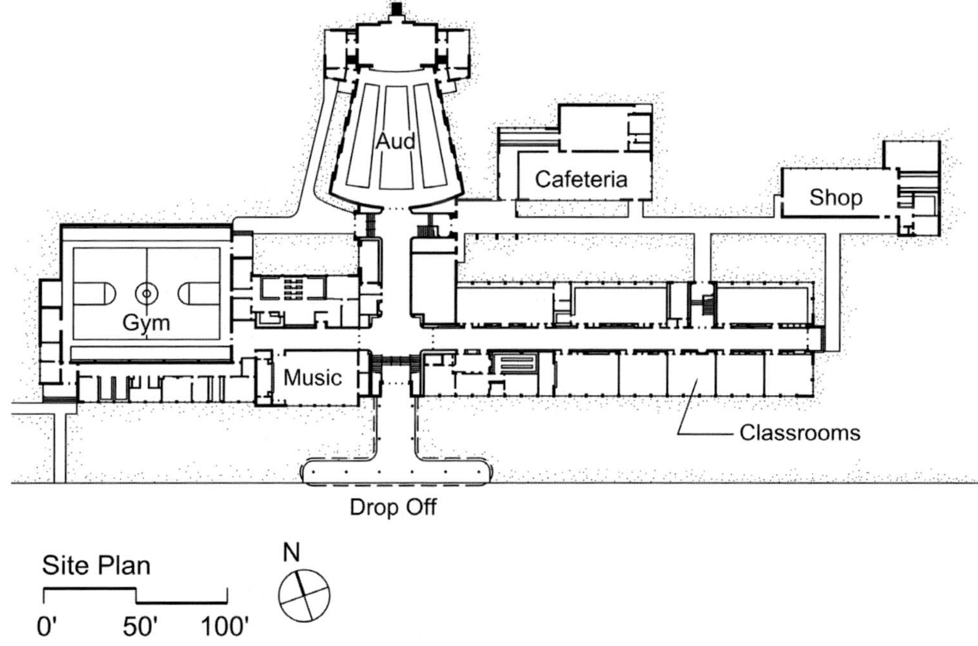

Bossier City High School, site plan. *Drawing by Guy W. Carwile.*

sides of a corridor, a pattern known as a double-loaded corridor. It runs west to east, and carries its banks of windows along its north and south walls. Sam deliberately sited the classroom building to receive light from the north and south. This broke from conventional wisdom, which held that classrooms should face east and west in order to receive sunlight part of the day. Sam disagreed. In siting a school, as he explained in an essay, "The Changing Classroom," for *American School Board Journal* in 1948, "I believe that the first consideration should be given to the orientation of classrooms. Most of the literature relating to school orientation seems to have been written for northern climates, and an east-west orientation is often advised."[5] In a southern climate this would overheat rooms. Moreover, north and south light would avoid the uncomfortable low angle of east and west sun. To protect Bossier High School's south-facing classrooms from heat and glare, Sam added two-foot-deep overhangs to shade the horizontal bands of windows.

Sam's use of a nine-foot modular scheme to lay out the entire school gives it an underlying sense of order. The floor beams of the reinforced-concrete frame meet at the support columns, which do double-duty as window mullions, and the window canopies are monolithic with the floor system. Further unifying the building is what each portion has in common—brick walls, bands of windows, horizontality, and angular forms. The rationality of the plan, the separation of units, and the geometric simplicity of the forms all show the profound influence of Bauhaus ideals on Sam's work. As requested by the school superintendent, classrooms are painted in different color combinations, two or three in each room, and furniture was movable, not anchored to the floor. This play of color and lightness is also expressive of European modernism. The school's asymmetrical composition and off-center entrance further emphasized the school's European sources. It is impossible to know to what extent the Bauhaus complex, with its buildings laid out and designed to best suit the school's purpose yet in a scheme that was completely unified, influenced Sam's Bossier High School.

By the late 1930s, school consolidation meant that transporting students from a town's increasingly expanding suburbs and rural areas had its own impact on school design. A place for the loading and unloading of students from buses is architecturally highlighted at Bossier with a 110-foot-long reinforced-concrete canopy to shelter vehicles and students from inclement weather. Supported on slender lally columns (steel filled with concrete), the canopy's sweeping curved ends and curved stepped soffit counter the strict angularity of the school's silhouette and add a notion of streamlined movement and speed.

While Sam's design conformed to tradition by giving the school a monumental facade, it broke with convention by setting the entrance off-center, eliminating traditional ornamentation, and partially veiling it by the arrival canopy. Emphasized instead is internal circulation. A vertical bank of operable windows rises above the entrance to illuminate the stairwell, another emblem of form following function and function becoming ornament. The prominent wall clock next to the stairwell window, although with slender rectangular digits indicating the hours rather than numbers, is a public gesture, as well as a reminder for students of where they should be and when. At Bossier, Sam creates a design of balance and proportion, a task more difficult when a building is not bilaterally symmetrical, and along with the school's long, clean lines it is an icon of the International Style.

Inevitably the school acquired additions and alterations over the years, but these have not lessened the body and character of Sam's initial design. For example, when the school added music to the curriculum in the 1950s, Sam's firm at the time, S. G. Wiener and Associates, designed a freestanding music building adjacent to the gymnasium and auditorium. The simple one-story structure's angular shape and brick walls match the earlier buildings.

HAUGHTON HIGH SCHOOL AND WINNFIELD ELEMENTARY SCHOOL

While Bossier High School was under construction, Sam was designing a high school for the nearby town of Haughton, which opened in 1940, and an elementary school of 1939 for Winnfield in Winn Parish. These gave him the opportunity to develop and refine his ideas about functional and progressive school design.[6]

The Haughton High School project consisted solely of an academic building that houses eight classrooms, a library, a laboratory, a study room, and a small assembly space. Students shared the use of a gymnasium and auditorium connected to an older elementary school already on the site. The building is two stories in height and, like Bossier High School, it features smooth brick walls over a concrete frame, crisp angles, a flat roof, continuous bands of horizontal windows placed above the seated pupils' eye level for visual comfort and shaded by reinforced concrete canopies, and a vertical window lighting the stairwell (see Plate 10). The linear plan with rooms on both sides of a central corridor is oriented to obtain north and south exposure.

New at Haughton was having adjustable interior partition walls between rooms. They could to be set against any of the mullions of the modular framing system and shifted as needed to adjust room sizes without changing the building's exterior appearance. Teachers then had the option of regrouping students according to the needs of the particular subject matter. This became an increasingly important aspect of school design as administrators and educators reassessed teaching methods, class organization, and class size. Flexibility became the catchword that dominated educational and architectural literature in the decades to come.

Entrance to the school is at the west end of the building and is recessed. Yet is has a significant presence because the building is small and the staircase's adjacent wraparound corner window draws attention to it, which adds a dynamic vertical accent. Decorative enrichment also is tied to structure as in the sheathing of the window mullions in a darker-colored red brick than that of the walls and by curving the corners of the mullion bricks to contrast with the building's sharp angles. In 1967 Bossier City architect Thomas R. Merideth added a cafeteria after the existing one was renovated as a library and a new gymnasium for the school (presently, the campus is over ten times the size of the original building designed by Sam).

Winnfield Elementary School.
Courtesy of LSU-Shreveport Archives and Special Collections.

Sam's design of 1939 for Winnfield Elementary School (now Winnfield Primary School) was featured in *The Nation's Schools* in 1946.[7] Winnfield, parish seat of Winn County, is a small town, but one that has played an outsize role in Louisiana's history as the birthplace of three powerful Louisiana governors—Huey P. Long, Earl K. Long, and Oscar K. Allen.

The school located on property adjacent to the high school included an auditorium to serve both schools, but a gymnasium was not necessary for the elementary students. With its reinforced-concrete frame, light-colored beige brick walls, horizontal massing, off-center entrance, linear plan with classrooms laid out on both sides of a central corridor, and long banks of windows, the school repeats features of both Bossier and Haughton high schools. The school's site, however, dictated that its double-loaded row of twenty-six classrooms face east and west. Their band of steel-sash windows were installed on the outer face of the wall to provide space for blinds on the interior, as well as to avoid water leakage, as Sam had used on the Wile House and William for the Weekend House on Cross Lake. But heat and sun glare inevitably were a problem and, lacking sheltering canopies, all the windows were subsequently covered with metal-louvered screens. The result confirmed Sam's opinion that a north-south orientation was preferable.

At Haughton, Sam had emphasized the entrance by recessing and highlighting it with an adjacent vertical window. For Winnfield Sam gives greater emphasis to the transition from outside to inside by developing the entrance area as a portal that rises almost to the roofline, and filling the space above the doors with a window and a clock. Embryonic here, the portal becomes a defining feature of his school designs in the 1940s, most impressively at Caddo Heights Elementary School. A reinforced-concrete, curved canopy stands in front of the entrance to shelter buses and vehicles. The auditorium extends at the rear of the entrance and could be shut off from the academic wing when used for community events. As at Bossier, the auditorium's wedge-shaped configuration reflects its internal organization.

In later years, Winnfield's flat roof was replaced by a gable roof, though fortunately its pitch is slight and does not significantly mar the design. More problematic is the decorative edging along the roof that replaced the original narrow band of metal flashing that served as a cornice. Despite these changes and the assortment of ancillary buildings that now dot the site, the essence of Sam's design survives.

Across the road from the school, the H-shaped two-story neoclassical Winnfield Intermediate School of 1928 by Herman J. Duncan of Alexandria demonstrates how much school design had changed in plan, flexibility, interior needs, and appearance in just over ten years. This solid and handsome brick school with its symmetrical and finite composition gave little allowance for easy modification of interior space or for expansion. As Sam wrote in his essay in *American School Board Journal,* "Designing along traditional lines will impose conditions on the interior that will make functional planning impossible, and there will result an unhappy compromise between what is needed for the interior use and the exterior appearance."[8] Sam's design for Winnfield's elementary school, along with Bossier and Haughton, shows how much he was determined to create a setting for modern educational practice. As well, all three schools visually expressed modernity and progress. Few communities in the United States had such modern buildings at such an early date, and those that did tended to be in California, where the climate encouraged outdoor instruction and architectural experimentation. There, Richard Neutra proved influential with his design for the Corona Avenue School of 1935 that incorporated glass walls along one side, which opened to a terrace for outdoor teaching, and a covered walkway in place of a traditional indoor hall. While California's climate encouraged outdoor classes, Shreveport's was not so accommodating. However, Sam and William introduced covered walkways in the 1950s in J. S. Clark (see Plate 12) and Woodlawn High School. In 1946 officials from the Ontario, Canada, school system visited Bossier, Haughton, and Werner Park schools to study their layout and facilities.

The Impact of World War II on School Design

Europe was already mired in World War II when these schools opened. Along with the war's devastating impact on European society, the rise and strength of dictatorships that had brought the Continent into conflict shaped a reassessment in the United States of the role the school could and should play in American life beyond the educational curriculum. In the broadest sense, the school building increasingly was seen as a locus for teaching values and citizenship in democratic society. Henceforth, the schools would become social centers for the neighborhood and provide multipurpose evening use as well. This, too, meant that these activity spaces would always require separate wings so that they could be locked off from the classrooms. During the Great Depression, such spaces as gymnasiums, auditoriums, and libraries had begun to be treated in such a way, and Sam's designs for Bossier and Winnfield schools made it clear how this could be done successfully for buildings of all sizes. In his design of 1941 for Werner Park Elementary School, he further underlined this community role.

WERNER PARK ELEMENTARY SCHOOL

Werner Park was a recently developed suburb on the western edge of an industrial section of Shreveport. From the 1920s, two one-story frame buildings had served elementary education. In 1941, the Caddo Parish school board, as Sam outlined in his article published in *American School Board Journal* in 1944, "decided to replace the old buildings with a modern fireproof building, dignified in design, and arranged and equipped for the present-day instructional program."[9] Sam collaborated with the superintendent and the assistant superintendent of schools in addressing the teaching and community requirements now expected of the building.

Oriented to receive north and south light, the two-story school had eleven classrooms, a cafeteria, and an auditorium. The plan is basically an ell, with the wedge-shaped auditorium at the east end and the cafeteria extending to the school's rear. While both spaces can be accessed from the school's lobby and closed off from the academic wing if used by the public, the auditorium has a separate public entrance at the exterior east end. This entrance, a monumental version of the more modest one for students at the front of the building, amplifies the school's role to the community. Reached from a broad flight of stairs flanked by low brick walls, the entrance's three doors are set between sweeping curved brick jambs and sheltered by a deep cantilevered canopy. The brick used for door and window jambs is flatter, longer, and darker in color than that of the walls, setting up a contrast in size and color that forms the ornamentation. Deeply raked mortar between the bricks enhanced the surfaces in sunlight and shadow.

Werner Park Elementary School.
Photo by Guy W. Carwile.

In his essay on the Werner Park design, Sam wrote that, ideally, a "design reduces all parts to the simplest form consistent with its function, and the use of unnecessary details and decoration is eliminated. The resulting masses and outlines are thus a fully functional expression of the construction and inner use areas rather than a conscious effort to design a building in a specific 'style.'"[10] This statement encapsulates his approach to the creation of appropriate spaces and was profoundly influenced by his travels in Europe a decade earlier. Yet in aesthetics this school is a departure from his previous International Style designs and, curiously at this late date, recalls in its details the work of Frank Lloyd Wright. Windows are narrow, vertical, clustered in groups of five, and set between horizontal bands of darker-colored brick. Although the building was designed after the Bossier, Haughton, and Winnfield schools, its combination of curved forms—the auditorium's public facade and the curve of the attached dressing room with its horizontal window band of glass block—gives it a slightly dated look. The effect is more streamlined than Sam's usual angular and strictly modernist forms, but that is part of its attraction, for it has a softer expression that perhaps makes it more approachable.

The Changing Classroom

Sam's essay "The Changing Classroom," published in 1948 in *American School Board Journal,* is a distillation of his experience in educational planning and offers suggestions for the future. Sam was convinced that flexibility in plan was essential in order to deal with potential changes in student numbers or activities, and a plan that could take additions if necessary. Consequently, he advocated a structural system that allowed extension and, for the interior, partitions between rooms that could be shifted as needed. To achieve the latter, spacing windows in long groups with small mullions between them would permit classrooms of varying lengths. In recommending a north-south orientation for schools in the South, he stated, "I cannot overestimate the importance of correct orientation and advise either a north or south exposure of all classrooms."[11] Direct sunlight was to be avoided, and ideally a classroom should receive daylight from both of its sides. The essay includes two diagrams, one showing how the movement of the sun might affect interior lighting and the other a cross-section illustrating a method of adding a clerestory window on a classroom's corridor side by lowering the corridor's roof below that of the classroom. Sam employed a similar system in Caddo Heights Elementary School, where the classroom block's wall is higher than that of the corridor to accommodate a clerestory window to bring light into the classrooms.

That form follows function was a guiding principle for modernist architects is iterated in his statement, "the functions of the rooms determine the form of the building, and the exterior will of necessity express the interior."[12] Sam urged architects and administrators not to force a building to conform to a traditional style: "In planning a school we must give primary consideration to creating the most desirable interior, rather than obtaining a monumental or picturesque exterior effect."[13] He was referring to the historic revival styles that were so popular in the 1920s and 1930s and which he also believed negatively governed the organization of interior space. Such massively scaled buildings were intimidating to children and, moreover, their interiors were drab.

In 1948 Sam participated in a symposium focused on school design, along with seven other firms whose practices included school buildings. Sponsored by *Progressive Architecture,* a summary of the participants' discussion was published in the magazine in April 1949. In a response to a question on problems encountered in dealing with clients in the educational field, Sam responded (encouragingly, according to the magazine), "so-called Gothic and Colonial are dead as far as schools are concerned in our locality. We have, however, had instances when it was difficult to convince the client that an unfamiliar plan or detail had the advantage we claimed for it."[14]

A student's well-being extended to interior furnishings, for "the classroom is the environment for a large part of every child's life, and it is our responsibility to make it pleasant as well as comfortable."[15] He recommended light colors for interior walls and added that it was his practice to paint each room in a different color scheme. However, he disagreed with those who advocated making the classroom look "homelike," for there was little in common between the requirements of the interiors of homes and school, and a schoolroom could be both efficient and attractive in its own way.

His essay concludes with an exhortation, "Let us realize that our old buildings belonged to an older order of education, and that the possibilities for improving our buildings in the future are as unlimited as the process in education and building technology."[16] Sam later served as advisory architect to the School Building Division of the U.S. Bureau of Education.

CADDO HEIGHTS AND PLANTATION PARK ELEMENTARY SCHOOLS

World War II had generated enormous material and manufacturing advances, and at its conclusion industrial companies were keen to find new clients for their products, from steel to glass, aluminum, and various new compound materials. School boards in turn were eager to use materials that were cost-effective, structurally sound, and permitted rapid construction. They were also beginning to realize that their older buildings and their problems such as poor organization and lack of sufficient lighting were having a negative effect on the children and instructors. Industry and school boards formed a perfect marriage, and one that offered opportunities for architects to rethink building types for modern needs.

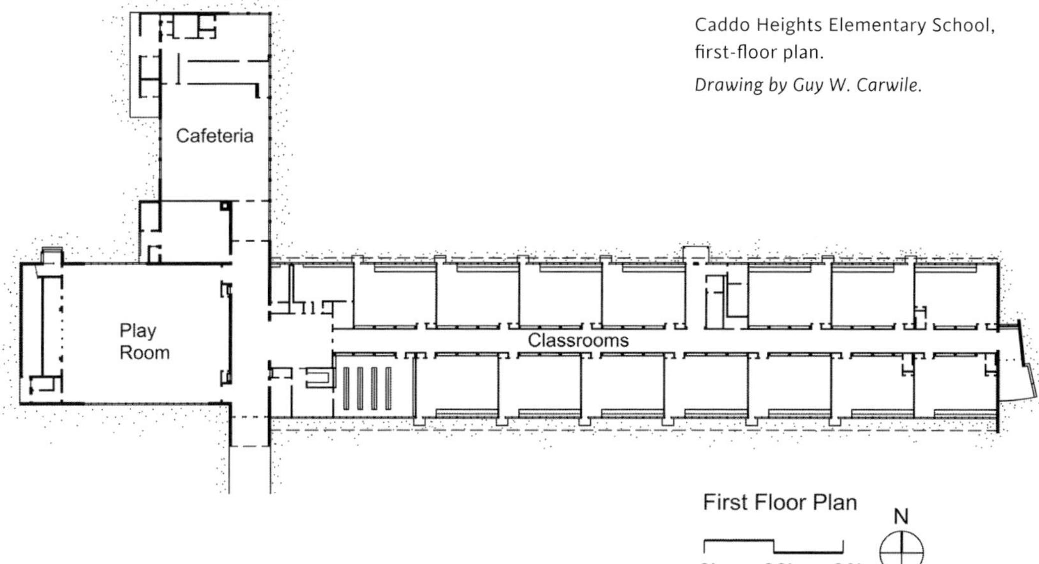

Caddo Heights Elementary School, first-floor plan.
Drawing by Guy W. Carwile.

Caddo Heights Elementary School, designed by Samuel G. Wiener and Associates, was the first elementary school constructed in Caddo Parish after the war. It was financed by a six-million-dollar bond issue passed in 1947 by the parish's voters for the purpose of building new schools. The school, which opened in 1949, was designed as a prototype in a study requested by the parish's school board to establish a new direction for its future educational facilities. The parish's building committee directed that the school should serve as a model or pilot for future parish schools and incorporate the most advanced ideas in planning, construction, light control, and community use.[17]

Intended for an eight-acre site, the plan clusters the auditorium and cafeteria at the west end of the classroom block, which faces north and south, an orientation the Caddo Parish School adopted for all new schools. A nine-foot module was used for the building's steel frame, and its support columns of the classroom wing were located so that partition walls between the fourteen classrooms could be easily shifted. Horizontal beams extended beyond the exterior walls to serve as supports for the window canopies, which on the south side are five-and-a-half feet deep

Caddo Heights Elementary School, building section.
Drawing by Guy W. Carwile.

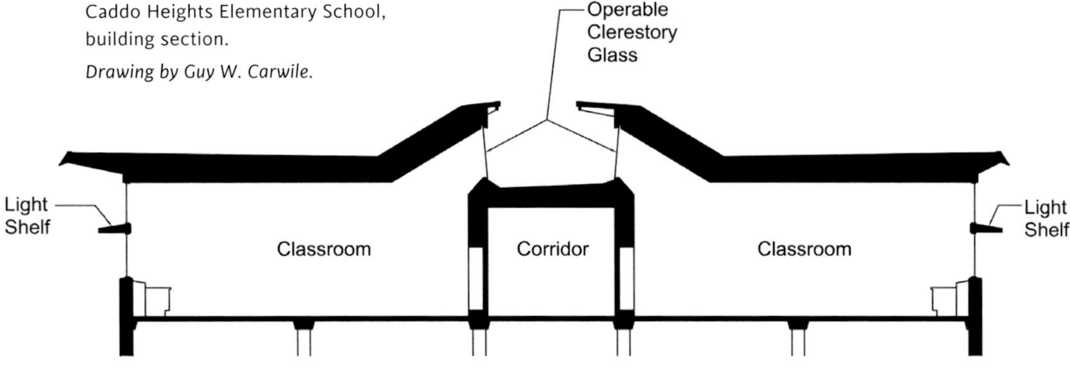

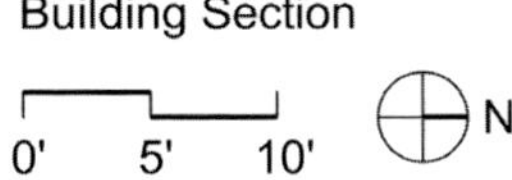

and effectively lowered room temperature in the summer.[18] Exterior walls are of light gray brick, and windows are steel-framed and fitted with ventilated sashes. The architects made scale models of a typical room to study natural illumination. For this school they achieved bilateral light by heightening the wall between the central corridor and that of the classrooms and filling the space with an operable clerestory window, thus also achieving light and cross-ventilation. In essence the concept draws on the traditional monitor roof used on many factory buildings. A similar system had been used by Baton Rouge architects Bodman and Murrell in the PWA-funded combined elementary and high school they designed in 1939 for Belle Rose in Assumption Parish, where they used a combined skylight and ridge ventilator above the corridor that was positioned to allow light and air into the flanking classrooms through transom windows.[19] When Caddo Heights Elementary School was later air-conditioned, the clerestory was closed, but the clerestory windows throughout the school still have the crank-and-gear hardware that operated them.

As in Sam's previous designs, the three major areas—academic wing, auditorium, and cafeteria—were accessible from the main entrance and admission to each was controlled. It is significant that only the cafeteria has a separate entrance, and the auditorium does not. The school's most striking feature is the monumental rectangular entrance portal. Nascent at Winnfield Elementary School, here it is enlarged to massive scale, rising higher than the attached classroom block and forming a transition to the tall auditorium on its other side. Its size and importance seem to repudiate Sam's admonition about obtaining a monumental effect. Yet, the portal's projecting framing walls envelop and give a sense of occasion to passage through its deep space. Sam's emphasis on the significance of transitional spaces from outside to inside is a theme in his work, whether created from hollowing out a building's mass as with the portico and screened porch in his own house, or wrapping an exterior in ornament to announce arrival as at the Municipal Auditorium, or moving from secular to sacred space as at B'nai Zion Temple. At this school, movement is from the brightly lit outside through the shady portal to a light and wide lobby lined with beige glazed tile. The glazed tiles, also used elsewhere in the building, have proved hard-wearing and economical in terms of maintenance, and have made it easy to keep the school clean. Placement of the school close to the sidewalk and street edge has proved problematic for circulation flow at students' arrival and departure times. Sam designed an addition to the school in 1967.

Three years after Caddo Heights Elementary School Sam restated the massive entrance portal in his design for Plantation Park Elementary School in Bossier City. Located north of Bossier City's downtown in a recently developed residential area adjacent to Barksdale Air Force Base, the school is similar in many other ways to Caddo Heights. It is single-story, has a double-loaded classroom block facing north and south shaded on both sides by a roof overhang, a separate auditorium, and a cafeteria. The design was highlighted in an article in *American School Board Journal* for its solution to light and the movement of air during Louisiana's hot and humid summer months.[20] As at Caddo Heights, the classroom walls are elevated to incorporate clerestory windows. One significant difference illustrating Sam's continuing inves-

Caddo Heights Elementary School. *Courtesy of LSU-Shreveport Archives and Special Collections.*

tigation into ventilation was making the auditorium and cafeteria freestanding and set at an angle to the classroom wing for better circulation of air. This placement also gave them separate entrances for nonschool use. In 1966 Sam designed a library and kindergarten for Caddo Heights.

Shreveport and the Baby Boom

The post–World War II baby boom made housing and school building two of the most important challenges for city governments, planners, and school boards. Enrollment nationwide in public schools from kindergarten through twelfth grade in the 1950 school year was 25.1 million. In 1955 it had jumped to nearly 30.6 million, and by 1960 it was 36.7 million. The number peaked in 1971 at 46.5 million, and then decreased until 1984. Caddo Parish, which experienced a population surge generated primarily by the oil and gas industry, saw student enrollment more than double between 1946 and 1966. In 1954 nearly 24,000 white students and just over 16,000 black students were enrolled in the parish's schools, and in Shreveport alone the number was nearly 19,000 white and just over 11,000 black.[21] Despite the *Brown v. Board of Education* Supreme Court decision of 1954 and the 1964 Civil Rights Act, which outlawed racial discrimination in schools and other public facilities, schools in Louisiana only began the process of desegregation following an order by the Supreme Court in 1969. The nearly forty new schools or additions to existing facilities constructed in Caddo Parish in the 1950s were thus segregated. Despite the concept of and lip service to separate-but-equal facilities for white and black students in the prewar period, those for black students had been decidedly inferior. In the postwar years the Caddo Parish School Board made some effort to improve them. For both white and black students the first priority after the war was for elementary schools, but by the late 1940s, middle and high schools were either under construction or being planned.

Linwood Junior High School.
Photo by Guy W. Carwile.

LINWOOD JUNIOR HIGH SCHOOL AND J. S. CLARK JUNIOR HIGH SCHOOL

The urgent need for schools brought work for many Shreveport architects. William with his firm of Wiener, Morgan and O'Neal designed two junior high schools in quick succession. Linwood Junior High School, in the fast-growing neighborhood of Cedar Grove, opened in 1949 for white students. J. S. Clark Junior High (now Middle School) for African American students opened in 1958 in the Allendale-Lakeside neighborhood of Shreveport. Both schools were designed for community activities as well as daytime academic use.

Linwood is composed of two rectilinear blocks, one with two floors of classrooms and an auditorium and the other with a cafeteria and workshops. This was William's first finger-plan school. The finger plan was widely used in the United States during the 1950s. At Linwood the two blocks, or fingers, are separated by a landscaped courtyard and linked by a covered walkway, but one deviation is the gymnasium that forms an ell from the cafeteria-workshop wing. The auditorium, cafeteria, and gymnasium are placed to facilitate use by the public in the evenings. They do not have separate entrances; instead the academic wing could be locked off from the auditorium by sliding gates. With the exception of four classrooms on the ground floor, all the instructional areas receive daylight and air from two sides, enabled through the central corridor's higher roof on the upper story. The grid of continuous steel-framed windows, the simple projecting slab that serves as a canopy over the entrance, and the sawtooth-shaped side walls of the auditorium with its narrow vertical windows establish an austere angularity.

Inside, everything was light and bright. Bill Wiener Jr. recalled: "my father and Jesse Morgan felt very strongly about the orientation and built a model with a flood light representing the sun which could be moved through a day on its vertical axis and further adjusted for declination for any time of the year in order to show the effect of proper orientation and sun control devices. They convinced the school board that all future schools should be designed with proper orientation. Many years later the school was air-conditioned and the fenestration was changed."[22] The school's cafeteria, corridors, and stairways were finished in glazed ceramic tile, and rooms were painted in cheerful colors.

J. S. Clark Junior High (now Middle) School, designed for fifteen hundred students, was named for Joseph Samuel Clark, the first president of Southern University, a historically black college located a few miles north of Baton Rouge. William created a compact campus plan for the J. S. Clark school, in part a result of the limited size of the site. Nevertheless the school's individual units have been split apart into a campus plan with each building or component clearly articulated. Bill Jr. has noted that J. S. Clark had the first campus plan in Caddo Parish.[23] The scheme, designed to more effectively serve both academic and community needs, is composed of a three-story classroom wing facing the auditorium, cafeteria, and workshop block across a paved and landscaped courtyard. The gymnasium, a separate structure, closes the end of the courtyard. All the units are connected by covered walkways constructed of reinforced cast-in-place concrete with a serrated profile to guide rain water to a drainage pipe encased in the concrete columns.

The school's modular configuration and concrete frame underpin light brown/red brick walls, and the bright blue insulated porcelain enamel panels and glass curtain walls of the academic wing. This wing has north-south orientation, but the plan of the school published in *Architectural Record* indicates it faces east and west, an error the magazine presumably introduced based on the orientation of most schools in the United States.[24] The upper two classroom floors are cantilevered over the ground story's administrative offices and the library, to provide a covered play and walk area. Ornamentation comes in two forms, one functional in the freestanding staircases at both ends of the classroom block, adding a bold sculptural note. Adjacent to the exterior staircase on the Hearne Avenue end wall is a sculpture of abstractly arranged metal squares in primary colors that recall the art forms of Europe of the 1920s. Students can also access the school through an entrance in the center from Ford Street to the north and, typically of many curtain-wall 1950s buildings, the entrance is decidedly low-key, not monumental. There is no hierarchy of parts or face for this building, and in this way the building reflects the aesthetic preferences of the 1950s. But it also means that there is no hierarchy between student or community use; all are equal here. The later addition of air-conditioning has made for some awkward units added to the school.

WOODLAWN HIGH SCHOOL

In 1949 the Caddo Parish School Board had engaged the services of the George Peabody College for Teachers in Nashville, Tennessee, to analyze the physical needs of the parish's school system. From the 1930s on, this prestigious school of education had conducted numerous similar surveys and reports for school districts in the United States, a practice it continued into the 1970s. The Peabody survey report, which was completed in 1950 for Caddo, recommended construction of a new high school for white students to be ready for the September 1960 academic term.[25] Taking into account the pattern of Shreveport's suburban growth, the report proposed that a site of at

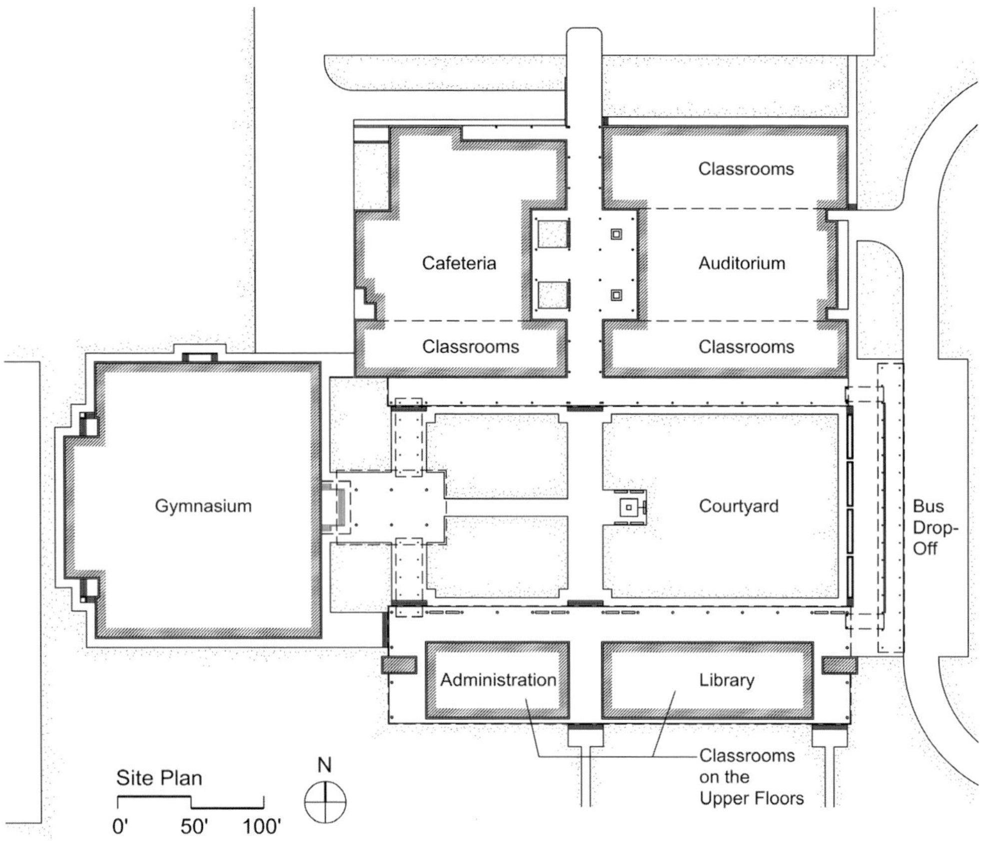

Woodlawn High School, site plan. *Drawing by Guy W. Carwile.*

least forty acres be acquired in the general area of Mansfield Road and West Seventieth Street, the Sherwood Park subdivision.

Woodlawn, the third of the schools designed by William for Wiener, Morgan and O'Neal and completed in time for the 1960–61 academic year, was the first high school constructed since completion in 1950 of Booker T. Washington High School for African American students, designed by Theodore Flaxman and Seymour Van Os (discussed in chapter 9). Woodlawn was planned for fifteen hundred pupils and for community use.[26] In plan and design, the school is a refinement of J. S. Clark School's campus plan, with separate structures grouped around a large landscaped courtyard dotted with shade trees. The three-story classroom block has a curtain wall of glass and blue spandrel panels, and its first floor is recessed to provide a covered walkway (see Plate 13).

The auditorium is situated between rooms designated for arts and crafts and for music. Entrance to the auditorium faces a wide covered breezeway that separates the auditorium's block from another that encompasses a cafeteria and rooms for workshops. The space between the auditorium entrance and that of the cafeteria is particularly spacious to accommodate crowds. But it is extraordinary in other ways, with the space flowing through the open-ended breezeway to brilliant light and landscape beyond. Two atria filled with plants are open to the sky (see Plate 14). The entire effect is more like something that would be found on a corporate campus than a school campus.

At the far end of the landscaped court that stands between the two building blocks is a gymnasium. Its presence and entrance are marked by a double-height portico supported on slender reinforced-concrete columns. The portico reaches deep into the courtyard, forming a processional route to the gymnasium. The ensemble brings to mind the ceremonial approach to and monumental quality of a Greek classical temple. It is classicism reduced to essential elements, which in many ways is the essence of modernism. As well, this clarity and honesty of form is echoed in the frank display of materials, not just the most obvious such as the brick and glass walls, but the reinforced-concrete waffle slab of the soffits and ceilings of the covered walkways, corridors, and gymnasium portico.

Artist Samuel G. Wiener Jr., Sam's son, designed the abstract mural on the classroom block's narrow end wall facing the street in an abstract pattern in blues and gray. The bus shelter is ornamented with glazed brick. Mosaic decoration and these colors were popular in the 1950s. As at J. S. Clark School, the school acknowledges the street and its neighborhood at its outside border line, not with an intimidating entrance or traditional facade, but instead with open arms to present the landscaped courtyard, making it fit comfortably in its residential environment.

Schools for a Postwar Society

In the late 1930s Sam revolutionized the school-building programs of the Shreveport region with his Bossier and Haughton schools. Starting from a reassessment of spaces that best suited contemporary educational programs and the needs of the school's larger community, he transformed the building's physical appearance. The result was progressive in all its dimensions, and in the post–World War II era the Caddo Parish School Board adopted a design program that reflected the reformist spirit embodied in Sam and William's work. They were lighter in appearance and emphasized horizontality, were more open and flexible in plan, provided honesty in structure and made use of new materials, provided better lighting and natural light and ventilation, were painted in bright colors, and incorporated open walkways and areas for outdoor activities.

Woodlawn High School, entrance to gymnasium.
Photo by Guy W. Carwile.

Sam and William designed more schools in the 1950s than those described here. For example, Sam designed Myra-Myrtis Road, Arthur Circle Elementary, and Ellerbe Road schools, and William, with Wiener, Morgan and O'Neal, was responsible for the Woolworth Road School. Shreveport's other modernist architects and architectural firms produced designs in the same spirit. Caddo Parish adopted the finger plan, a scheme composed of parallel rows of single-story linear units, for its elementary schools, and the firm of Van Os and Flaxman used it for Herndon Elementary (now Herndon Magnet School), north of Shreveport. The finger plan, which worked well for daylight and for cross-ventilation in the days before air-conditioning, was employed for Judson, Mooretown, and Summer Grove elementary schools, all designed by the firm of Neild and Somdal (Edward F. Neild and Dewey A. Somdal). Other architects, whatever their personal aesthetic preferences, produced designs in the same spirit, among them W. S. Evans who produced Sunnybrook Elementary and the Eighty-first Street School, and the firm of Annan and Gilmer which designed Hollywood Heights and Northside Elementary.

The social role that schools played did not disappear at the conclusion of the war, but instead took on another responsibility, that of a weapon against Communism. In a special issue of *Life* magazine focused on schools, renowned historian and educator Henry Steele Commager published a short essay, "Our Schools Have Kept Us Free."[27] In reference to World War II and the Cold War, he wrote, "To our schools went the momentous responsibility of inspiring a people to pledge and hold allegiance to these historic principles of democracy, nationalism, American values and egalitarianism." The role of schools were thus conceived as having a higher purpose than merely the acquisition of knowledge, for education promised to bring a good society, which generated good government.

Philip and Clara Lieber House.
Photo by Guy W. Carwile.

9

MODERNISM AND MODERNISTS IN SHREVEPORT AND BEYOND

In their designs of the 1930s, Sam and William introduced the new European forms to Shreveport, setting a new direction for architecture in the city. They were able to realize their ideas by having clients who held similar views and aesthetic sense. Their contemporaries in the city only occasionally had the fortune to have clients willing to be as innovative. The circumstances of the Great Depression, though, limited everyone to what might have been accomplished. After World War II, clients and architects alike embraced the technology and materials of modernism, if not always the aesthetics.

Jones, Roessle, and Olschner

In September 1931, the firm of Jones, Roessle, Olschner and Wiener was actively seeking federal-funded projects under the Public Works Administration (PWA). Other than the Municipal Incinerator and Bossier High School, they had little success, securing only a couple of school additions. They were competing against other Louisiana architects and firms—J. W. Smith of Monroe; Weiss, Dreyfous and Seiferth of New Orleans; and Neild-Somdal Associates in northwest Louisiana—with far more influential political connections beyond the state and particularly within it.

Clarence Olschner, who with Sam constituted the Shreveport branch of the firm, possessed neither the Shreveport connections nor the financial means to survive in an independent practice during the Great Depression. When his collaboration with Sam on the Municipal Incinerator concluded in 1935, Olschner found a position with the Federal Emergency Relief Administration as a resident engineering inspector. Based in Fort Worth, Texas, his job was to advise and verify compliance with federal contract requirements. In 1940, he returned to New Orleans, the city of his youth, in the employment of the Housing Authority of the Federal Works Agency. The Great Depression had brought to an end the remarkable professional association between Olschner and Sam.

Ernest W. Jones and Rudolph B. Roessle remained in New Orleans and formed a partnership with Frederick V. von Osthoff, who from 1922 to 1929 had worked in the office of Jones, Roessle and Olschner. In 1929 von Osthoff joined the New Orleans practice of Weiss, Dreyfous and Seiferth, a firm that was awarded a remarkable number of PWA and WPA commissions during the Depression. In 1947, von Osthoff rejoined Jones and Roessle's firm, which after Jones's death in 1955 was renamed Roessle and von Osthoff. Their projects in New Orleans included the Calliope Street housing development and commercial buildings, including the F. W. Woolworth stores, which had a somewhat streamlined corporate style. Roessle died in New Orleans in 1967.

Theodore A. Flaxman

Sam and William defined modern architecture in Shreveport in the 1930s, and while there was no one to match them, Theodore A. Flaxman came as close as he could and arguably closer than anyone else. Flaxman shared Sam's ideas about architecture and had traveled with Sam and Marion for part of the time when all three were in Europe in 1931. Interviewed in 1983, Flaxman gave all credit to Sam for the architectural revolution in Shreveport:

> Here in Shreveport the only person who contributed to what we would call architecture was Sam. He led the way. I was greatly influenced by him. When I came back [from Europe] at the end of 1931, there was nothing [modern] in Shreveport or anywhere else. During the 1930s and the Depression, Sam began to do things. No question about that we were tremendously influenced by the Bauhaus. We didn't know of [Erich] Mendelsohn until we got there. In those days architecture was taught on one system only—Beaux-Arts. Sam and I saw what we thought were necessities [and] we had the urge to clean ourselves of classical training. To change, took a real effort on the part of a young architect, established architects wouldn't and didn't. Sam was the first.[1]

Born in Houston, Flaxman (1901–1986) graduated with a BA from Rice Institute (now Rice University) in 1923 and undertook graduate studies at Columbia University in New York City from 1924 to 1925. In the year between Rice and Columbia, Flaxman was a draftsman in the office of Jones, Roessle, Olschner and Wiener, where he worked under Sam's supervision. Upon completing his studies at Columbia, Flaxman was employed from 1925 to 1926 as a draftsman for the prestigious firm of Trowbridge and Livingston in New York City, after which he moved to Shreveport and collaborated on some projects with Edward F. Neild. In 1933, Flaxman set up his own practice.

Flaxman's architecture resonates with the inspiration he found in the work of the European modernists, most notably that of Erich Mendelsohn. The dramatic sweeping curve that Sam gave Big Chain Broadmoor in 1940 was inspired in part by Mendelsohn's work, but previous to that Flaxman's design for the Masonic Temple at Creswell Avenue and Wichita Street was the Shreveport building that best exemplified that source. Flaxman had seen several of Mendelsohn's buildings, including the curved Schocken department stores in Stuttgart and Chemnitz, the Universum Cinema in Berlin, and, while in the company of Sam and Marion, the Einstein Tower in Potsdam. The Masonic Temple reflects these sources and is arguably Flaxman's most significant work. The temple presents a symmetrical facade with walls of cream-colored brick on a dark brown base that curves inward to a recessed central entrance (see Plate 15). Lower wings flank the building. The dark base gives a slight impression that the building is elevated above the ground. When built, a glass-block window filled the area above the entrance, but this was later replaced by a plate-glass window containing a Masonic symbol. The horizontality of the sweeping curves of the walls is emphasized by projecting rows in the brick walls and narrow bands of glass-block windows. They give texture to the surface, and the play of recession and projection, shadow and light, is also found in Mendelsohn's work. The sweeping forms are bold, particularly for clients who tended toward more traditional styles, but the symmetry of the building conveys a sense of Beaux-Arts order. Altogether the building is easy to enjoy. Of Flaxman's plan for landscaping in front of the temple, a low retaining wall between a pair of steps that leads up from Creswell Street survives. However, the wall and steps show that the building was not conceived as an isolated object but as part of an urban setting.

Flaxman acknowledged that he was overwhelmed by Mendelsohn's work and that the temple was his working out of this obsession. In an unusual display of honesty for a designer, however, Flaxman said about the temple, "I didn't think it was very good then. I did it very badly but did it as well as I could as a young man."[2] He recalled that he was criticized for the modern design and queried why he did not design a "nice colonial house." Flaxman explained that it came into being because he knew the head of the temple's building committee and persuaded that person to accept the modern design, who then "bullied people into it."[3]

Most of Flaxman's work during the Great Depression consisted of small commercial projects and residences in Shreveport and neighboring towns. Among the houses he designed were the Coleman House of 1938 at 123 East Preston Avenue for a client who wanted something "modern, non-stylistic." The L-shaped one-story house has an entrance portico cut deeply into one corner that is supported on a pair of slender steel columns, a corner steel-framed casement window, and a rectangular red-brick chimney, vaguely reminiscent of the chimneys Frank Lloyd Wright used for this houses, that is tucked into the reentrant angle of the ell and rises high above the flat roof. Two features of the house are particularly noteworthy: one is the porthole window next to the entrance, a feature he borrowed from European buildings, and the other is the massive attic space. The attic extends beyond the white-painted walls to shade them and the windows and serves as an insulation space, similar to that of the Cross Lake Weekend House. As Flaxman observed, "We were struggling in those days with how to ventilate [and cool] a house."[4] The attic finishes at the roof line with two narrow cornice bands that give the house a nautical flavor, which of course is heightened by the porthole window.

Flaxman's other projects in the 1930s include a one-story flat-roofed house on Ratcliff Avenue (now altered). The addition of a game room to Philip and Clara Lieber's house (Seymour Van Os designed the house in 1935) at 660 Slattery Boulevard is glass-block shaped in a bold curve. As Flaxman remembered, "I couldn't get it [the curved shape] off my mind."[5] He used the curve again for an addition to a house on McCormick Street.

In 1939, Flaxman formed a partnership with Seymour Van Os under the name Van Os and Flaxman and opened their office in Suite 311 of the Ricou-Brewster Building. Much of their practice in the postwar years was devoted to schools in the massive school-building campaigns undertaken by parishes throughout the state. Their most important commission was Booker T. Washington High School in 1947 for Caddo Parish School Board. Located at 2104 Milam Street, this school for African American students was the first high-school building since Central Colored High School, which opened in 1917, with approximately 140 students. By 1940, Central High had 1,600 students and, despite the addition of buildings in 1926 and 1939, it was impossibly overcrowded (the school also drew students from east Texas, who boarded in Shreveport during the school year). The school became a junior high when Booker T. Washington opened. The latter was intended to ameliorate the substandard level of educational facilities for the parish's black students. Schools in Louisiana and the South in general were segregated by race. Wedged into a sloping site, the school is mostly two stories, though it increases to three on the eastern side of the property in response to the topography. It is a thoroughly modern building of brick with a glass-curtain wall. Photographs of the school featured in *Life* magazine in 1950 in a special issue on schools focused on the educational program, specifically the trade and manual classes

Booker T. Washington High School.
Photo by Guy W. Carwile.

that traditionally played a significant role in the education of African American students.[6] The photographs showed students hand-setting type for a printing press as well as the auto-repair and bricklaying workshops. The school was one of the reasons *Look* magazine gave an All America City award to Shreveport in 1953, in recognition of the improved schools, housing, and medical facilities for its black population.

Van Os and Flaxman designed several more schools, including Phillips Junior High and the High School for African American students in Minden (1952–1964), Webster Parish High School and an elementary school in Minden, and Many High School (1956), all now altered. They also designed several buildings at Barksdale Air Force Base. Their most significant work in the 1950s was the new temple for B'nai Zion, which they designed with Sam, and can be counted as one of the finest buildings with which Flaxman was involved as an architect.

Seymour Van Os

Seymour Van Os (1893–1974), with whom Flaxman formed a partnership in 1939, was born in New Orleans and graduated from Tulane University in 1913 with a BS in architecture (the school of architecture was not yet established as a separate unit with its own degrees). After employment in various New Orleans offices, including that of S. S. Labouisse, he came to Shreveport in 1915, where he worked with architect John Y. Snyder. In 1917, Van Os entered the U.S. Army and, after the war, he accepted a reserve commission in the Corps of Engineers, which later in December 1940 led to his being recalled to duty as a major. He established an architectural office in Shreveport in 1919, working on small projects, mostly houses, and on the Municipal Auditorium.

Van Os designed in a variety of styles as suited the client, fashioning such popular residential styles of the time as Colonial Revival and Mediterranean, though usually with a slight twist so that they were not formulaic. His design for his own house (720 Slattery Boulevard) is best described as Spanish Mission, but he designed an impressive streamlined Moderne house for Philip and Clara Lieber in 1935. The late 1930s show Van Os's skill in various interpretations of Art Deco and Moderne. The three-story former Salvation Army Building (1932) at 710 Crockett is Art Deco, while his design for the historic Agudath Achim Synagogue (1938), now Rutherford House, at 1707 Line Avenue, is Moderne. Both buildings emphasize the textural qualities possible with brick construction, and the former synagogue, a solid blocky building with massive tower-like forms framing the entrance, emphasizes the sense of weight and strength that can be conveyed with the material. Van Os's work became thoroughly modern after he partnered with Flaxman in 1939, but this was also because they had the clients that were receptive to contemporary design. In the postwar period, Van Os designed a house for his son Herman Van Os at 3510 Madison Park Boulevard. The house's plan fully emphasizes the centrality of the automobile to modern living, for it is the driveway that rises from the street to the residence, which spreads out on its higher elevation. A path from the garage runs parallel to the front of house to the entrance door.

In an interview in 1972, Van Os was asked what buildings gave him particular pride. He cited two postwar schools—Booker T. Washington and Eden Gardens Elementary (1966) at 626 Eden Boulevard.[7] Van Os described the former as being the first building in the city "in the modern manner," by which he meant a tall building with a curtain wall of glass, and the latter for the use of precast and prestressed concrete. It is illuminating that he selected two buildings dependent on the improved technologies and materials of the postwar period. Van Os was one of the founders of the Shreveport chapter of the American Institute of Architects, which was established in large part in response to the fee-cutting that affected architects in the 1920s.

Dewey A. Somdal and Edward F. Neild

Dewey A. Somdal (1898–1973) an Illinois native, attended the University of Illinois but never completed the program, instead joining the Corps of Engineers in 1918 and then serving in World War I. He relocated to New Orleans in 1921 to work for the Saenger Amusement Company, founded by Shreveport brothers Julian H. and A. D. Saenger, who had offices in New Orleans. And Somdal also served as a draftsman in the prestigious New Orleans office of Favrot and Livaudais. In 1923, Somdal moved to Shreveport to join the office of Edward F. Neild, a position that in 1934 evolved into a partnership, Neild-Somdal Associates, which lasted until Neild's death in 1955.

Neild was one of Louisiana's busiest architects over the course of his forty-seven-year career, responsible for buildings in Arkansas, Texas, and Missouri as well as in Louisiana. Born in 1884 in Shreveport, he studied engineering and graduated with a BS from Tulane University, after which he returned to Shreveport and in 1908 estab-

Louisiana State Exhibit Building.
Photo by Guy W. Carwile.

lished his firm. The Caddo Parish Courthouse, a massive Beaux-Arts classical pile of 1928, is the most prominent of Neild-Somdal's projects in the city. After Harry Truman, who was then a judge in Kansas City, Missouri, saw the building while on a trip inspecting courthouses throughout the United States to get inspiration for a design for the Jackson County Courthouse in his home city, he appointed Neild to work with a group of Kansas City architects to design the Jackson courthouse (1934). Later, when Truman was president, he sought out Neild to assist in the design of the Truman Presidential Library in Kansas City, which was completed in 1957. Neild died in 1955 while in Kansas City consulting on the project.

In the somber years of the 1930s, Neild-Somdal did relatively well, getting several PWA projects, mostly for school additions and alterations. From the evidence of Neild's work, he favored buildings infused with classical forms and details, and this mode was where he had achieved considerable success. By the late 1930s, modernism, probably under the influence of Somdal and Neild's son, Edward F. Neild Jr., who joined the firm in 1936, inflected the firm's work, resulting in the stripped-down versions of classicism that became favored for civic and institutional buildings. Their most sophisticated and original design, and the one that comes closest to a modern ideal, is the PWA-funded Louisiana State Exhibit Building (now the Louisiana State Exhibit Museum) completed in 1939 at the fairgrounds on Greenwood Road.[8] This smooth-surfaced reinforced-concrete-framed building is composed of a one-story circular pavilion wrapping a central courtyard bookended by symmetrical one-story wings. The central entrance is formed of a severe rectangular portico with two elliptical, dark pink, granite columns without bases or capitals. Exterior ornamentation is the building's name carved across the top of the portal, below which is a carving of the state seal and the names of Louisiana's sixty-four parishes on the wings. Within the portico the building is brought alive by artist Conrad Albrizio's brilliantly colored frescoes of Louisiana's agriculture and industries that so stunningly contrast with the stark monochrome exterior.

Among Neil-Somdal's other notable designs of the 1930s were the State Capitol Annex (1939) in Baton Rouge and the sparely ornamented seven-story office building of 1939 for the United Gas Corporation in Shreveport, which received a twelve-story addition in 1954.

Their postwar work, however, was thoroughly up-to-date and of its era. In 1949 they reinvigorated Jordan and Booth, a men's clothing store at 421 Texas, with a new fashionable facade. William had done the same for Rosenblath's men's store in the mid-1930s. These stores thrived, in part because they catered to a particular clientele. Jordan and Booth, just half a block from the courthouse and nestled among high-rise banks and commercial buildings, could count on the men who ran these institutions for their customers. The shop has a dynamic asymmetrical facade, with an entrance set deep between a large curved glass display window on one side and a smaller angled one on the other, all set within a glossy pinkish-gray marble rectangular frame.

Neild-Somdal also designed a new department store for Selber Bros., completed in 1955, on the southwest corner of Milam and McNeil streets. Similar to the facelift that Sam and William gave the Palais Royal store in the late 1940s, this five-story box-like brick-and-limestone-faced building was fully air-conditioned, with window openings limited to the street level for display and one window that rose above the central entrance to the roofline. Feibleman's Department Store had already taken the windowless route, when Sears, who then owned it, bricked up the windows in the 1940s. Selber Bros.'s name was attached in 1950s-style print and script across the top corner of the facade.

By the 1950s, Neild and Somdal had fully adopted the austere forms of that decade as seen in the three-story former Young Women's Christian Association (YWCA) building of 1954 at 710 Travis Street, where smooth cream-colored brick walls have windows grouped in horizontal rectangular frames and a sweeping kidney-shaped canopy wraps the building's corner. The small garden beside the building demonstrates the importance of landscaping to buildings of this era, though its original large holly tree has been replaced. Neild and Somdal also designed the twenty-four-story steel-framed Henry C. Beck Building (1956), with its glossy glass and aluminum curtain wall. Beyond Shreveport in Ruston, the Lincoln Parish Courthouse (1950) is an asymmetrical composition of rectangular box-like forms with windows placed to create what seem like abstract patterns across the salmon-red walls, but which respond to the spaces within.

After Neild's death in 1955, Somdal and Neild Jr. continued the architectural practice. Somdal was always involved with city planning issues and, in 1940, when the Shreveport City Planning Commission was reactivated, he was appointed chair. This gave him considerable influence on many of Shreveport's urban improvements, including zoning, subdivision regulations, and traffic. The commission was reconstituted in December 1954 as the Metropolitan Planning Commission. Somdal remained on the committee. Contractor W. Murray Werner, whose firm built several of the Wieners' buildings, was appointed a member. Somdal served on the city's committee for the long-range Greater Shreveport Master Plan, which was adopted in 1957.

Henry Schwarz

Born in Janesville, Texas, Henry Schwarz (1894–1966) attended Tulane and Columbia universities, graduating from the latter in 1917, and moving to Shreveport in

A. A. Mason House.
Photo by Guy W. Carwile.

1921. Like other architects, including Flaxman and Somdal, he came to Shreveport in the boom years following World War I when the growth of the oil and gas industries offered the potential for many new buildings. His early designs were generally in historic styles, but in the 1930s he often employed a blocky modern expression with minimal decoration. His commissions included two funded by the PWA. One, a fire station (1934–35) at Hearne and Kings Highway, has been demolished, and the other is the two steel-framed buildings of 1934 for the Farmers' Market at 2139 Greenwood Road, with facades banded horizontally in bands of light and dark colors of brick. Around 1939 Schwarz designed the control building for KWKH radio station, on US 71 north of Shreveport. This plain, rectangular flat-roofed building, with a reinforced concrete ground level and two upper floors of brick, was painted white except for the band of red that slices across its middle floor. Its International Style appearance is more a result of economy than sophisticated design.

Julian Peter Sokoloski

The only European-born architect of the Shreveport-based modernists was Julian Peter Sokoloski (1887–1954). Raised and trained in Germany, he was the municipal architect for the city of Berlin in the 1920s, but lost that position when Hitler came to power. In 1933, he immigrated with his wife Margarete to Shreveport, aided by their Shreveport relatives Bernard Sokoloski and Emanuel Phelps. Sokoloski became a friend of Sam, presumably in part because of their shared firsthand knowledge of European modernism. In 1935 Sokoloski designed a single-story International Style house for his family at 626 McCormick. The wooden house, an asymmetrical composition of rectangular forms painted white, has had some alterations. Sokoloski, like many architects who had small practices, maintained his office in his house. He gave the A. A. Mason House (1937) at 103 Ardmore Avenue a lively curved front of white-painted brick, and steel-casement windows (later replaced by glass-block windows), and ventilated the house with an attic fan that like those used by Sam and William in the early 1930s. Sokoloski designed the addition of 1951 to Jones, Roessle, Olschner and Wiener's Kings Highway Christian Church and added the tower that was part of Sam's original design.

Lester C. Haas

Though he was younger than the other Shreveport architects, Lester C. Haas's (1913–2004) career belongs to the decades after World War II. Haas's education was broad in focus and wide in geographical range. He began with two Baltimore institutions, Johns Hopkins University and the Maryland Institute of Design, before transferring to the University of Pennsylvania, where he earned a BA in architecture in 1936. He attended the Ecole des Beaux-Arts, Fontainebleau, in 1939 and the American Academy in Rome a year later. Haas also traveled widely in Europe in 1939 on a fellowship. In the summers of 1934 and 1935, he worked for Henry Schwarz. After service in the war, he returned to Shreveport and in 1946 set up his office. Haas designed various commercial and institutional buildings, including the KTBS-TV/Radio Studios in 1948, and a house in 1950–51 at 6120 Arden Street for E. Bernard Weiss, who was co-owner of Goldring's Department Store. The brick house spreads out on its elevated site, and while in many ways is similar to ranch-style houses elsewhere in its overall form and the foundation landscaping, it has a strong flavor of Frank Lloyd Wright in its low-hipped roof and grouping of windows.

One of Haas's most interesting buildings was La Sands Western Hills Hotel of 1957 in Bossier City, unfortunately now demolished, in which he worked with engineer E. M. Freeman, who had collaborated with Sam on the Municipal Airport.[9] The two-story 130-room motor hotel was six-sided in plan with all the rooms facing a kidney-shaped swimming pool and a landscaped garden. The hotel's ground-floor rooms each had a private patio garden, and the second-story rooms had balconies. All the rooms were air-conditioned and had televisions. The hotel was full-service with a restaurant, a coffee shop, a bar-lounge, and a gift shop. The restaurant and bar-lounge opened to terraces. The hotel also offered a babysitting service and free ice. Parking was on the perimeter of the six-sided hotel, and St. Louis–based Stuart M. Mertz was the landscape architect. Other than a few projects in St. Louis and Florida, little is known about Mertz's career. However, he was a fellow at the American Academy in Rome in 1940, the same year Haas was there, and presumably the two remained acquainted. For the hotel he bordered the swimming pool's surrounding terrace with curved beds of low shrubs and a large lawn to one side.

La Sands Western Hills Motel.
Courtesy of Guy W. Carwile.

The hotel was colorful with bright red, white, and blue accents to add a festive or holiday note and to attract passing motorists.

Richard Neutra and Shreveport

The most renowned modernist architect who designed a building in Shreveport was not homegrown, but European-born Californian Richard Neutra. In the postwar period an architect-designed modern house was a sign of culture among those who valued and could afford such luxury and, while the Wieners were the favored architects among many such Shreveport clients, occasionally some set their sights in a different direction. In 1949, businessman James O'Brien and his wife, Nora, commissioned California architect Richard Neutra to design their house on Richmond Avenue after seeing a cover story on him in the August 15, 1949, issue of *Time* magazine.[10] The couple wanted a so-called "name" architect, someone nationally recognized. They had first considered hiring Frank Lloyd Wright but, upon visiting him in his workshop and house at Taliesin, Wisconsin, they found him too inflexible for their taste. Neutra, born in Vienna in 1892, had immigrated to the United States in 1923. After working first briefly at Talieson, he relocated to Los Angeles. Unlike Sam and William, Neutra had spent his early years in the midst of the architectural revolution occurring in Europe and was therefore not compelled to make a pilgrimage to see modern buildings. This was the only building Neutra designed in Louisiana.

Set far back on its lot and screened by existing pines and oaks, the single-story O'Brien House is set perpendicular to the street. The house is sheathed in redwood and has a flagstone floor and random ashlar chimney. Its original plan (the house has been added to) was binuclear with private spaces separated from the more public by a flagstone path into two separate units.[11] The two parts, however, were visually linked by roof overhangs and the chimney, which rises between the dining and living rooms. The principal bedrooms and the living room formed the private unit, and the dining room, kitchen, utility rooms, and guest room occupied the other. The living room, which opens via a sliding glass door to a screened porch overlooking the garden, faces south, and that side is sheltered by the extension of the gently sloped roof. This element, which had a long history with the Wieners, was not normally incorporated into Neutra's designs.

In a letter of 1952 from Neutra to Mrs. O'Brien (in the possession of the house's current owners), shortly after her husband's death he informed her of his receipt of the award at the "National Convention of Architects in New York last month."[12] According to Neutra, he was told by one of the jurors "that the jury was impressed by giving two prizes to me for California structures and they decided that not such a majority [of prizes] should go to California and something must go to other states. They unanimously decided on your house, and had long faces

James and Nora O'Brien House. *Photo by Guy W. Carwile.*

when they opened the envelope and saw my name as the architect—also in Louisiana."

Beyond Shreveport

Although the Wieners' fellow architects each had only a few clients in the 1930s willing to accept new forms, between them they did produce a significant number of modern buildings. Beyond Shreveport, modern buildings were rare. Perhaps there might have been more if the economy had permitted. One of the few firms with an active practice during the Great Depression, the New Orleans–based practice of Weiss, Dreyfous and Seiferth did absorb and render some of the attributes of modernism, though their versions tended to be more mainstream. In large part this was due to their institutional and commercial clients.

As Governor Huey Long's favorite architects, the firm designed the Art Deco Louisiana State Capitol (1932), the most prominent of their designs. Weiss, Dreyfous and Seiferth always attempted to design to please their clients, and when Long asked them for something modern, they interpreted the demand as a streamlined New York City skyscraper with setbacks. Their design for Lakefront Airport in New Orleans, which was completed in 1934 (and beautifully restored in 2013), is the most lavishly decorated of their Art Deco buildings, enriched with sculpture and marble, and abounding in the relatively new material of aluminum. Weiss, Dreyfous and Seiferth were awarded more substantial PWA- and WPA-funded projects in the 1930s than any other firm in Louisiana. Their numerous commissions to add buildings to the state's colleges and universities began with Huey Long and his goal to improve the state's educational facilities. While many of these buildings are in a variety of historic styles, there are also some that are handsomely Moderne, notably those completed in 1940 at McNeese State University in Lake Charles.

The one Weiss, Dreyfous and Seiferth building that can accurately be described as modern is the house in Metairie, just outside New Orleans, constructed in 1938 for James K. Feibleman, relative of the Feibleman family. James Feibleman, inspired by the houses Walter Gropius designed in Germany, requested the architects for a residence that represented the most modern forms of the time. The plan was worked out between the architects and the client. It is a streamlined European-inspired creation of intersecting geometric volumes, brick walls painted white, and bands of horizontal windows, yet despite the correct forms, it has a weighty, grounded appearance that puts it slightly at odds with the lightness seen in European work. Feibleman began his career as an author but soon became an assistant manager of the New Orleans Feibleman's store. In 1930 he was vice-president of the Feibleman Realty Company and, after the war, he taught English and philosophy at Tulane University.

The Weiss, Dreyfous and Seifeth firm broke apart after the principals were implicated in the scandals of the Huey Long era, and each formed new partnerships after the war. Their role in Louisiana's architectural culture was never as significant as it was in the 1930s. Instead, the postwar period saw a new generation of Louisiana architects, many in New Orleans, and that city began to catch up architecturally with Shreveport to fully embrace the twentieth century.

From Shreveport to New Orleans

It took a few years for modern architecture to firmly establish itself beyond Shreveport to cities throughout Louisiana. Bodman and Murrell in Baton Rouge made the shift from the more popular Art Deco to an undecorated modernism beginning in the 1940s, particularly for the schools they designed in the city. When modernism (or, as architects then preferred to describe their work, contemporary architecture) did emerge around 1950, it occurred most notably in New Orleans. There a spirit of postwar progressivism made that city look to the future rather than to the past, and in this climate architects found clients receptive to their ideas. Perhaps the most notable firm and certainly the most prolific was that of Curtis and Davis (Nathaniel C. Curtis and Arthur Q. Davis), which was formed in 1947. Both architects were raised in New Orleans, and both had studied architecture at Tulane University, but Davis continued his studies at the Harvard Graduate School of Design, where Walter Gropius, Marcel Breuer, and others were dispensing the aesthetics and technologies of modernism. Among Curtis and Davis's extant mid-twentieth-century houses, the most notable are the Steinberg House (1957) in New Orleans, with rooms arranged around a central courtyard and grouped according to use, and the Curtis House (1962), organized into public and private areas and open space. They also designed many other modern houses, churches, and institutional buildings in New Orleans and beyond.

A variation on the binuclear house plan was the pavilion plan, a scheme that more decisively separated a family's activities. New Orleans–based Charles Colbert of Colbert-Lowrey-Hess-Boudreaux Architects designed a house (1960) of four separate pavilions for physician Henry G. Simon in New Orleans in which each structure, separated by courtyards, accommodated a different function. Pavilion plans had only a brief popularity, mostly in the 1960s. Moreover, outside of Southern California, such weather phenomena as rain, heat, and snow demanded at least a covering canopy to link the individual units. Colbert had a major impact on the design of the parish's schools in his position of supervising architect for the Orleans Parish School Board in the 1950s, analogous to Sam's influence with his prototype design for Caddo Heights Elementary School. Colbert personally designed several of New Orleans's schools, as did Curtis and Davis, all of which were modern in style and sensitive to the city's climate. Several of them were demolished in the city's rebuilding after Hurricane Katrina.

New Orleans–native architect and interior designer James Lamantia also undertook graduate studies at Harvard in the mid-1940s, and with the firm of Burk, Le Breton and Lamantia, and later independently, designed houses, schools, and interiors infused with the eye of modernity. The Wieners called on Lamantia to design the furniture for the Shreveport Municipal Airport. Lawrence and Saunders (later Lawrence, Saunders and Calongne) was another important firm. In the 1950s, they created two houses in the Lake Vista neighborhood of New Orleans. This neighborhood has modernist houses by several other New Orleans architects. Unfortunately, the 1951 house Sam Wiener designed there for the Cahn family has been demolished. Lawrence, who served as dean of Tulane's architecture school from 1959 to 1971, further encouraged a curriculum shift to modern design. For several years in the 1950s Tulane students had been taken on an annual trip to Shreveport to see the Wieners' buildings.

Although born in Denver, Colorado, John Desmond moved to New Orleans as a youth. He opened a practice in Hammond in 1953 and in Baton Rouge in the early 1970s. He gave both cities many extraordinary contemporary buildings that draw their beauty from his sensitivity to structure, modern materials, and spatial richness. His own house (1960) in Hammond was composed of a cluster of separate pavilions linked by covered hallways.

Modernism Arrived

Sam and William had set a new direction and standard for architects and architecture in the 1930s, and their continued innovations in the postwar period continued to inspire local architects. While the brothers had clients in the 1930s willing to break with tradition, not all of their contemporaries were as fortunate so often. The postwar period, however, ushered in a forward-thinking spirit that enabled both the established and an emerging generation of architects to enrich Louisiana with numerous modern buildings for whom the Wieners had paved the way.

Samuel G. and Marion Pfeifer
Wiener House.
Courtesy of LSU-Shreveport Archives and Special Collections.

CONCLUSION

It is sometimes asserted that modernism arose in the United States in the 1930s in the wake of exhibitions and immigrant architects. It is a misconception that stubbornly clings. The notion is based on an exhibition, "The International Style," held at the Museum of Modern Art in 1932, and the subsequent book of the same name, which almost exclusively featured European buildings. At that time Los Angeles did have a concentration of modern buildings designed by immigrant architects Richard Neutra and Rudolf Schindler, and they are generally recognized as the earliest proponents of European-inspired modernism in the United States. The houses they designed made modern architecture and California synonymous. Of the wave of immigrant architects fleeing Nazi Germany, who arrived from the mid-1930s, it was only after World War II that they had a substantial impact on American architecture. Although Walter Gropius built a Bauhaus-inspired house in 1938 for his family in Lincoln, Massachusetts, he shaped American architecture primarily through the budding architects he taught at Harvard's Graduate School of Design (GSD) in the 1940s and 1950s. Marcel Breuer, who also taught at the GSD until 1946, had significant influence on the shape of residential design through the houses he designed. His work became widely known through publications. Within a few years after Gropius and Breuer started teaching at the GSD, their ideas and influence on architectural education reverberated through American design programs and schools. Mies van der Rohe, who had been the last director of the Bauhaus in Dessau, Germany, immediately before it was closed by the Nazi regime, introduced modernist ideals to Chicago. Yet the commonly held view that modern architecture was born with these immigrants is increasingly seen as simplistic.

While modernism in the United States only became a strong movement in the 1940s and 1950s when it became a "national style" for commercial and institutional buildings and many new residential developments, credit for its beginnings and the shift from historicist styling cannot solely be ascribed to the European immigrant architects. American architects were already producing modern buildings in towns throughout the country. A handful of American-born architects have been recognized, notably Arkansas-born, New York City–based Edward Durell Stone, who designed a couple of modernist houses in the 1930s. George Fred and William Keck of Chicago, who worked in the Midwest, are principally known through the idiosyncratic houses they created for the 1933 Century of Progress Exposition in Chicago. Yet there were other less-known American-born architects designing in a modernist idiom based on their experience of traveling through Europe to visit its innovative buildings. Just as architects in the eighteenth and nineteenth centuries had taken the so-called Grand Tour to examine the monuments of Greece and Rome, in the twentieth century a number of Americans deliberately set sail for Europe to see firsthand and to meet and talk with the architects of the buildings they saw illustrated in the architectural journals. This history is now being corrected as evidenced by recent scholarship and such publications as that on Barry Byrne in Chicago.[1] An exhibition called "Designing Home: Jews and Midcentury Modernism," held in 2014 at the Contemporary Jewish Museum in San Francisco, has also given a fuller, more accurate, and more complex picture of mid-twentieth-century American architecture.[2]

Sam and William Wiener were at the forefront of this quiet architectural revolution. Sam, who had first been inspired by Eliel Saarinen's innovative ideas about city planning and design while he was a student at the University of Michigan, went to Europe, as did William, to seek out the buildings and the architects. What they learned about construction methods, materials, and formal qualities became a framework for their designs. For them it was not merely an aesthetic or a method or system, but a way of looking at, embracing, and building for modern life.

The Architecture of Sam and William to 1940

The 1930s was the decade when Sam and William's body of work was the most avant-garde. The buildings of that decade were anchored at each end by more mainstream work, though always in contemporary styles and current—and sometimes ahead of their time—in materials, construction methods, and forms. In the 1920s, when Sam began his career and became a partner in the firm of Jones, Roessle, Olschner and Wiener, his projects were in a variety of styles, from palatial Renaissance for the Feibleman store, to Italian Romanesque for the Kings Highway Christian Church, to the newly fashionable variants of Art Deco for the Municipal Auditorium, Big Chain Fairfield, and the Downtown Airport, though for each building the style helped denote its function as well as satisfying the client. Then in 1931 Sam took his second trip to Europe, and everything changed. At the same time, William began his career. While William had visited Europe for several months in 1927, little is known about what he saw. Fortunately, testimony exists of Sam's 1931 voyage, recorded in conversations with Sam's widow Marion Wiener and with architect Ted Flaxman, with whom Sam and Marion traveled for part of their European explorations, and the postcards and correspondence between Sam and Flaxman.

The Wieners' work of the 1930s is exceptional, not merely within the context of Shreveport or Louisiana, but nationwide. The buildings they designed in this decade, rooted as they were in European and Bauhaus modernism, were radical for America, and especially for the South. Their designs emphasized the extended horizontal plane of the walls, the roof, the bands of windows, and sometimes the extension of an entrance canopy to create an airy portico. While the extraordinary Weekend House at Cross Lake of 1933 was lifted off the ground and seemed to deny gravity, it was an exception, for their subsequent houses were grounded. Sam sometimes emphasized the parallel lines of ground and building base in the lower-floor brick walls, making a connection with the earth in material, weight, and color. The contrast of red brick with the smooth planar white stucco walls above is deliberate, for it made the upper floor appear to be weightless and free-floating. In Sam's own house the projection of the second floor added to the effect. The Municipal Incinerator, with its insistent horizontal lines, also seemed to hover above the lower-level receiving doors. These were buildings fully in the spirit of European modernism, as was the sweeping unadorned curve of Big Chain Broadmoor.

The Architecture of Sam and William after 1940

If European modernism and the Bauhaus formed the Wieners' center of gravity in the 1930s, from the 1940s their work began to take a different turn. As ever, they employed the latest in structural and surface materials and in technological innovation, but in style they were not breaking new ground to the extent they had in their prewar work. In general their designs now were matched by a modernism finally accepted in the United States. For the house designs of the 1940s and 1950s, Sam and William abandoned stucco in favor of a different expression of lightness or lack of weight, now achieved through sheets of plate glass and wood (see Plate 16). The 1930s stuccoed surfaces were of their time, and innovations of the 1940s and beyond lay in the technological advances generated by World War II. The commitment to the expression of natural materials integral to Sam and William's earlier work remained and was now satisfied by the extensive use of wood both inside and out, exposed brick on interiors as well as exteriors, and, at the Municipal Airport, the richly colored and mottled marble for its interior.

The postwar years brought numerous commissions, many of them large and complex. Clients now were primarily institutions or businesses, limiting their ability to be as stylistically inventive as they were in the 1930s. Or perhaps their aspirations for a modern expression were realized. Both architects, however, continued exploring planning and structural issues. This was as true of William's structural and framing experiments with modules and modular parts to increase efficiency, cost, and design as it was for the several schools they created for the Caddo Parish School Board. The planning and engineering issues inherent in such contemporary complicated and large building types as the Municipal Airport, highway motels, and the greatly expanded shopping centers that define the vigorous consumerism of the postwar years offered challenging opportunities.

Sam and/or William

Again, it can be difficult to identify or separate Sam's designs from William's. Although the surface differences can be small, they exist. Bill Wiener Jr., William's son and an architect, believes that, while his father and uncle adopted the International Style ahead of most other American architects, Sam was more pure and faithful to Bauhaus ideals.[3] Further, William deviated from the purism as suited the project and was more sensitive about adapting to the northern Louisiana climate. Certainly the Cross Lake Weekend House played with Le Corbusier's Villa Savoie prototype to create something dynamic rather than static, while resolving local climatic conditions. Bill Jr. sees these trends particularly in William's postwar houses in the experiments with modular design, family-oriented entrances, and pitched roofs to better respond to solar and weather issues.

Despite Sam's adherence to Bauhaus ideals, he never lost his passion for the tactile and textural qualities intrinsic to brick construction. His early visit to Italy and Venice embedded in him a deep appreciation of the craft of building and the role of ornament in architecture, not ornament in terms of decorative applied work, but enrichment achieved through the surface and subtle patterning of bricks and contrasts in color and materials—brick, steel, wood, and glass. In the 1940s that is evident, for example, in the brickwork at the Werner Park Elementary School.

Clients and Commissions

Sam and William could not have achieved their design ambitions without willing clients. In that respect, they were extraordinarily fortunate in the 1930s to have clients who were sufficiently adventurous or willing to stand apart from convention and sometimes be the recipients of unkind critical comments on their taste in residential design.

Marion Wiener recalled that her and Sam's house was described as looking like a Coca-Cola factory.[4] In Shreveport the unusual coming together of designer and client was to a large extent based on a small community of like-minded people whose sense of identity was not rooted in the region's historic building patterns or traditional styles. According to Marion, Sam did not accept every potential client who approached him, turning away those who did not have a similar aesthetic vision.[5]

The majority of the Wieners' clients for their house designs were relatives or friends. They were also Jews, who wished to make a clear and firm statement of their forward-thinking and vibrant cultural identity. Certainly Marion Wiener thought that was so, and Bill Jr. has expressed similar sentiments. And perhaps for Sam and William another consideration, and one that strengthened the link, was that so many of the European modernist architects whose works they had seen and admired were of Jewish descent—Bruno Ahrends, Peter Behrens, Marcel Breuer, Pierre Chareau, Erwin Gutkind, Erich Mendelsohn, and Bruno Paul, and immigrant architects Richard Neutra and Rudolf Schindler. Within a few years after Sam and William toured Europe, visiting buildings and meeting architects, modernism was stifled in Germany and its architects scattered. Many of them reconstituted their ideas in America, where they found fertile ground and accolades for their designs. Yet Sam and William had already introduced many of the concepts and forms of the new architecture to the South.

The Architects' Legacy

Sam and William's legacy is most profound on their hometown of Shreveport and northern Louisiana, not only for the designs they produced but their activities in their profession and their community. Both were members of the American Institute of Architects (AIA), and both were recognized and made fellows of the organization, Sam in 1950 and William in 1961. Sam was the first president of the North Louisiana Chapter of the AIA, and he served for fifteen years on the Louisiana State Board of Architectural Examiners, being appointed by four governors. He participated in many civic organizations, including the boards for the Shreveport Chamber of Commerce, the Shreveport Airport Advisory Committee, Goodwill Industries, the Shreveport Jewish Federation, and B'nai Zion Temple. At a national level he was on the National Committee of Industrial Relations for the AIA and an advisory architect for the School Building Division of the U.S. Bureau of Education.

Similarly, William's involvement in state and regional architectural associations included the Northern Louisiana AIA, where he served a several committees, and in the 1940s and 1950s variously as president of the Louisiana Architects Association and of the Shreveport Chapter of the AIA, which split off from the Northern Louisiana Chapter in 1956, and as director of the Gulf States Region, AIA. Locally he was involved in numerous civic and business activities, including committees of the Chamber of Commerce, the Shreveport Beautification Foundation, and the United Way. He, too, was a member of the B'nai Zion congregation.

Sam and William's architectural influence beyond the materiality of their buildings and their professional associations was limited, notably where teaching was concerned. Both acted as critics for students' design work at Tulane University's School of Architecture in New Orleans, and in 1951 Sam taught a few architectural design courses at Tulane, though he never held a permanent position, or apparently wanted to. Thus neither Sam nor William extended their influence through students anywhere close to a level achieved by Gropius and Breuer at Harvard or Mies in Chicago, and consequently never acquired numerous acolytes to spread their names far and wide. Their impact was through the buildings themselves. For several years from the late 1930s, groups of Tulane's architecture students were taken to Shreveport to tour the Wieners' modern buildings that were so much more original than almost anything then built in New Orleans. Architect Buford L. Pickens, head of the architecture program at Tulane University from 1946 to 1953, had described Shreveport as "the capital of modern architecture" in Louisiana.[6] The Northern Louisiana and then the Shreveport chapter of the AIA sponsored and paid the expenses of the tour after the war.

Yet, given how many of their buildings were published in the major architectural journals from the 1930s through the 1950s, why are Sam and William and their designs not better known? Not only were their projects published in all the major American journals, they were also featured in European magazines. Moreover, photographs of the Municipal Incinerator were exhibited and recognized internationally as a great modern building. It was one of the thirty-seven American buildings illustrated in Alberto Sartoris's 1941 revision of his massive and celebrated 1935 book on modern architecture from around the world (thirty-one of the other thirty-six American buildings featured were designs by William Lescaze and Richard Neutra).[7] Instead, the Wieners, like American-born architects in other regional centers, have been outshone by architects who already carried name recognition or the prestige of European birth and early practice. One reason may be that most histories of architecture have been written by scholars working in or studying outside of the South. Another cause might lie in the interests and habits of historians needing and then perpetuating architectural icons—both architects and buildings. Once an icon is established—Frank Lloyd Wright comes to mind as the most obvious example—that icon gets studied and restudied. Elizabeth Mock's influential book, *Built in USA: 1932–1944,* published in 1944 by New York's Museum of Modern Art, is still cited as a source for understanding the scope of American modernism to 1944. But this book gives the impression that modernism was limited to Wright and to the Chicago area, the Northeast, and the West Coast, and it only travels as far south as Tennessee. The Wieners are not included.

It is fortunate, then, that two major journals from the 1930s through the 1950s had editors eager to promote new architecture. *Architectural Forum* began to include American and European modern architecture in the 1930s, and this was the journal that published most of the Wieners' work in that decade. During the 1940s and 1950s the Wieners' work was showcased most often in *Architectural Record.* It may be no coincidence that Herbert L. Smith, who began working at the journal in 1949, had grown up in Shreveport and would have been familiar with the Wieners' buildings of the 1930s. Smith also initiated and was editor of the annual publication *Record Houses,* which included some of Sam and William's designs. This is not to diminish the inherent importance of the Wieners' work, but speaks to the power of editors and writers in establishing the reputation of buildings and architects.

However, the lack of national recognition beyond the years of their practice also has a lot to do with Sam and William themselves. Although their work was featured in the journals and Sam published a few articles, neither architect appears to have been overly concerned with their heritage. Sam's writings were not to promote himself, but to explain the genesis of or the features to consider in the design of a particular building type. Nor did they take as much care in preserving the documents of their work as one would have liked. While many of the Wieners' design drawings are archived in the Noel Memorial Library of Louisiana State University in Shreveport, these are primarily working drawings, not perspectives. Moreover, these projects do not represent their entire body of work, for other drawings, perhaps left in the ownership of clients, have been lost over time and, unfortunately, not one of the models they made during the preparation of their designs appears to survive.

Sam and William's principal legacy resides in the buildings themselves. What they reveal is that Sam and William's designs are far from formulaic, but creations derived from and responsive to the modern world as expressions of their age. Their body of work also shows that modern architecture, especially that of the 1930s, was not the province of a few iconic architects and that it had a greater geographic range than is usually assumed. Modernism was never a fixed orthodoxy or dogma, unbending in its rules or parts, but instead diverse in form and in its adaptation to American lifestyles and regional characteristics, and it could be created equally as well by American-born architects as by European immigrants.

APPENDIX: SELECTED CHRONOLOGY OF THE WIENERS' BUILDINGS

Timeline of Identified Works designed by Samuel G. Wiener and William B. Wiener

The buildings listed in this timeline are works discussed in this book. The list indicates architect(s) responsible and the building's date and location. If a building has suffered a major alteration or has been demolished, that information is noted. Additional buildings the architects designed or may have designed, but for which there is incomplete information, are not included. This list is a work in progress, and buildings by the Wieners are still being discovered and documented. The Ginsburg House, for example, only came to our attention in 2013. The date for each building indicates the design. All locations are Shreveport unless otherwise noted.

ABBREVIATIONS

JROW Samuel G. Wiener with Jones, Roessle, Olschner and Wiener
SGW Samuel G. Wiener
WBW William B. Wiener

1923 Feibleman's Department Store, 624 Texas St. JROW
1925 Kings Highway Christian Church, 806 Kings Hwy. JROW. 1952 addition, Julian Sokoloski
1926 Bossier City Municipal Building, 630 Barksdale Blvd., Bossier City. JROW
1927 Municipal Memorial Auditorium, 705 Elvis Presley Ave. JROW with Seymour Van Os
1928 Big Chain, Fairfield, 1500–1530 Fairfield Ave. JROW (altered)
1929 Municipal Airport (Downtown). JROW (demolished)
1930 Andress Motor Company, 717 Crockett St. JROW
1931 El Karubah Club House, Cross Lake. JROW
1933 Weekend House, Cross Lake. WBW and SGW (demolished)
1933 Wile House, 626 Wilder Place. JROW. 1938 addition, JROW; 1952 addition, WBW; 1957 addition, WBW and Associates
1934 Preston House, 222 Jordan St. WBW
1935 Boatner House, 1040 Delaware St. JROW
1935 Municipal Incinerator, 1731 Kings Hwy. JROW (demolished)
1936 Flesh House, 415 Sherwood Rd. WBW
1936 Rosenblaths Store, 403 Texas St. WBW (demolished)
1936 Ramsey Garage/Apartment, 2012 Dillingham Pl. WBW
1936 Orthopedic Clinic (Children's Clinic), Line Ave. at Margaret Pl. WBW and SGW (demolished)
1937 Samuel G. Wiener House, 615 Longleaf Rd. SGW

1938 Mayer House, 907 River Rd. WBW (altered)
1938 Levy House, 835 Margaret Pl. SGW (altered)
1938 Badt House, 721 Longleaf Rd. SGW and WBW
1938 Bossier City High School, Coleman St. at Mansfield St., Bossier City. JROW
1939 Haughton High School, 201 E. McKinley St., Haughton. SGW
1939 Winnfield Elementary School, S. St. John St. at Lafayette St., Winnfield. SGW
1939 Commercial National Bank, Texas St. at Edwards St. McKim, Mead and White with SGW
1939 Udes House, 722 Unadilla St. SGW and WBW
1940 Big Chain Store, Broadmoor, 3900 block of Youree Ave. SGW and WBW (demolished)
1941 Jacques Wiener House, 622 Longleaf Rd. SGW and WBW
1941 Werner Park Elementary School, 2715 Corbitt St. SGW
1946 Big Chain Store, Lakeshore, Lakeshore Dr. at Jewella Ave. SGW and WBW (altered)
1947 Palais Royal Department Store remodeling, Milam St. at McNeil St. SGW and WBW
1947 Zigzag Shops, Ockley Dr. at Youree Ave. WBW
1948 Gamm House, 1 Longleaf Ln. SGW and WBW
1948 Fairfield Building, 1600 Fairfield Ave. SGW and Associates
1948 Caddo Heights Elementary School, 1702 Corbitt St. SGW and Associates
1948 Linwood Junior High School, 401 W. 70th St. WBW
1949 Davidson House, 6336 Querbes Dr. WBW
1949 Shreveport Municipal Airport, Interstate Dr. SGW and E.M. Freeman and Associates (altered)
1949 Confederate Memorial Medical Center, Kings Hwy. at Linwood Ave. SGW with Neild and Somdal, and Van Os and Flaxman
1950 East Building, P&S Hospital, Jordan St. at Line Ave. SGW and WBW (altered)
1950 Fellman Clinic, 2515 Line Ave. SGW and WBW (altered)
1950 Herold House, 1050 Ontario St. WBW
1950 W. and C. Wiener House, 228 Ridge Dr., Jackson, MS. WBW and SGW; 1957 addition, WBW
1950 William B. Wiener House, 2 Longleaf Ln. WBW
1951 Ginsburg House, 3860 Bellaire Cir., Fort Worth, TX. SGW and WBW. 1962 addition, SGW (demolished)
1951 Simon House, 543 College Ln. WBW
1951 Plantation Park Elementary School, 2410 Plantation Pk. Dr., Bossier City. SGW and Associates
1953 The Shreveporter Highway Hotel, Greenwood at Broadway. SGW and WBW (demolished)
1954 B'nai Zion Congregation Temple, 245 Southfield Rd. SGW with Theodore Flaxman and Seymour Van Os
1954 Tullos House, 3118 Country Club Dr. WBW and Associates
1954 Levy House, 3402 Madison Park. SGW
1954 Muslow House, 6025 Arden St. SGW and WBW. 1956 addition, WBW and Associates
1955 Big Chain Store and Uptown Shopping Center, Line Ave. at Pierremont Rd. SGW and WBW (altered)
1957 J. S. Clark Junior High School, 351 Hearne Ave. Wiener, Morgan and O'Neal
1958 Woodlawn High School, 7340 Wyngate St. Wiener, Morgan and O'Neal
1959 J. and K. Wiener House, Jackson, MS. SGW and WBW

NOTES

INTRODUCTION

1. "Week-end House, Cross Lake, La.," *Architectural Forum* 61 (October 1934): 234–35.

2. Henry-Russell Hitchcock and Philip Johnson, *The International Style: Architecture Since 1922* (1932; rpt., with foreword by Henry-Russell Hitchcock, New York: W. W. Norton and Co., 1966), 119–23.

CHAPTER ONE

1. Bill Wiener Jr., telephone interview with Karen Kingsley, August 7, 2014.

2. Ibid.

CHAPTER TWO

1. Marion Wiener, interview with Karen Kingsley, Shreveport, April 27, 1983.

2. "Feibleman's to Open Doors of Palatial Home Here to Public Saturday," *Shreveport Times,* October 3, 1924, 1.

3. Ibid.

4. *Times Picayune,* November 1, 1931, 1, 5.

5. "Kings Highway Christian Church, Shreveport, La.," *American Architect* 131 (April 20, 1937): 517–23.

6. Samuel Wiener, *Venetian Houses and Details* (New York: Architectural Book Publishing Co., 1929).

7. Bill Wiener Jr., interview with Karen Kingsley, Shreveport, June 2001.

8. "The Municipal Auditorium, Shreveport, Louisiana," *Southern Architectural Review* 2, no. 1 (January 1, 1937): 10–13.

9. Clarence E. Olschner, letter to Sam Wiener, January 16, 1974, Samuel G. Wiener Collection, 083, Box 5, Louisiana State University, Shreveport (LSUS), Archives and Special Collections.

10. In reference to Big Chain, John Hussey, interview with Guy Carwile, Shreveport, May 2014; for the Municipal Auditorium, Bill Wiener Jr., interview, June 2001.

11. George Malcolm, "'Big Chain' Typifies Trend to the Complete Market," *Chain Store Review* 3 (February 1930): 40.

12. *Chain Store Age* (April 1930): 47.

13. Malcolm, "'Big Chain,'" 51.

14. Ibid., 49.

15. Ibid., 51.

16. Richard Longstreth, *The Drive-In, the Supermarket, and the Transformation of Commercial Space in Los Angeles, 1914–1941* (Cambridge, Mass.: MIT Press, 1999), 150.

17. John Groves, letter to Samuel G. Wiener, April 20, 1931, Samuel G. Wiener Collection, 083, Box 6, LSUS.

18. *Pencil Points* (July 1931): 545.

CHAPTER THREE

1. Hitchcock and Johnson, *The International Style,* 11.

2. Marion Wiener, interview, April 27, 1983.

3. Theodore Flaxman, interview with Karen Kingsley, Shreveport, July 16, 1983.

4. Marion Wiener, interview with Karen Kingsley, Shreveport, March 21, 1983.

5. Flaxman, interview, July 16, 1983.

6. "El Karubah Club House, Cross Lake, Louisiana," *Architectural Record* 76 (July 1934): 38–39.

7. "Week-end House, Cross Lake."

8. Bill Wiener Jr., interview with Karen Kingsley, Shreveport, August 1983; and Bill Wiener Jr., telephone interview with Kingsley, October 12, 2014.

9. Bill Wiener Jr., interview, August 1983.

10. Emily (Mimi) Wile Hussey, interview with Guy Carwile, Shreveport, October 2012.

11. "House of I. E. Wile in Shreveport, Louisiana; Jones, Roessle, Olschner and Wiener, Architects," *Architectural Record* 76 (October 1934): 252–53.

12. Bill Wiener Jr., interview, August 1983.

13. "House for John S. Preston, Shreveport, Louisiana, William B. Wiener, Architect," *Architectural Forum* 63 (October 1935): 376–77.

14. Lois Rosenfield, interview with Guy Carwile, Shreveport, February 2014.

15. Samuel Wiener, "People, C Factor and Architecture," *Southern Building* (January 1952): 5–6.

16. "House for Samuel G. Wiener, Shreveport, La.," *Architectural Forum* 70 (February 1939): 121.

17. Ibid., 121.

18. Marion Wiener, interview, April 27, 1983.

19. Bill Wiener Jr., letter to Kingsley, August 1983.

20. Wiener, "People, C Factor and Architecture," 6.

21. *Architectural Forum* 66 (April 1937): 292.

22. "House Remodeled for Yandell Boatner, Shreveport, La.," *Architectural Forum* 65 (October 1936): 290.

CHAPTER FOUR

1. U.S. Congress, *National Housing Act: Hearings before the Senate Committee on Banking and Currency,* 73rd Congress, 2nd sess. (Washington, D.C.: U.S. GPO, 1934), 168.

2. Samuel G. Wiener Collection, 083, Box 6, LSUS.

3. Ibid. At this date the Jones, Roessle, Olschner and Wiener firm was composed of the principals and William Wiener, draftsmen Carl L. Olschner and Andrew Schneider, engineer L. H. Roeger, superintendent George Thompson, and Dallas-based consulting mechanical engineer R. F. Taylor. The letter was used to enquire after at least one other potential commission because Morgan City is handwritten over Alexandria. An architect in the architectural office of the U.S. Treasury designed the Morgan City post office, and Edward F. Neild was awarded the contract for the Alexandria building.

4. Ibid.

5. Ibid.

6. C. W. Short and R. Stanley-Brown, *Public Buildings: A Survey of Architecture of Projects Constructed by Federal and Other Governmental Bodies between the Years 1933 and 1939 with the Assistance of the Public Works Administration* (Washington, D.C.: Public Works Administration, U.S. G.P.O., 1939), 471.

7. C. E. Olschner, "The Design of Municipal Incinerators." *The American City* 50 (October 1935): 47–49.

8. Olschner, letter to Sam Wiener, January 16, 1974.

9. "Municipal Incinerator, Shreveport, Louisiana," *Architectural Forum* 63 (November 1935): 483.

10. Samuel G. Wiener Collection, 083, Box 5, LSUS.

11. Lewis Mumford, "The Skyline: The Golden Age in the West and the South," *New Yorker* (April 30, 1938): 50–51, 50.

12. Ibid., 50.

13. Samuel G. Wiener Collection, 083, Box 5, LSUS.

14. Ibid.

15. Louise Matthews Hewitt, *Days of Building: History of a Jewish Community (*Shreveport: Jewish History Committee of Shreveport, Louisiana, 1965); Beverly S. Williams, "Anti-Semitism and Shreveport, Louisiana: The Situation in the 1920s," *Louisiana History* 21, no. 4 (Autumn 1980): 387–98.

16. Bill Wiener Jr., interview, August 1983.

17. Richard Baudouin, letter to Karen Kingsley, December 28, 1983.

18. Ibid.

19. Samuel Wiener, "No American Jewish Architectural Style," *National Jewish Post and Opinion* (Friday, July 1963): 9.

20. Ibid., 9.

21. Ibid.

22. "Clinic for Dr. Guy A. Caldwell, Shreveport, Louisiana," *Architectural Record* 81 (May 1937): 23.

23. "Optometric and Dental Clinic in Shreveport," *Architectural Record* 113 (1953): 180–84.

24. Gabrielle Esperdy, *Modernizing Main Street: Architecture and Consumer Culture in the New Deal* (Chicago: University of Chicago Press, 2008).

25. "Remodeled Men's Store, Shreveport, La.," *Architectural Forum* 67 (July 1937): 14.

26. Godfrey M. Lebhar, "Current Comment," *Chain Store Age* (September 1941): 25.

27. T. J. Campbell, "Shreveport Super Has Ultra Modern Features," *Super Market Merchandising* (June 1941): 16.

28. Ibid., 17.

29. Geoffrey Baker and Bruno Funaro, *Shopping Centers: Design and Operation* (New York: Reinhold Publishing Corporation, 1951), 59, 73, 143–46.

30. "Windowless Super-market Opens as Showplace of South,"

Chain Store Age (September 1941): 26–27; Campbell, "Shreveport Super," 16–19.

31. Samuel G. Wiener Collection, 083, Box 2, LSUS.

32. Ibid., Box 3, LSUS.

33. Ibid.

34. Guy W. Carwile, "$2.50 and up with Radio and Fan: The Hotel Palomar Courts," *SCA* [Society for Commercial Archeology] *Journal* 21, no. 2 (Fall 2003): 4–11.

CHAPTER FIVE

1. Samuel G. Wiener Collection, 083, Box 6, LSUS.

2. Doris Wheeler, design librarian, Louisiana State University, Baton Rouge, letter to Karen Kingsley, January 11, 1985.

CHAPTER SIX

1. Todd Hebert, "New Homes for Shreveport: Suburban Development, 1945–1955," *North Louisiana Historical Association Journal* 20 (1989): 115.

2. "Entirely Architect Designed: Municipal Airport, Shreveport, La.," *Architectural Record* 113 (February 1953), 123.

3. William B. Wiener, interview by William Evans and Joe Middleton, tape recording, Shreveport, 1972, LSUS Archives and Special Collections, LSU Shreveport.

4. U.S. Civil Aeronautics Administration, *Airport Design* (Washington, D.C.: G.P.O., 1949).

5. Walter Prokosch, "Airport Design: Its Architectural Aspects," *Architectural Record* 109 (January 1951): 112.

6. "Entirely Architect Designed," 129.

7. Baker and Funaro, *Shopping Centers,* 22.

8. "Southern Highway Hotel: The Best Is None Too Good," *Architectural Record* 119 (January 1956): 192–95.

9. Samuel G. Wiener Collection, 083, Box 10, LSUS.

CHAPTER SEVEN

1. "Residence of Mr. and Mrs. William B. Wiener House," *Architectural Record* 112 (November 1952): 183.

2. Peter Blake, *Marcel Breuer: Architect and Designer* (New York: Museum of Modern Art, 1949), 87.

3. Ibid., 87.

4. "Astute Design and Orientation Produce a Distinguished House," *Architectural Forum* 90 (March 1949): 98.

5. "Week-end House, Cross Lake," 234.

6. "Bayou Beauty," *Popular Home* (Late Fall 1956): 10–11; "Architects Design Complete Home," *The Second Treasury of Contemporary Houses* (New York: F. W. Dodge Corporation, 1959): 146–50.

7. "Bayou Beauty," 11.

8. James Muslow Jr., interview with Guy Carwile, Shreveport, September 2014.

CHAPTER EIGHT

1. Robert D. Leighninger Jr., *Building Louisiana: The Legacy of the Public Works Administration* (Jackson: University Press of Mississippi, 2007), 71.

2. Drawing, Samuel G. Wiener Collection, 083, LSUS; Leighninger, *Building Louisiana,* 87.

3. Samuel G. Wiener, "Bossier Looks to the Future in Building New High School," *American School Board Journal* (November 1941): 33.

4. Ibid.

5. Samuel G. Wiener, "The Changing Classroom," *American School Board Journal* (January 1948): 23.

6. "Haughton High School, Haughton, Louisiana," *Progressive Architecture* 27 (June 1946): 70–71.

7. "New Elementary School Provides for Modern Educational Needs," *The Nation's Schools* 37, no. 3 (March 1946): 38–40.

8. Wiener, "Changing Classroom," 22.

9. Samuel G. Wiener, "The Werner Park School, Shreveport, Louisiana," *American School Board Journal* (September 1944): 37.

10. Ibid., 39.

11. Wiener, "Changing Classroom," 23.

12. Ibid., 22.

13. Ibid.

14. "Fields of Practice: School Design. A Symposium," *Progressive Architecture* 30 (April 1949): 61–62, 61.

15. Wiener, "Changing Classroom," 22.

16. Ibid., 23.

17. "Meeting Enrollment Needs and the Educational Program," *American School Board Journal* (July 1951): 32.

18. Ibid., 35.

19. "Belle Rose School, Assumption, Louisiana," *Architectural Record* 13 (March 1948): 125.

20. "The Plantation Park Elementary School: The Bossier City, Louisiana, Complete Elementary School," *American School Board Journal* (May 1955): 51–53.

21. "Enigma of the Crowded Classroom," *Shreveport Magazine* (December 1955): 15.

22. Bill Wiener Jr., letter to Karen Kingsley, September 11, 2000.

23. Ibid.

24. "J. S. Clark Junior High School, Shreveport, Louisiana," *Architectural Record* 129 (August 1960): 195.

25. "Progress Report and How the Peabody Survey Pinpointed a Need," *Shreveport Magazine* (September 1958): 24; *Public Schools of Caddo Parish, Louisiana* (Nashville: George Peabody College of Teachers, Division of Surveys and Field Services, 1950).

26. "A Budget Campus Scheme Replete with Murals." *Architectural Record* 130, no. 4 (October 1961): 166–67.

27. Henry Steele Commager, "Our Schools Have Kept Us Free," *Life* (October 16, 1950): 56.

CHAPTER NINE

1. Flaxman, interview, July 16, 1983.

2. Ibid.

3. Ibid.

4. Flaxman, interview, April 28, 1983.

5. Ibid., July 16, 1983.

6. "Some Get a Factory Look," *Life* (October 16, 1950): 86.

7. Seymour Van Os, interview by Lester Haas and Joe Middleton, tape recording, Shreveport, 1972, Archives and Special Collections, LSUS.

8. "Louisiana's Permanent Exhibit Building," *Architectural Record* 87 (February 1940): 38–41.

9. "Louisiana Luxury Resort," *Architectural Record* (April 1958): 226–27.

10. Karen Kingsley, *Buildings of Louisiana* (New York: Oxford University Press, 2003), 358.

11. "James O'Brien House, Shreveport, La., Richard J. Neutra, Architect," *Architectural Record* 117 (May 1955): 170–71.

12. Richard Neutra, letter to Mrs. J. C. O'Brien, August 16, 1952. The letter came with the contents of the house when sold by the estate of Mrs. O' Brien.

CONCLUSION

1. Vincent L. Michael, *The Architecture of Barry Byrne* (Champaign: University of Illinois Press, 2013).

2. "Designing Home: Jews and Midcentury Modernism," Contemporary Jewish Museum, San Francisco, 2014.

3. Bill Wiener Jr., telephone interview, August 7, 2014.

4. Marion Wiener, interview, April 27, 1983.

5. Ibid.

6. "Shapers of the City," *Shreveport Magazine* (January 1955): 18–21, 18, 19. Marion Wiener in an interview, April 27, 1983, said these visits began in 1939.

7. Alberto Sartoris, *Gli Elementi dell'Architettura Razionale,* 3rd rev. ed. (Milano: Hoepli, 1941), 796.

BIBLIOGRAPHY

The most comprehensive resources for the architecture of Samuel G. and William B. Wiener and their contemporaries are in Louisiana State University, Shreveport, Archives and Special Collections in the Noel Memorial Library, which holds drawings and documents of the architects' work. The archive also contains taped interviews with several of the architects. Other important repositories are the National Register nominations. The files are available at the Division of Historic Preservation, Louisiana Office of Cultural Development, in Baton Rouge, and final reports on individual buildings are available online at www.crt.la/cultural-development/historic-preservation/. Several buildings (Big Chain Broadmoor, Municipal Memorial Auditorium, Samuel G. Wiener House, I. Ed Wile House, James Muslow House, and Hotel Palomar Courts) have been documented for the Historic American Buildings Survey (HABS) by Guy W. Carwile and his students at Louisiana Tech University, Ruston. These can be consulted at memory.loc.gov/ammem/collections/habs_haer. Documentation of northern Louisiana's buildings for HABS is an ongoing project, and more will be added in the years to come. Other useful resources are *Shreveport Magazine, Shreveport Times,* and local newspapers, all of which frequently published articles on buildings and city planning issues. The works listed below include only those that substantially focus on the buildings and topics of this book.

SHREVEPORT AND LOUISIANA GENERAL

Brock, Eric J. *Eric Brock's Shreveport.* Gretna, La.: Pelican Publishing Co., 2001.

Carruth, Viola. *Caddo: 1,000; A History of the Shreveport Area from the Time of the Caddo Indians to the 1970's.* Shreveport, La.: Shreveport Magazine, 1970.

Chujo, Ken. "The Negro Division: Public Education Policy for Black Louisiana, 1916–1941." In *Education in Louisiana,* ed. Michael G. Wade (Lafayette, La.: Center for Louisiana Studies, 1999): 300–325.

Hebert, Todd. "New Homes for Shreveport: Suburban Development, 1945–1955." *North Louisiana Historical Association Journal* 20 (1989): 113–24.

Hewitt, Louise Matthews. *Days of Building: History of a Jewish Community.* Shreveport: Jewish History Committee of Shreveport, Louisiana, 1965.

Kingsley, Karen. *Buildings of Louisiana.* New York: Oxford University Press, 2003.

——. *Modernism in Louisiana: A Decade of Progress, 1930–1940.* New Orleans: School of Architecture, Tulane University, 1984.

Leighninger, Robert D., Jr. *Building Louisiana: The Legacy of the Public Works Administration.* Jackson: University Press of Mississippi, 2007.

Louisiana: A Guide to the State. Compiled by Workers of the

Writers' Program of the Works Progress Administration in the State of Louisiana. New York: Hastings House, 1941.
McLaurin, Ann M., ed. *Glimpses of Shreveport.* Natchitoches, La.: Northwestern State University Press, 1985.
"Shapers of the City." *Shreveport Magazine* (January 1955): 18–19, 50.
"Shreveport, Louisiana." In *Encyclopedia of Southern Jewish Communities.* isjl.org/history/archive/la/shreveport.htm
Thomson, Bailey, and Patricia L. Meador. *Shreveport: A Photographic Remembrance, 1873–1949.* Baton Rouge: Louisiana State University Press, 1987.
Williams, Beverly S. "Anti-Semitism and Shreveport, Louisiana: The Situation in the 1920s." *Louisiana History* 21, no. 4 (Autumn 1980): 387–98.

GENERAL ARCHITECTURE

"Airport Terminal Building." *Progressive Architecture* 113 (May 1953): 69–121, 129–35.
Baughn, Jennifer V. Opager. "A Modern School Plant: Rural Consolidated Schools in Mississippi, 1910–1955." *Buildings & Landscapes: Journal of the Vernacular Architecture Forum* 19, no. 1 (Spring 2012): 43–72.
Blake, Peter. *Marcel Breuer: Architect and Designer.* New York: Museum of Modern Art, 1949.
——, ed. *Marcel Breuer: Sun and Shadow: The Philosophy of an Architect.* New York: Dodd Mead & Co., 1956.
Caudill, William Wayne. *Toward Better School Design.* New York: F. W. Dodge Corp., 1954.
Commager, Henry Steele. "Our Schools Have Kept Us Free." *Life* (October 16, 1950): 56.
Esperdy, Gabrielle. *Modernizing Main Street: Architecture and Consumer Culture in the New Deal.* Chicago: University of Chicago Press, 2008.
Longstreth, Richard. *The American Department Store Transformed, 1920–1960.* New Haven: Yale University Press in association with The Center for American Places at Columbia College, 2010.
——. *The Drive-In, the Supermarket, and the Transformation of Commercial Space in Los Angeles, 1914–1941.* Cambridge, Mass.: MIT Press, 1999.
Michael, Vincent L. *The Architecture of Barry Byrne.* Champaign: University of Illinois Press, 2013.
Ogata, Amy F. "Building for Learning in Postwar American Elementary Schools." *Journal of the Society of Architectural Historians* 67, no. 4 (December 2008): 562–91.
Prokosch, Walter. "Airport Design: Its Architectural Aspects." *Architectural Record* 109 (January 1951): 112–33.
Short, C. W., and R. Stanley-Brown. *Public Buildings: A Survey of Architecture of Projects Constructed by Federal and Other Governmental Bodies between the Years 1933 and 1939 with the Assistance of the Public Works Administration.* Washington, D.C.: Public Works Administration, U.S. G.P.O., 1939.
Stone, Edward Durell. *The Evolution of an Architect.* New York: Horizon Press, 1962.
U.S. Civil Aeronautics Administration. *Airport Design.* Washington D.C.: G.P.O., 1949.

PUBLICATIONS BY SAMUEL G. WIENER

Wiener, Samuel G. "The Changing Classroom." *American School Board Journal* (January 1948): 21–23.
——. "No American Jewish Architectural Style." *National Jewish Post and Opinion* (Friday, July 1963): 9.
——. "People, C Factor and Architecture." *Southern Building* (January 1952): 5–6.
——. "Poblacion, Factor C y Arquitectura." *Arquitectura* 20, no. 226.
——. *Venetian Houses and Details.* New York: Architectural Book Publishing Co., 1929.

INSTITUTIONAL AND RELIGIOUS BUILDINGS

"An Attractive Incinerator?" *Louisiana Architect* 4, no. 8 (June 1965): 6–7.
"Clinic for Dr. Guy A. Caldwell, Shreveport, Louisiana." *Architectural Record* 81 (May 1937): 23. [Orthopedic Clinic.]
"El Karubah Club House, Cross Lake, Louisiana." *Architectural Record* 76 (July 1934): 38–39.

"Kings Highway Christian Church, Shreveport, La." *American Architect* 131 (April 20, 1927): 517–23.

"Louisiana's Permanent Exhibit Building." *Architectural Record* 87 (February 1940): 38–41.

Mumford, Lewis. "The Skyline: The Golden Age in the West and the South." *New Yorker* (April 30, 1938): 50–51. [Municipal Incinerator.]

"The Municipal Auditorium, Shreveport, Louisiana." *Southern Architectural Review* 2, no. 1 (January 1, 1937): 10–13.

"Municipal Incinerator, Shreveport, Louisiana." *Architectural Forum* 63 (November 1935): 482–88.

Olschner, C. E. "The Design of Municipal Incinerators." *The American City* 50 (October 1935): 47–49.

"Optometric and Dental Clinic in Shreveport." *Architectural Record* 113 (1953): 180–84. Rpt. in Paul H. Kirk and Eugene D. Sternberg, *Doctors' Offices and Clinics: Medical and Dental.* New York: Reinhold, 1955, 174–77. [Fellman Clinic.]

Reneval, Pierre. "L'Architecture et L'Urbanisme aux Etats-Unis." *La Revue Moderne* 38, no. 1 (Janvier 15, 1938): 20. [Municipal Incinerator.]

Sartoris, Alberto. *Gli Elementi dell'Architettura Razionale.* 3rd rev. ed. Milano: Hoepli, 1941. [Municipal Incinerator, 796.]

"Shreveport Points with Pride to Stainless Trimmed Garbage Plant." *The Enduro Era* 4, no. 8 (August 1935): 2. [Municipal Incinerator.]

"Usine d'Incinération des Ordures à Shreveport." *L'Architecture d'aujourd'hui* 11 (1940): 69–70. [Municipal Incinerator.]

Weeks, Marcus D. "Modern Municipal Incinerator." *Manufacturers Record* (August 19, 1935): 25, 58.

COMMERCIAL BUILDINGS

"Activities of Gulf States Regional American Institute of Architects." *Southern Building* (May 1952): 8. [Fairfield Building.]

American Architect. (July 5, 1928): 69–70. [Feibleman's Department Store.]

Baker, Geoffrey, and Bruno Funaro. *Shopping Centers: Design and Operation.* New York: Reinhold Publishing Corp., 1951. [Big Chain Broadmoor, 59, 73, 142–43, 146; Big Chain Lakeshore, 73, 143–46.]

"Big Chain Buildings, Shreveport, La." *The American Architect* (July 5, 1928): 68. [Big Chain Fairfield.]

"Broadmoor Shopping Center, Shreveport, Louisiana." *Brick and Tile* 5, no. 9 (September 1948).

Campbell, T. J. "Shreveport Super Has Ultra Modern Features." *Super Market Merchandising* (June 1941): 16–19. [Big Chain Broadmoor.]

Carwile, Guy W. "$2.50 and up with Radio and Fan: The Hotel Palomar Courts." *SCA* [Society for Commercial Archeology] *Journal* 21, no. 2 (Fall 2003): 4–11. [Hotel Palomar Courts.]

"Crossroads Modern Style." *Shreveport Magazine* (August 1955): 16–17, 32–33. [Big Chain Uptown.]

"Louisiana Luxury Resort." *Architectural Record* (April 1958): 226–27. Rpt. in *Motels, Hotels, Restaurants and Bars,* 2nd. ed. (New York: McGraw-Hill, 1960): 108–9. [La Sands Hotel.]

Malcolm, George. "'Big Chain' Typifies Trend to the Complete Market." *Chain Store Review* 3 (February 1930): 49–51. [Big Chain Fairfield.]

"Remodeled Men's Store, Shreveport, La." *Architectural Forum* 67 (July 1937): 14. [Rosenblaths.]

Sawyer, Ray. "How a full-Service Motel Efficiently Handles Advance Reservations." *Tourist Court Journal* 30, no. 5 (February 1967): 11–20. [Shreveporter Hotel.]

Scott, J. L. "Overnight fire destroys Broadmoor landmark." *The Times* [Shreveport] (March 27, 2003):

"Southern Highway Hotel: The Best Is None Too Good." *Architectural Record* 119 (January 1956): 192–95. Rpt. in *Motels, Hotels, Restaurants and Bars,* 2nd ed. (New York: McGraw-Hill, 1960): 16, 110–13. [Shreveporter Hotel.]

"Windowless Super-market Opens as Showplace of South." *Chain Store Age* (September 1941): 26–27. [Big Chain Broadmoor.]

HOUSES

"Architects Design Complete Home." *The Second Treasury of Contemporary Houses.* New York: F. W. Dodge Corp., 1959. 146–50. [Muslow House.]

Architectural Forum 66 (April 1937): 292. [Ramsey Garage/ Apartment.]

"Astute Design and Orientation Produce a Distinguished House." *Architectural Forum* 90 (March 1949): 97–99. [Gamm House.]

"Bayou Beauty." *Popular Home* (Late Fall 1956): 10–11. [Tullos House.]

Decorative Art 1940: The Studio Yearbook. London: Studio Publications, 1940. [Samuel G. Wiener House, 34–35, 91.]

"Economical House: Result of Good Planning." In Jean Graf and Don Graf, *Practical Houses for Contemporary Living.* New York: F. W. Dodge Corp., 1953. 30–31. [Simon House.]

Ford, Katherine Morrow, and Thomas H. Creighton. *The American House Today: 85 Notable Examples.* New York: Reinhold Publishing Corp., 1951. [Davidson House, 16; Gamm House, 153, 178–79.]

"Fun and Convenience are Part of This Design." In Jean Graf and Don Graf, *Practical Houses for Contemporary Living.* New York: F. W. Dodge Corp., 1953. 152–57. [William B. Wiener House.]

Graf, Jean, and Don Graf. *Practical Houses for Contemporary Living.* New York: F. W. Dodge Corp., 1953. [William B. Wiener House, 152–57.]

"House for John S. Preston, Shreveport, Louisiana, William B. Wiener, Architect." *Architectural Forum* 63 (October 1935): 376–77.

"House for Samuel G. Wiener, Shreveport, La." *Architectural Forum* 70 (February 1939): 120–21.

"House of I. E. Wile in Shreveport, Louisiana; Jones, Roessle, Olschner and Wiener, Architects." *Architectural Record* 76 (October 1934): 252–53.

"House Remodeled for Yandell Boatner, Shreveport, La." *Architectural Forum* 65 (October 1936): 290.

"James O'Brien House, Shreveport, La., Richard J. Neutra, Architect." *Architectural Record* 117 (May 1955): 170–71.

Manning, Amanda. "Less is More." *Portico* [Jackson] (December 2010): 50–55. [Julian and Kathryn Wiener House.]

"Residence of Mr. and Mrs. William B. Wiener House." *Architectural Record* 112 (November 1952): 183–87. Rpt. as "Designed for Entertainment" in *A Treasury of Contemporary Houses.* New York: F. W. Dodge Corp., 1954. 153–57.

"Week-end House, Cross Lake, La." *Architectural Forum* 61 (October 1934): 234–35.

AIRPORTS

"Administration Building, Municipal Airport, Shreveport, La." *Southern Architectural Review* 1, no. 2 (September 1936): 16–17. [Downtown Airport.]

"L'Aeroporto Municipale di Shreveport." *Vitrum* (May 1954): 10–12.

"Entirely Architect Designed: Municipal Airport, Shreveport, La." *Architectural Record* 113 (February 1953): 123–31.

"Greater Shreveport Municipal Among Finest in the Nation." *Aviation News* 1, no. 5 (August 1961): 1.

"New Airport and the Carriers." *Shreveport Magazine* (August 1949): 12–13, 26.

"Shreveport: America's Latest Municipal Airport." *Airports and Air Transportation* 7, no. 104 (January–February 1954): 137–38.

Shreveport Magazine. (April 1955): 18–19, 30. [Municipal Airport.]

SCHOOLS

Architectural Record 89, no. 2 (February 1941): 101–3. Rpt. in *School Planning: The Architectural Record of a Decade.* Compiled by Kenneth Reid. New York: F. W. Dodge Corp., 1951. 43–45. [Bossier High School.]

"A Budget Campus Scheme Replete with Murals." *Architectural Record* 130, no. 4 (October 1961): 166–67. [Woodlawn High School.]

"Caddo Heights Elementary School, Shreveport, Louisiana." *Modern Brick Builder.* (1950–51): 7–8.

"Enigma of the Crowded Classroom." *Shreveport Magazine* (September 1955): 15, 30.

"Fields of Practice: School Design. A Symposium." *Progressive Architecture* 30 (April 1949): 61–62.

"Haughton High School, Haughton, Louisiana." *Progressive Architecture* 27 (June 1946): 70–71.

"J. S. Clark Junior High School, Shreveport, Louisiana." *Architectural Record* 129 (August 1960): 194–95.

"Meeting Enrollment Needs and the Educational Program." *American School Board Journal* (July 1951): 32–35. [Caddo Heights Elementary School.]

"A Music Building for Bossier High School." *American School Board Journal* (April 1957): 70.

"New Elementary School Provides for Modern Educational Needs." *The Nation's Schools* 37, no. 3 (March 1946): 38–40. [Winnfield Elementary School.]

"Planned for Instructional and Community Use." *American School Board Journal* (November 1951): 41–44, 91. [Linwood Junior High School.]

"The Plantation Park Elementary School: The Bossier City, Louisiana, Complete Elementary School." *American School Board Journal* (May 1955): 51–53.

"Progress Report and How the Peabody Survey Pinpointed a Need." *Shreveport Magazine* (September 1958): 23–24.

"Some Get Factory Look." *Life Magazine* (October 16, 1950): 86. [Booker T. Washington High School.]

Wiener, Samuel G. "Bossier Looks to the Future in Building New High School." *American School Board Journal* (November 1941): 32–35.

——. "The Werner Park School, Shreveport, Louisiana." *American School Board Journal* (September 1944): 37–39.

INDEX

Note: page numbers in *italics* refer to illustrations; those followed by "n" indicate endnotes; Plates are found after page 80; projects by architects other than Sam and William are attributed in parentheses.